THE OFFICIAL BIOGRAPHY OF RANGERS

THE OFFICIAL BIOGRAPHY OF RANGERS

RONNIE ESPLIN
&
GRAHAM WALKER

hachette
SCOTLAND

First published in 2011 by
HACHETTE SCOTLAND, an imprint of Hachette UK

1

Cataloguing in Publication Data is available from the British Library

ISBN 978 0 7553 1918 3

Typeset in Din and Bosis by Avon DataSet Ltd,
Bidford-on-Avon, Warwickshire

Printed and bound in Great Britain by
Clays Ltd, St Ives plc

HACHETTE SCOTLAND
An Hachette UK Company
338 Euston Road
London NW1 3BH

www.hachettescotland.co.uk
www.hachette.co.uk

ACKNOWLEDGEMENTS

We would like to thank Sandy Jardine, Craig Whyte, Ally McCoist, Walter Smith, Bobby Russell, Steven Thompson, Robert McElroy, Andy Kerr, Gary Ralston, Mary 'Tiny' Gallacher, Iain Duff, David Edgar, Steve Clark, Alex Anderson, Iain McColl, Elaine Sommerville, Davie Wilson, Aileen Wilson, Carol Patton, Gordon Hay, Peter Drury, Iain Patterson, Jim Loughran, George Wells and Stephen Smith.

Thanks also to Bob McDevitt for his support, encouragement and patience. Thanks also go to Julian Flanders.

CONTENTS

Foreword xi

Chapter 1 A New Era 1

Chapter 2 Founders and Early Years 9

Chapter 3 Bill Struth – Man and Manager 25

Chapter 4 Struth's Teams 34

Chapter 5 The Blue Riband 45

Chapter 6 All the Way to America 54

Chapter 7 Ruling Britannia 60

Chapter 8 War and a Visit from the Dynamos 64

Chapter 9 'Ritchie, Shearer, Caldow . . .' 69

Chapter 10 Cold War Conquerors 80

Chapter 11 Dark Domestic Decade 89

Chapter 12 Treble Kings 106

Chapter 13 Permanent Revolution 118

Chapter 14 Nine-in-a-Row 132

Chapter 15 Foreign Managers 148

Chapter 16 Alex McLeish – The Manager of Transition 169

Chapter 17 Smith Returns 175

Chapter 18 European Nights 194

Chapter 19 European Finals   207
Chapter 20 Ibrox   222
Chapter 21 Days of Tragedy   234
Chapter 22 The Fans   252
Chapter 23 The Boardroom   267
Chapter 24 Ally McCoist   276

Bibliography and Other Sources   285
Managers Appendix   289
Index   305

 FOREWORD

I was very proud and privileged to play for Rangers and was lucky enough to enjoy a successful career at Ibrox and play with so many great players. I've witnessed many changes at the club and in football since I first travelled through to Ibrox from Edinburgh as a teenager in 1964. I made my debut under Scot Symon the week after the infamous defeat by Berwick Rangers in 1967 and played in Willie Waddell's side which won the European Cup-Winners' Cup in 1972, beating Moscow Dynamo in the Barcelona final, having played in the final against Bayern Munich in 1967.

After finishing with the club in 1982, I returned to the commercial department at Ibrox in 1996 and witnessed Walter Smith guiding Rangers to nine-in-a-row and admired Walter's work during his second stint as manager where he guided the club to the 2008 UEFA Cup final and won eight out of 12 domestic trophies realistically available to him, culminating in 2010–11 with another SPL championship victory.

Rangers are now entering another new era following the

tenure of Sir David Murray, the most successful chairman in the club's history.

Under new owner Craig Whyte, we all hope the club can continue its success and meet the challenges we will face in the future.

However, the past is also important to the fans, especially at Ibrox. The club's history, heritage and traditions are what make Rangers unique. I was well aware of that as a player but it has been confirmed to me on a daily basis since I followed on from the great Willie Thornton as custodian of the Ibrox Trophy Room and club memorabilia.

More recently, with the help of Robert Carmichael, I have updated the club's archives and our match/player data is now comprehensive, covering every match from 1872 up to the present day. I am delighted that some of these statistics are included in *The Official Biography of Rangers* which will be a welcome and valued addition to the club's archives.

There have been around 300 books written about Rangers but this one is of the highest quality, a well-researched and well-written book chronicling 140 years of our glorious past and giving a valuable insight into our history.

It brings back many great memories for me as a former player and I would thoroughly recommend this to any Rangers fan.

Sandy Jardine

1
A NEW ERA

A new era at Rangers began on Friday 6 May 2011, when Craig Whyte became the club's new owner. After six months of protracted negotiations, and well-publicised scepticism from some members of the sitting Ibrox board, the Motherwell-born businessman acquired Sir David Murray's 85.3 per cent majority shareholding in a deal worth £52.5 million.

A statement released to the Stock Exchange confirmed that Whyte had paid Murray £1 for his shares which had cost the steel magnate £6 million in 1988. Murray bowed out with dignity after handing the torch on. 'From a personal perspective, today is the end of an era,' he said. 'I have had the privilege of being the majority shareholder of our great football club for over 22 years. During this time, we have seen many highs and lows together, and I trust that the successes will continue for many years to come.'

The new owner immediately became involved in an SPL title race that was to go to the last day of the season. The following day Whyte was mobbed outside Ibrox by excited and grateful supporters before the 4–0 win over Hearts. Afterwards he said: 'It was an exciting day for me after six months of negotiation with Sir David Murray. It was a tremendous feeling to walk through the front door as owner of Rangers. Being able to bring my father, Tom, to Ibrox was something special. He used to bring me to the Copland Road end to watch Rangers 30 years ago. The only thing different is that now I can't sing in the directors' box.'

On the Tuesday night he watched Rangers keep themselves ahead of Celtic by one point with a 2–0 home win over Dundee United and on the following Sunday he travelled to Rugby Park with thousands of other Light Blues fans to see a 5–1 win over Kilmarnock to keep the title at Ibrox for the third successive season, and the last trophy for the retiring manager Walter Smith before he gave way to his assistant, Ally McCoist. In due course, there were several boardroom changes, as expected, and former SFA chief executive and ex-Rangers player, Gordon Smith, was recruited as the director of football.

Whyte acknowledged the achievements of Murray as 'tremendous' while describing the contribution of Smith as 'amazing' and he knows he follows in the footsteps of other legendary figures at the club such as William Wilton, Bill Struth and Willie Waddell. 'When you walk around Ibrox, you see that it is an amazing place,' says Whyte. 'The history of the club is fantastic and I have to pinch myself when I think "I own this now". It is incredible. It will take time to sink in. It was a hectic start and winning the championship within nine days of me taking over was amazing. We had expected to be second, all our business models were based on that, all the way until Inverness beat Celtic with a few games remaining and so it was tremendous to win it. In the short term, we've got access to the Champions League and if you get to the group stages it means £17 million for the club. Celtic would have had that if they had qualified and that is the thing about Scottish football, not only does it give you a huge financial advantage if you win, it takes that advantage away from your rivals, especially this season where there is only one club from Scotland in the Champions League. So you can't underestimate the value of a title win.'

Hitherto Whyte was an unknown figure to the Ibrox support and the general Scottish public. Born in 1971, his life as a venture capitalist began as a 15-year-old at Kelvinside Academy in Glasgow when he traded stocks and shares, reputedly making a £20,000 profit before he left to start work in his dad's plant hire firm. Whyte's portfolio expanded over the years and he now boasts business interests in Britain and overseas, including financial services, commodities trading, transportation and property.

He surrendered his anonymity in November 2010, when he confirmed to the Stock Exchange that he was considering making an offer for the Govan club. However, it was only in the weeks preceding the conclusion of the deal that he fell under the media spotlight and he admits the rapid increase in profile was 'surreal'. 'After parking the car at Ibrox after we won the title at Kilmarnock, I thought I could walk in through the crowd but I quickly found out that I couldn't,' he says. 'That was a fantastic experience but you realise you have to make some changes to your life, which I didn't want to do. And that is the biggest change for me. Arriving for the game against Hearts and walking around Edmiston Drive the reality hit home then, it was amazing. It is strange to walk around the streets and be recognised. I live in London and was quite distant from it all. It is all a bit surreal to me. For the first few days when people were asking for an autograph, I thought they were winding me up. You have to deal with that. I don't live in Glasgow so that might make life easier. I would hope that the focus will return to the team and manager and the owner can have more of a low profile – but maybe that's wishful thinking. I understand it goes with the territory and it has to be dealt with. It's not something that has been part of my life before. In financial terms it wasn't a huge deal but it is a life-changing deal and there is no other option but to cope.'

Whyte's buyout has allayed serious fears among Rangers

fans about the club's financial plight, which had some talking about possible administration. Increasing debts built up over the years led, controversially, to bank intervention in 2010 and while costs were being cut, the club still owed around £22 million before Whyte wiped the slate clean and promised £25 million of investment over five years.

Whyte knows all too well that expectations still run high at Rangers. However, he also knows that the big-spending days of the previous two decades brought the club to the brink of ruin. Consequently, he is keen to stress his desire to keep Rangers in rude financial health during his tenure. 'When I first started watching Rangers, John Greig was the boss and there was Davie Cooper playing,' he says. 'And when Graeme Souness was the manager we had players like Terry Butcher, Chris Woods and Graham Roberts. That was a fantastic team to watch and when Walter took over we had Laudrup and Gazza, they were great days for Rangers and it was great to watch them do nine-in-a-row and those are my memories. We want to get the best players here that we can but in terms of paying English Premiership salaries of £100,000 or £200,000 per week, it is not financial reality for Rangers or any other club in Scotland. There may be changes in the future but right now we are where we are. We are in the Scottish League, we don't have television income to speak of, and so to bring the top players up here is pretty difficult. Nothing is impossible and we will look at a lot of things going forward but it is going to be pretty difficult getting back to those days.

'The fans want us to spend as much as possible but we have to manage expectations,' Whyte continues. 'There will be investment but the club has to pay its way. There is no way we will be making big losses here. I think there is an understanding these days that you can't throw silly money about. We have got to run this as a business. I have said that from day one. And for the long-term future you need a long-term business plan. Expectations are huge but I don't think anyone is expecting us to run this business in any other way than as a commercial operation. They have seen what has happened in the past when Rangers overspent – it caused real difficulties and until this takeover went through the club was in financial difficulty. People don't want to see that happen again. I have an obligation to leave the club in a good shape. It is paramount that we do that.'

Increasing the earning potential of Rangers is key to Whyte's plans for the future and he will be going all out to push the club's name abroad, while trying to maximise the facilities available at Ibrox. 'I do think we have a fantastic brand which is recognised worldwide and we have to find out how to capitalise on it and we will be working on that,' he says. 'We also have fantastic facilities here at the stadium and so have a lot of commercial opportunities. I think we can do better in that aspect. So I do think there is an opportunity here to run, if not a hugely profitable business then a long-term, financially sustainable business. If we are in the Champions League we can make a profit. If we are not then we aim to break even. It is not easy to invest and make a profit but as long as the team is performing and we are getting into the group stages of the Champions League and the fans continue to fill Ibrox, then we can make a profit. We had the best team in the league last season and have to build on that but we have to do it shrewdly, buying and selling players. But I think the fans understand that.'

To that end, Whyte feels that the youth system at Murray Park will have to bear more fruit in the future, with the club's scouting system under pressure to unearth some hidden gems. 'Everything has to be geared up for bringing our own players through,' he says. 'The more we can do that, the more successful the club is going to be. Murray Park is hugely important and I would like to see players coming through who know what it is like to play for Rangers, to play for the jersey, rather than bringing in foreign players who don't understand what it means to play for a club like this and who are here just for the money. Although last season you saw some players here on loan who got quite passionate about the club. Scouting players who are under the radar is also hugely important and we have to be better at buying and selling them.'

Whyte's takeover came near the end of a season when the tensions between the Old Firm were running higher than usual due, in part, to the unusually high number of meetings – seven – between the clubs. A summit meeting was convened by First Minister Alex Salmond in Edinburgh following the Scottish Cup replay at Parkhead in March 2011. At the end of an ugly encounter, which saw three Rangers players handed red cards in a 1–0 defeat, Celtic manager Neil Lennon clashed with McCoist and the fall-out, overblown as it was, inspired government intervention. Representatives from both clubs, the SFA and Strathclyde Police attended the meeting after which Rangers and Celtic agreed measures to improve behaviour surrounding the volatile fixture, which was even being blamed for an increase in domestic violence.

While such co-relations were debated, it was obvious that the rivalry between the two clubs had spilled out of the football arena. Lennon was sent bullets and parcel bombs in the post and had to have 24-hour security at one stage. Celtic players Niall McGinn and Paddy McCourt were also targeted along with high-profile Celtic fans Paul McBride QC and former MSP Trish Godman, which added, albeit indirectly, to the enmity between the two clubs and their respective supporters. Whyte hopes to restore respect and relations between the Glasgow giants but insists the blame for the wider troubles of society cannot be laid at the door of the Old Firm. 'I don't think the Old Firm rivalry is a bad thing,' he says. 'The fans enjoy it. I think the media over-hyped it but obviously the off-field things that were happening – bombs being sent to Celtic people – were disgraceful. However, it had nothing to do with football or with Old Firm rivalry.

'I think the way the club is projected and its image is very much our responsibility,' continues Whyte. 'We want to present the club in a certain way and play our part in Scottish society but we can't control what a few idiots do. Rangers and Celtic need each other. There is a good commercial relationship between the clubs at the moment and I am happy to talk to any of the Celtic directors and see how we can all build that relationship going forward.'

If trying to re-establish good with relations with the neighbours wasn't enough for Whyte, he will also be tasked with dealing with other issues such as league reconstruction, which remains high on the agenda. SPL chief executive Neil Doncaster spent most of the season unsuccessfully pushing a proposal that would see the league reduced from 12 teams to ten. Former First Minister Henry McLeish authored the SFA-commissioned report into the future of Scottish football, a broad and wide-ranging document that also claimed that a ten-team top division was the most financially viable model for the SPL.

However, the self-interest of owners and chairmen prevented a consensus being reached, to the frustration of many in the game. Whyte retains an open mind on the subject of league sizes but admits he is keen on the long-held dream of most Old Firm fans – a move to England. 'I think there has to be change,' he says. 'I know the club was in favour of a ten-team league before I took over but I haven't looked at it closely. I want to do the best for Rangers and I think we need a more exciting league which can generate more media income. And what is good for Rangers and Celtic ultimately should be good for Scottish football. But the idea of the Old Firm playing in England never goes away. If someone said we could be in the English Premier League tomorrow and playing Manchester United, Spurs and Arsenal we would jump at the chance, obviously. But whether it is going to happen is another matter. I think it is a long-term project to get in to a set-up like that but if the opportunity is ever there, it is something that we would be very interested in.'

The inability of the top clubs to get together and plot a way forward for the game was one of just one of many problems bedevilling the Scottish game when Whyte picked up the keys to Ibrox. The doom-mongers point to falling crowds, dwindling standards and disappearing coefficients, issues that brought many to ask why anyone would want to buy a football club in Scotland. But Whyte believes Rangers have 'an exciting future' and states with some optimism, 'I bought the club because I am a fan and I think I can run it as a business and do well.'

However, he is determined not to replicate the experience of his predecessor who once said that the club provided him with a fraction of his income while taking up the majority of his time. 'I am definitely trying to guard against that,' the London-based tycoon says. 'It is all about having the right team around me to run the business. In the first year I am going to very involved because it is a learning curve for me as well. I will be hands-on but I do have other business interests and I can't spend all my time here. I have no plans to move to Glasgow but I will be spending a lot more time here. Actually, the last time I lived in Glasgow was in 1997 – I had forgotten how much it rained here!'

2
FOUNDERS AND EARLY YEARS

The story of Rangers Football Club is beginning to emerge in more fascinating detail due, mostly, to an organic growth of interest in the club's early history in recent years. Though it has been well known for many decades that four teenagers from the Gareloch, Moses McNeil (16), brother Peter McNeil (17), Peter Campbell (15) and William McBeath (15), founded the Glasgow club, surprisingly little has been known about them or their lives.

That has all changed. Former player Sandy Jardine has beavered away for years within the Ibrox archives to improve the overall understanding of the club's history, and more recent research from outside has thrown even further light on the Gareloch boys' part in its foundation, growth and development.

In 2006 Light Blues fan Iain McColl began researching the club's founders which led to him mapping out the Founders Trail, a trip around Glasgow to places of historical interest for Rangers fans with a narrative emphasising the part played by the four youngsters. 'Many years ago I read *The New Era* by

Willie Allison and was immediately drawn to the four boys who had famously formed Rangers,' said McColl. 'Unfortunately there was little real information about the lads in terms of what had inspired them, where they worked, lived, or what became of them. So around 2006 I started my own research into their lives. During this work, I became aware of many locations around Glasgow relating to where they spent their time, including homes, business addresses, where Rangers played their early games and where they socialised. I would often stroll around the sites wondering if anyone else would be interested. Two years later I received a call from journalist Gary Ralston, who was also researching the story for his own book. He had almost completed his work and we had a mountain of information and stories to share. Two other fans, Gordon Bell and Neil Stobie, had also been in touch with me expressing a particular interest in the geography of Rangers' history.

'Between us we drew up a Founders Map and in September 2009 we took a group of supporters around Glasgow on foot, visiting the sites we had come up with. The starting point, of course, was Flesher's Haugh on Glasgow Green, where that month in conjunction with the club we'd had a plaque erected within the Football Centre celebrating the four boys. The plaque was unveiled by Heather Lang, granddaughter of founder Peter McNeil, whom Gary Ralston had located. The walk proved extremely popular, so in March 2010 we decided to organise another tour but this time on an open-top bus. The popularity of the project has astounded us. The bus has a capacity of 70 and every seat has been taken on the monthly trips that we've run regularly since that first one. It continues to grow with the help of supporters' clubs who are now making block bookings. We're also advertised on various Glasgow historical websites and plan to approach the official Scottish tourist organisations with a view to incorporating the tour into the mainstream tourist trade.

'The whole tour is fascinating, particularly for local people: the humble beginnings of the club, the ages of the boys, the fact that this whole rags-to-riches story was played out on the streets of Glasgow at locations people walk past every day.

'We approached the club earlier in 2010 with our plans and now the Founders Trail ends with a tour of Ibrox. There is a painting depicting the four founders, which takes pride of place at the top of Ibrox's marble staircase. There's also a website which is regularly updated [www.gallantpioneers.co.uk]. Our research is on-going and we already have three new locations identified for next year, a house just off Paisley Road West belonging to Tom Vallance being one of them.'

Gary Ralston's research culminated in the book *The Gallant Pioneers*, which was published to critical acclaim in 2009. It added hugely to what had already been published on the club's early days. 'I wanted the book to be the starting point for people to research Rangers,' said the *Daily Record* journalist. 'I didn't set off with a zealous drive to demystify Rangers or show the fans the light. I was simply intrigued by the four young boys – and Tom Vallance – and wanted to know what became of them. I wanted to satisfy my own curiosity. When Rangers were formed in 1872, it was in the infancy of the game and there wasn't a sporting press as such, that didn't come until a few years later. What helped me with my research has been the advent of the Internet. There is nothing better than getting your fingers dirty in libraries and archives, looking at the primary resources, but the Internet allows part-time historians to look at archives and indulge themselves in genealogical research. I didn't find anything surprising but my work did provide some detail and colour and reaffirmed of the club's humble beginnings and the sporting reasons behind its formation.

'There are a number of people who still believe Rangers was formed as a Protestant club. This is nonsense and I am surprised about the number of people who purport to know about football who believe that. There was no great connection between religion and Rangers although, of course, we assume that the boys who formed the club were Protestants. The most pleasing aspect has been the amount of people who have said,

"I didn't know that" and who now look at the club in a different way.'

While interest in the history of Rangers is developing quickly, Robert McElroy, editor of the *Rangers Historian* magazine, has been researching the subject for many years. His work has produced a number of books about the Light Blues, of which *Rangers: The Complete Record* is a 'must-have' publication for any contemporary football writers or students of Scottish football. He remembers when interest in the story of Rangers was minimal even for some of those within the club's inner echelons. 'The recent interest in the club's history has to be welcomed and the Internet has helped that along,' he said. 'When I was writing my early books, at times it was like banging your head against a brick wall. I remember talking to a director of the club in the early 1990s when I was working on a book and the one question he had was, "How many photographs are going to be in it?"'

Of course, research is not always accurate. In fact the first full-length history of the club, John Allan's *The Story of the Rangers*, published in 1923, caused immense confusion by stating that Rangers was formed in 1873. No one knows for sure the reason behind the incorrect date but one theory is that the publication of the Govan club's 'jubilee' history was late and thus it may have simply been expedient. The club appeared happy to play along with the inaccuracy for decades, even celebrating its centenary in 1973. But the early *Scottish Football Annuals* all give the date of the origin as 1872, the year confirmed in a famous article, 'The Rangers FC' written by an early player, William Dunlop, under the pseudonym of 'True Blue'. In addition, the early club handbooks all state the foundation date as 1872.

What is irrefutable, however, is that the McNeil brothers, Campbell and McBeath were the boys who decided to form the club and it was Moses who suggested it be called Rangers after seeing the name in a book about English rugby. Although Glasgow Green, in the east end of the city, is the registered birthplace of Rangers, conception took place in West End Park (later renamed Kelvingrove Park) where the four teenagers discussed how to take forward their interest in association football which was sweeping Victorian Britain and which, according to Dunlop, had been fostered by the excitement of watching games involving Queen's Park, Vale of Leven and Third Lanark Volunteers.

It should be noted that Glasgow, nowadays a vibrant, modern and cosmopolitan city, was at that time a very different place. For its part in facilitating the Industrial Revolution, Glasgow was known as the Second City of the Empire. It was on its way to a population peak of over a million, many of those immigrants from the Highlands and from Ireland. A dark, grimy city was characterised by its heavy industries such as shipbuilding, steel and engineering. When workers in those labour-intensive industries were allowed a Saturday afternoon off, the game of football began to flourish but the early days of the sport were disorganised and amateurish in every sense of the word.

Those four founding fathers had to find fellow enthusiasts to make up a team for Rangers' first game, which took place towards the end of May 1872, two months after the inauguration of the club, against Callander at Flesher's Haugh. The home team played four 'ringers' to make up the eleven. The quintet of players who were acquired from other clubs – Harry McNeil (brother of Moses, Peter and Willie) and Willie McKinnon both of Queen's Park, and John Hunter and Willie Miller of Eastern – were the only ones to strip, the rest played with their day-to-day clothes on.

The game ended goalless but in their second fixture Rangers beat Clyde (not the present Clyde of Cumbernauld) 11–0 and the club soon began to take shape. The first general meeting was held and new office bearers elected with training nights organised. The early enthusiasm generated by the fledgling football club would see Peter McNeil getting to Glasgow Green early on match day to secure the pitch until Rangers' reputation grew to the extent that the best part of the ground became by popular consensus 'their pitch'.

One of the most significant figures in Rangers' history, Tom Vallance, joined the club in the spring of 1873. He would have a long career as player and administrator – eventually becoming president of the club – his influence spanning several decades. Vallance was an internationalist, a fine athlete and rower as well as a fine full back. He even had the distinction of having two paintings accepted by the Royal Scottish Academy, perhaps a unique honour for a Scottish footballer.

Rangers had left it too late to apply for membership of the Scottish Football Association in 1873–74 and had to watch as interested spectators as Queen's Park won the inaugural Scottish Cup competition. But with William McBeath installed as the first president of the club for the start of the following season, Rangers took their first real steps in Scottish football. On 12 October 1874 Rangers played their first competitive match. Captained by Peter McNeil, the Light Blues faced Oxford in the first round of the Scottish Cup at Queen's Park Recreation Ground with a team that read: John Yuil, Tom Vallance, Peter McNeil, William McNeil, Willie McBeath, Moses McNeil, Peter Campbell, George Phillips, James Watson, David Gibb, John Campbell. Goals by Moses McNeil and Gibb gave Rangers victory, but they exited the competition in the next round to a disputed goal against Dumbarton, one of the most successful teams of the Victorian era, in a replay at Boghead.

Rangers, growing in popularity and with ambition plentiful, moved to the first ground they could truly call their own at Burnbank, on the south side of the Great Western Road near the Kelvin Bridge. The first game there, against Vale of Leven on 11 September 1875, ended in an encouraging 1–1 draw. The club stayed north of the River Clyde for just one season before moving to Kinning Park from where they launched a Scottish Cup campaign that ended in their first appearance in the final in 1877. Opponents that day, Vale of Leven, were one of the best teams in Scotland but the Light Blue upstarts pushed them close. After two 1–1 draws, Rangers lost 3–2 in the second replay but emerged with their reputation and popularity enhanced.

Moses McNeil, however, went to his grave believing that Rangers should have triumphed in the first replay. In a *Daily Record* article published in 1935, he said: 'Only a few minutes remained [in extra time] when a melee occurred in the Vale goal. The keeper, W.C. Wood, cleared his lines but we claimed the ball had passed over the goalline. The referee disallowed our claim, but I still maintain to this day that it was a perfectly good goal and that Rangers name should have been inscribed on the cup that season.'

Two years later Rangers played the same opponents in the final again. Again the match ended in a 1–1 draw and again the Kinning Park club had a goal disallowed in controversial circumstances. This time, however, Rangers were so incensed that they refused to turn up for the replay and Vale of Leven were awarded the trophy.

As the decade came to a close there were changes to be made on the pitch as key players like Peter Campbell and Hugh McIntyre departed the scene. But Rangers' growing pains seemed far from troublesome; success on the pitch was matched by the club's growing popularity and at the AGM in 1879 it was claimed that the club had never been in better shape.

However, the new decade brought with it some major setbacks. One of the club's founders and its first Scottish international Moses McNeil moved across the city for a spell at Queen's Park, although he soon returned to the fold, and in 1882 Tom Vallance left to work in India. Although he too was to return a year later due to ill health, his best days as a player were behind him. Another departure followed with the tragic death from typhoid fever of 26-year-old president Archie Harkness that same year. Although vice-president George Goudie moved up to take his place, the club was plunged into an era of destructive internal politics. Rangers fell under the sway of John Wallace Mackay, a controversial and unpopular figure, whose tenure as match secretary coincided with one of the gloomiest periods of the club's history. Despite the popularity of the team and its players, attempts to build up membership had been neglected and income was in short supply. According to the *Rangers Handbook* of 1955–56, Goudie's first task was to loan the club £30 to keep it afloat. The club faced an eviction notice from its Kinning Park ground, which in any case was frequently in a bad state on account of drainage problems. The early 1880s saw much concern over finance and there were regular rows over expenditure within the committee that ran the club. It was not until 1886 that Mackay's influence began to wane and he was finally forced to resign.

Despite all the financial woes, Rangers still managed to run a second team ('The Swifts') and a third team ('The Shields') and continued to travel long distances to England to play challenge matches. Indeed for a time in the mid-1880s it looked like Rangers would join the English league but the matter of English teams playing professional players at this time proved an obstacle. For a short period Rangers also played in white shirts but in 1883 it was agreed that they revert to the 'old colours', namely royal blue jerseys and white knickers.

Although the club had been successful in friendlies and in the Scottish Cup, Rangers' first silverware had been secured in the Glasgow Charity Cup in 1879 when they defeated Vale of Leven 2–1 in the final at Hampden. But already they had their sights fixed on bigger prizes. In 1885-86 Rangers had decided to enter the English FA Cup. This was not unusual at the time for Scottish clubs, although costs of travel and shortage of time often proved problematic. But they refused to play their first round match against Rawtenstall because the English club fielded professional players. However, they entered the competition again the following year, pulling off a shock 1–0 win against Everton at Goodison Park in the first round, thanks to a goal from Charlie Heggie. Subsequent victories against Church, Cowlairs and Lincoln City saw them drawn at home to Old Westminsters in the quarter-finals. In what turned out to be the last match played at Kinning Park, Rangers won 5–1 to advance to a semi-final against Aston Villa.

The club's ten-year lease on their ground had come to an end in 1886 but the club were unsure of their next home and were in discussions about extending the lease. They were finally forced out in February 1887 having secured use of a new piece of land at nearby Ibrox, close to where the current ground is situated. Kinning Park was officially closed on 26 February 1887, with a match between the 'Ancients' and 'Moderns'.

Eight days later Rangers faced the mighty Aston Villa at Nantwich Road, Crewe, confident that two victories over the Birmingham side in recent friendlies would give them the edge. However, the match ended in a 3–1 defeat and Villa went on to win the cup that year, beating West Bromwich Albion 2–0 at Kennington Oval in London.

Despite their extraordinary FA Cup campaign, it was abundantly clear that Rangers still had work to do before they could consider themselves an established and stable Scottish club. The first step, however, was a move to the 15,000-capacity Ibrox Park, complete with grandstand and pavilion. The cost of construction, undertaken by Fred Bradby & Co, totalled £833.8/6d, and the stadium was opened on 20 August 1887 with a game against top English side Preston North End, popularly known as the 'Invincibles'. An 8–1 defeat was not an auspicious start.

The significance of 28 May 1888, when the first match against newly formed Celtic took place at Celtic Park, would only become clear in time. Around 2,000 people turned up for the home side's first ever match and saw Neilly McCallum, a former Rangers player, score the first goal for Celtic in a 5–2 win for the team from the east end of the city. A few months earlier McCallum had played for Rangers against Aston Villa in Birmingham. The relationship between Rangers and Celtic was initially friendly, and after their first meeting players and staff from both clubs returned to nearby St Mary's Hall for a convivial night's entertainment. It was not until the early part of the 20th century that the clubs' rivalry would become bitter and split along religious lines of which much has been written since.

However, while Celtic's DNA was unashamedly Irish and Catholic, Rangers was not formed as a Protestant club, even though this was at a time when many famous-to-be clubs in Scotland and England did spring up with church associations. The statement of a Rangers vice-chairman in 1967 that they had begun life as a 'Presbyterian Boys Club' was incorrect and can perhaps be considered an attempt retrospectively to rationalise the solidly Protestant character the club had by then acquired.

However, there may have been no Old Firm, as Rangers and Celtic would come to be known in time, had the Light Blues not recovered from yet another perilous position in the wake of their derby defeat. Season 1888–89 brought unprecedented on-field woe to the Ibrox club who played 39 matches in which 19 were lost and seven drawn. A 6–1 home defeat to Celtic in the Glasgow Cup was compounded by a second-round defeat to Clyde in the Scottish Cup. At times the club struggled to find eleven players to make up a team and as a consequence Rangers were again close to going out of business with large debts built up over the matter of the new ground.

However, Rangers survived near bankruptcy to take their place in the newly formed Scottish League of 1890–91 which included Celtic, Third Lanark, Heart of Midlothian, St Mirren, Dumbarton, Renton, Cowlairs, Cambuslang, Vale of Leven and Abercorn. The notable absentee was the country's top club, Queen's Park, the Hampden amateurs refusing to join a league that would ultimately involve professional clubs. In a thrilling season the Light Blues came close to becoming Scottish foot-all's first undisputed champions. The Gers' first league game was played on 16 August 1890 and resulted in a 5–2 home victory over Hearts. By the end of that inaugural league campaign, Rangers had played 18 games with 13 wins, three draws and two defeats. However, those losses had been at home to Celtic (2–1) in the penultimate fixture and earlier in the season away to Dumbarton (5–1) with whom they would eventually share top place with 29 points apiece. It was decided that a play-off would take place at Cathkin Park to decide the title. Rangers took a 2–0 lead but Dumbarton fought back to make it 2–2 and the 1890–91 championship was shared for the only time in Scottish League history.

The formation of the Scottish League ensured that the Scottish game was soon professionalised. The rapid growth and commercialisation of the sport drove such a development, and there was the influential example of England where professionalism had been accepted in 1885. Rangers, like other Scottish clubs, needed to pay players to prevent them going to England to make a living. The issue of professionalism had dogged Rangers' relations with the game in England, most notably in 1885 when the club pulled out of their FA Cup match against Rawtenstall FC under threat by the Scottish authorities over the English club playing professionals. For failing to honour the fixture Rangers were subsequently fined by the English FA.

Rangers grew in strength and the following decade would see an accumulation of honours at Ibrox. They finished runners-up in the league in 1892–93, 1895–96 and 1896–97, and on 17 February 1894 it was a case of third time lucky in the Scottish Cup when they defeated Celtic 3–1 in the final. Success bred success and two more Cup final triumphs followed, Rangers beating Dumbarton 5–1 in 1897 and retaining the trophy the following season with a 2–0 win over Kilmarnock.

In 1897 the *Scottish Sport* newspaper commented as follows about the team's style of play: 'Seen in their very best swing, they are a combination of clever, graceful exponents of the purest type of play, with the requisite resource and sufficient judgement to make them as formidable as they are fair. The colours of the club were never worn by a finer team, and in consequence the club bank-book was never so bulky.' The same journal also regularly referred to Rangers as 'Scotia's Darling Club', an indication of the club's popularity and renown in the country as a whole even at this early stage in their history. While football was, of course, the club's *raison d'être*, its reputation as an institution was also bolstered by the Rangers Sports events, which it staged at Ibrox. Noting the one held in August 1897, the paper stated: 'It was a dainty dish that the Rangers served. Moreover, it is one that will vastly enhance their reputation as sports caterers, and, at the same time, enrich by a very handsome sum their already well-filled exchequer.' Around 10,000 people attended this event, and although other clubs attempted to emulate Rangers none succeeded in putting on such popular events. The Rangers Sports indeed continued as an annual summer happening when the club moved to the present Ibrox ground, and it was even made grander when Bill Struth, who had been a runner before becoming a football trainer, was team manager. Some of the world's most famous athletes made appearances including Olympic runners Eric Liddell and Sydney Wooderson.

In 1897 the *Scottish Sport* also referred to Celtic as Rangers' 'strongest' and 'keenest' rivals, though there was certainly no hint of the religiously charged rivalry that was to develop a few years later. In fact, the journal's preview of the New Year Rangers v Celtic match at Ibrox devoted much of its space to describing the antics of a 'weather prophet' from Kirkcudbright who at half-time and full-time was to 'scientifically cause to be discharged with a loud report, synchronously with the referee's whistle, his world-renowned patent automatic GUN, ingeniously constructed on new and novel clockwork lines, and encompassed within the limited precincts of what he himself describes as "a small house (portable), three feet square".' The prophet and his time gun certainly drew the crowds – the takings were a record for the Glasgow League (which took place between January and May) and only slightly under the Scottish League record (August to February) – but the newspaper concluded that his contraption 'need not just yet be included amongst the indispensable appurtenances of the game'.

Rangers made great strides on the field and in terms of the club's finances during the 1890s. Perhaps more significant than their shared title win of 1891 and Scottish Cup successes was the league campaign of 1898–99 when Rangers won every match. Eighteen games, 18 victories and 79 goals scored at an average of more than four a game. It was a feat that has never been equalled, the club's first outright league championship victory and the first of four successive title wins. Stalwarts of this and other great sides of the decade included John McPherson, a player who served the cause in virtually every position in team, and who would go on to serve as a director from 1907 until his death in 1926. Another important and constant presence was left back Jock Drummond who formed a formidable full-back partnership with Nicol Smith.

Flushed with success the club moved onwards and upwards. Previous woes, it seemed, had been discarded and there was a structure in place from which to build future success, underpinned by another colossus in the club's history, William Wilton. He had joined Rangers as a player in September 1883 but had failed to make the first team. In fact Wilton's talents lay off the field. He had taken charge of the reserves, the Swifts, and they enjoyed considerable success during his tenure. He had been appointed the club's match secretary in 1889 and had played a big part in Rangers' preparations for the newly formed Scottish league and the advent of professionalism in Scottish football.

When Rangers Football Club became Rangers Football Club Ltd on 27 May 1899, the first board of directors were appointed and Wilton, hitherto honorary match secretary, was appointed manager and secretary with James Henderson becoming chairman. The capital of the company was £12,000, divided into 600 Proprietary shares of £5 each, and 9,000 Ordinary shares of £1 each.

The start of the 1900s saw the increasingly professional Rangers, whose first-team players were on £2 per week, build and grow as a team and as a club. However, the growing confidence of the burgeoning Govan club was severely dented by the first Ibrox Disaster. In 1902, during a Scotland v England match, a section of the mostly wooden western terracing collapsed under sheer weight of numbers, leaving 25 people dead and over 500 injured. It was a blow to the club whose new stadium, designed by Glaswegian architect Archibald Leitch, had been the source of some pride. Sadly, it was not to be the last tragedy at the stadium (see chapter 21).

Rangers' rivalry with Celtic intensified as the Parkhead club superseded the Light Blues' four-in-a-row with six straight title wins from season 1904–05 to 1909–10. However, despite that rivalry, fans of both clubs joined together to take part in an infamous Hampden riot, following the drawn 1909 Scottish Cup final replay. The term 'Old Firm' had originated during the early years of the century as a jibe at the financial benefits both clubs enjoyed from their frequent meetings, many of which had been drawn games, particularly in cup competitions. During the build-up to the replay – the first game had been a 2–2 draw – there was much press speculation that the teams might contrive another draw in order to force another lucrative replay. Gate receipts of over £4,000 from the two matches, watched by a combined attendance of 130,000 people, heightened suspicions. Certainly that appeared to be the collective view of some Rangers and Celtic fans after the replay at the national stadium ended 1–1. It was incorrectly thought that there would be extra-time. When it became clear there would be a second replay instead, fans stormed the pitch, set fire to turnstiles and fought with the Fire Brigade when they arrived to help restore order. The riot lasted three hours during which time 130 people were injured, six seriously. The SFA decided to withhold the cup that season and fined both clubs £150. Despite this the Old Firm's stranglehold on the Scottish game was set to tighten. Third Lanark won the First Division title in 1903–04 but the championship trophy would have green or blue ribbons on it until Motherwell won it in 1931–32.

Until his tragic death in a boating accident on 2 May 1920, the day after Rangers had won the title back from Celtic, Wilton, helped latterly by assistant Bill Struth, had laid the foundations for a period of dominance which was to last until the Second

World War. Season 1919–20 had seen the Govan club firmly impose themselves on the Scottish game. They won 31 of their 42 league games, drawing nine and losing just two. But it was the manner of those victories that really impressed. Rangers scored 106 goals and conceded just 25 during a season that bore favourable comparison with the clean-sweep league campaign of 1898–99.

Wilton had been a major force at the club. John Allan's book, *The Story of the Rangers*, paid him this fitting tribute: 'The ideals for which he strove are still sought after by those who are left in custody of the cherished traditions of the club.' In his book on Rangers' managers author David Mason summed up Wilton's contribution with these words: 'It is doubtful whether Rangers would have become the club that it is today without the endeavours of William Wilton. He established the organisation of the club, seeing it through the traumas of disaster and war, and guiding it towards not just success but also prominence in the game throughout Scotland.' By the time he was swept to his death off the deck of a friend's yacht off the Inverclyde coast, Rangers had gone through almost five decades of trials and tribulations to take their place at the top table of Scottish football.

It had all become possible due to the four men known as the Gallant Pioneers and Vallance. Ralston's painstaking research adds greatly to their stories by unearthing some fascinating and tragic facts. 'Peter Campbell drowned, Peter McNeil was fragile when he died in 1901 and William McBeath's work took him away down south, his life took a different turn. I got the impression Moses was happier just contributing as a player than behind the scenes. The biggest executive role he performed at Rangers was that of honorary secretary in 1877. But the club outgrew him. One of the saddest things was that his death in 1938 went unrecorded apart from a paragraph in the *Daily Record* a week after he died. Moses' relationship with Rangers in his latter years was intriguing. He sent his apologies for missing the club's Jubilee Dinner in 1923. Maybe he was ill, we don't know, but perhaps by then there was a distance between him and the club. He would have been at the top table and been treated probably more respectfully than Tom Vallance although Vallance deserves all the praise he gets. He wasn't there when the four boys took that walk in the park and dreamed up the foundation of Rangers Football Club but he is possibly the most significant figure in the club's history. He helped Rangers make its reputation and contributed more off the park than on it. After his playing career was finished he assumed a patriarchal role at the club, guiding it through some severe financial times, the sort of which were not experienced again until recent years. As president, he took Rangers to Ibrox when newspapers were wondering if the club would ever survive if it left Kinning Park. He was a well-known figure around Glasgow, president of the Restaurateurs and Hoteliers Association and would organise regular gatherings and reunions. Vallance remained close to the club until he died in 1935 and Struth and Jimmy Bowie were at the funeral. It was the football equivalent of a state funeral. Interestingly, in 1898, at an event at his Glasgow restaurant to mark the 21st anniversary of the Scottish Cup final defeat by Vale of Leven, he bemoaned football, saying it had been reduced to a mercenary matters. Who knows what he would have made of it now?'

3

BILL STRUTH – MAN AND MANAGER

Following Wilton's death the club wasted no time in appointing a successor and announced that Bill Struth was to take over as manager. It was one of the finest appointments in the club's history. If one individual has come to personify Rangers above all others it is William 'Bill' Struth. His record is unsurpassed: between seasons 1920–21 and 1953–54 he led Rangers to 18 league championships, ten Scottish Cups, two Scottish League Cups and many other domestic trophies. The official record even omits several tournaments won in the war years of 1939–45. It is a matter of great regret that he was not around to manage Rangers in European competitions, which did not begin until the mid-1950s.

Struth displayed a sign in his office bearing the message that no man was greater than the club itself. However, it is hard to exaggerate the importance of Struth's contribution to the development of Rangers from a successful Scottish club into a famous institution of international renown. Struth was involved in all aspects of the club's business, shaped its character from within as well as superintending its successes on the playing field. Stories of his authoritarianism abound; under him players took a big chance on their careers if they stepped out of line. Despite this he invariably gained the loyalty and affections of his players. Testimonials to him have come from numerous players, all of them cognisant of how he brought the best out of them and gave them an imperishable pride in what they did. It is easy to make fun of the mores of a different and earlier age, yet the insistence on a certain dress code – including the regulation bowler hat – on punctuality, on first-class travel and even on sitting in the best seats in the cinema during their time off all instilled vital self-esteem and confidence, and the rewards were reaped on the pitch.

Struth's approach to management was distinguished by his meticulous attention to detail. Like legendary managers who came after him, Struth made it his business to know everything about his players. Bob McPhail recalls that he would surprise certain players by commenting on the pubs they were seen drinking in; he would even know if McPhail, who hailed from a religious family, had been in church on a particular Sunday. He would engage in psychological ploys to get the reaction from players he was looking for, often convincing them they could play and play invincibly when far from fully fit. Tommy Muirhead, a Rangers captain in the 1920s, said Struth had 'the discerning eye of a detective and the sure and nimble fingers of a surgeon'. While players who did not do their jobs could expect to feel his wrath – goalkeeper Bobby Brown was rapped painfully with Struth's walking stick after conceding a bad goal in the Scottish Cup final and told to 'pay attention to your work!' – he would always defend his team against any outside detractors with the full force of his intimidating persona. He was a driven man and he drove Rangers with a relentless desire to be the best.

Undoubtedly Struth's words and his direction carried conviction partly on account of the times; this was a Scotland in which community values centred on respectability and self-respect, and institutions like churches still wielded a powerful social and cultural influence. The 'work hard, play hard' ethic and the moral righteousness of the day were shared by all political parties, left and right. Authority figures, whether policemen, ministers, priests, or teachers, were given their place. Even the maverick inside forward Torry Gillick, one of the players who found total obedience hard to maintain, could only acknowledge the genius of his boss. Reflecting on the day he signed for the club in May 1933 he said, 'Mr Struth gave me the impression that I wasn't signing for a football club, but that I had entered the most magnificent organisation in the world. I did not know it then. But he was right.'

The dour and forbidding image of Struth that has passed into history was in a sense cultivated by the man himself but belied an often kind and thoughtful man. Celtic fan Hugh Savage was an apprentice plumber on a job at Ibrox in the 1930s, and he recalls in his memoir *Born up a Close* that it was obvious from what he saw that Struth commanded the respect of all around him, besides giving the young plumber some complimentary tickets. During the war while Willie Thornton was fighting abroad, Struth would send money regularly to his widowed mother, a fact like many others, which casts him in a very different light and one which he did not wish to become known. His personal foibles are, however, better known: the rack of suits in his office and the sartorial changes he would make during a normal working day; the canary which was his companion in his office from the 1930s and received a regular tipple of whisky from him to encourage it to sing; the mania for the players to take brisk walks around the Ibrox track in their suits before changing to their training gear.

It has often been noted that Struth's background was in athletics rather than football; he had been a champion sprinter and half-mile runner. As Rangers' first historian, John Allan, put it, Struth was 'a man well versed in the theories of preparing athletes for supreme tests of endurance'. His football experience consisted of a few years as trainer at Clyde before he was taken on in the same capacity at Rangers in 1914. He had built quite a reputation at Clyde and the 'Bully Wee' were reckoned to have become an exceptionally fit bunch of players during his time there. Rangers had, in fact, tried unsuccessfully to poach him in 1910. Throughout the First World War Struth worked effectively with team boss William Wilton. It was a formidable combination: Wilton with high standards, administrative acumen and a vision of the future, and Struth with his rigorous methods and an eye for the right players at the right time. Wilton's death was traumatic for the club; fortunately Struth was on hand to take over. A strong hand was needed to build on the remarkable foundations laid down by Wilton; Struth took to the task immediately.

Struth had learned a great deal from Wilton and he went on learning once he had taken the reins himself. Despite his stress on discipline and standards, Struth was not a one-trick pony. His managerial prowess accommodated a range of skills and insights. He was shrewd and aware at all times.

What Struth lacked in personal experience of playing football at an advanced level he made up for in man management. He always formed a close relationship with the team captain and entrusted him with carrying on to the pitch the values for which he stood, good sportsmanship not least. He also depended on the captain of the day to make the right decisions and organise his players during games. Struth famously held weekly tête-à-têtes with Davie Meiklejohn, the club captain for much of the 1920s and 1930s, and picked his brains about football matters including the strengths and weaknesses of the next opponents. Later, he would similarly depend on the strong presence and football know-how of 1940s skipper George Young. It was perhaps this very willingness to accept that his knowledge was limited in certain regards and to draw on the expertise of others that was an essential part of Struth's greatness as a manager. Nevertheless, he was by no means unschooled in the more technical aspects of the game, and he was to prove astute time and again in his choice of which players to sign, and which players to select in an effort to surprise and disorient the opposition. His first signing, in June 1920, was Queen's Park winger Alan Morton, a player destined to become one of the greatest Scottish internationals of all time.

The managers with whom Struth was most often compared were his Celtic counterpart and personal friend, Willie Maley, and the Arsenal boss, Herbert Chapman. Struth emerges well from such comparisons. His record relative to Maley's speaks for itself. Rangers racked up 14 championships to Celtic's four in the time when the two were in direct opposition, each winning six Scottish Cups in these years. Maley's status at Parkhead was akin to that of Struth at Ibrox – both were powerful characters that guarded the reputations of their respective clubs. However, behind the scenes there seems to have been doubts around the wisdom of Maley's judgement, while his mean-spirited treatment of Hoops legend Jimmy McGrory has seriously lowered his standing even among Celtic historians. Maley's style was on the face of it avuncular and folksy and in distinct contrast to Struth's sternness, but in both cases this was simply the public image. Moreover, Maley was pushed out of Celtic in 1940, and remained bitter about it. Struth certainly drew fire from critics for prolonging his stay in the manager's chair, but there was, nonetheless, a dignified handover to Scot Symon in 1954, and a genuine outpouring of sorrow on Struth's death two years later. His name has been conjoined with that of Rangers ever since, and if anything his place in the club's history has been burnished still more. As his obituary in the club handbook stated, 'He LIVED Rangers.'

As for Chapman, Struth shared the Englishman's vision for the progress and promotion of the game. Struth would periodically lament the low standard of competition in Scotland, not out of arrogance or conceit, simply concern about the value for money for the public, and the need for all good teams to be tested to their limits in order to improve still further. Hence Struth was eager to accept the challenge of matches against Chapman's Arsenal (see chapter 7), and crack continental outfits like Rapid Vienna and the Moscow Dynamos. The wins over Arsenal in 1933 perhaps gave him most pleasure in a managerial career studded with trophies and achievements.

What is not commonly known is that Struth might have been Chapman's successor. From what Willie Maley wrote in an article paying tribute to his rival and friend it seems that both he and Struth 'were sounded on the matter of being his [Chapman's] successor and the old tag of "East, West, Hame's best" worked on our respective feelings till we both declined with thanks . . .'

It is only really fair to assess managers, and players, in the context of their time and against their contemporaries and an examination of the men that have managed the club since Struth's retirement in 1954 is revealing. There could never be another Struth, although Rangers found in his successor, Scot Symon, someone who carried on the traditions of a restless quest for excellence on the field, and an all-round sense of dignity and class. However, the manner of Symon's dismissal in 1967 (see chapter 11) threatened to damage the club's standing as never before. The cruel treatment of a manager with such a distinguished record and a gentleman to boot disgusted a wide range of Scottish public opinion well beyond the ranks of Rangers fans. It was not considered in keeping with the standards set by the club.

Symon was greatly respected, and many players paid tribute to him for his work. However, he did have his critics among the playing staff. Some players, such as Eric Caldow and Billy Simpson, have not been reticent in criticising him. They accused Symon of being blatantly favourable to certain players, normally ones that he himself had signed after Struth had resigned, such as Sammy Baird. Both Caldow and Simpson had been recruited by his predecessor. This situation was an inevitable product of the changeover between Struth and Symon, and such was Struth's longevity that this kind of issue never arose.

But it is interesting to note that Struth had his favourites too; he was just more careful not to let anyone know about it and not to allow factions and cliques to develop. It is, indeed, an outstanding feature of Struth's career as manager that he appears to have enjoyed universal respect and loyalty within the dressing room. Certainly there were fractious episodes over wages and bonuses, such as the famous 1949 stand-off between captain George Young and the club, which was resolved in the club's favour with no ground given. But even these confrontations did not leave any lasting, injurious, impression.

Other Rangers managers to whom Struth has been compared include Willie Waddell, Jock Wallace, Graeme Souness, Dick Advocaat and Walter Smith. All left deep imprints of their personalities on the club. All took a Struth approach on matters of discipline and the upholding of the club's good name. Waddell, indeed, deliberately invoked the memory of his old boss in his quest to rescue the club's fortunes and reputation in 1969, although he did so with insufficient recognition of the changing times and the social and cultural effects of a turbulent decade. However, Waddell and then Wallace can be said to have restored pride, and wrung from less than great teams some truly great performances and achievements, the European Cup-Winners' Cup triumph of 1972 being the ultimate example. It might be added that Waddell resembled Struth significantly in the way he became the only figure who mattered at Ibrox and was, in effect, beyond the control of the board. This was never true of Symon, Wallace, Souness (at least after the arrival of David Murray), Advocaat or Smith.

Souness's drive, aspirations and determination were also in the Struth mould, although the controversies that surrounded him in a much more media-intrusive age often embroiled the club in unseemly rows, and his own indiscipline on the pitch in his early days as player–manager likewise tarnished the club's reputation. But it was Souness who had the courage, supported by Murray, to grasp the nettle of the sectarian question with the signing of Maurice Johnston (see chapter 13), and that courageous quality would have commended itself to Struth whatever the imponderables around the matter itself. Struth seems to have had no personal commitment to Rangers' all-Protestant character during his time as manager. He is on record as approaching Catholic players with a view to joining the club and seems only to have been dissuaded by the desire of the players themselves to leave things be. When Struth was trainer the club engaged the services of at least two Catholic players.

Advocaat's reputation as a disciplinarian was well founded, and he greatly admired and respected the club's history and traditions. However, in the late 20th and early 21st century world of astronomical transfer fees, players' agents and dressing room tantrums, he was not as successful as Struth in getting his way, and even when he did it could have debilitating consequences. In addition, Advocaat's credentials for bringing top-class players to Ibrox, much in evidence in his first two seasons, were seriously dented by some of his later acquisitions.

Finally, there might be said to be something of Struth in Walter Smith, a man who grew up listening to the folklore surrounding the club's greatest figure and imbibing what Rangers meant to its supporters and the wider world. In his two spells as manager Smith has achievements of Struth-like consistency to point to, and he has been a dignified ambassador for the club. Unfortunately for Smith, his second period in charge coincided with the gravest financial threat to the club since the 1880s, a state of affairs that Struth, happily, never had to contemplate.

There is, however, one blot on the Struth copybook, and that was his deep involvement in the divisive boardroom struggle in 1947 (see chapter 23) that saw long-time Rangers servant James Bowie ousted and Struth himself retain the post of manager and be named as a director of the club. Despite his failing health and losing a leg to gangrene in 1950 when he was 74, Struth carried on as manager until resigning in 1954. No manager as successful or as long-lasting as Struth could be without a certain ruthlessness and keen instinct for self-preservation. Nevertheless, this was an unedifying episode in Rangers' history, and the club may have suffered much more from it in a time of greater investigative scrutiny by the press and of a more lurid style of reporting. In fact this was a time when the difficulties of getting any information or news out of Ibrox were simply accepted as the way it was. In his construction of an aura of mystique around the club, the better to enhance its fascination to outsiders, Struth also cultivated a virtual cult of secretiveness. There was an 'untouchability' about the players and officials which was on another level entirely from other clubs.

Shortly before he retired, Struth was presented with a portrait of himself in oils, painted by the artist Charles Chapman. A presentation ceremony was conducted by the Glasgow Lord Provost, Tom Kerr, a Rangers fan of long standing, who told Struth that he was 'a Napoleon who had never met his Waterloo'. In his speech of thanks Struth uttered these unforgettable words:

'To be a Ranger is to sense the sacred trust of upholding all that such a name means in this shrine of football. They must be true in their conception of what the Ibrox tradition seeks from them. No true Ranger has ever failed in the tradition set him.

'Our very success, gained you will agree by skill, will draw more people than ever to see it. And that will benefit many more clubs than Rangers. Let the others come after us. We welcome the chase. It is healthy for all of us. We will never hide from it. Never fear, inevitably we shall have our years of failure, and when they arrive, we must reveal tolerance and sanity. No matter the days of anxiety that come our way, we shall emerge stronger because of the trials to be overcome. That has been the philosophy of the Rangers since the days of the gallant pioneers.'

Little wonder that these words still adorn supporters' emblems today, and are still recited by those who wish to guard Struth's secret.

4
STRUTH'S TEAMS

The mark of a great football manager, as Sir Alex Ferguson has shown over more recent years, is to build championship teams and keep them at a high level while all the time building new ones. Thus Bill Struth built and rebuilt Rangers' teams for more than 30 years, amassing the biggest single contribution of any Gers manager to the club's world-leading collection of trophies and honours. From his first season in 1920–21 through to his retirement in 1954 Rangers were almost constantly winners of titles and cups. Struth knew a thing or two about getting players to knit together as a group, about team spirit, about different capacities and styles complementing each other in a balanced unit, about when to introduce new players and leave out experienced ones, and about driving his players on to produce that extra ounce of effort and flash of magic to win the day.

It is worth stressing that Struth inherited a strong team after the tragic death of his predecessor William Wilton. Players who had been mainstays of the team under Wilton, such as James

Bowie, Bertie Manderson, Andy Cunningham and Sandy Archibald, all remained to serve Struth. However, it was under Struth that Davie Meiklejohn, a local Govan lad, blossomed into one of the finest half backs Scotland has ever produced. Within a few years of Struth taking over 'Meek' had become captain both of club and country. Moreover, he was the fulcrum of Struth's Rangers in the 1920s and 1930s and he would earn the trust and the faith of his boss like perhaps no other player. Meiklejohn would carry on to the park his manager's values and ambitions. He was equally respected and trusted by his teammates. One of them, Alan Morton, put it perfectly when he said at Meiklejohn's funeral in 1958 that 'No cause was ever lost when Davie was behind you.' It was, of course, Meiklejohn who took the responsibility of taking the penalty at a vital moment in the 1928 Scottish Cup final, a score that shattered the infamous cup 'hoodoo' (see chapter 5). It was also Meiklejohn who, sensing the seriousness of Celtic goalkeeper John Thomson's injury in the Old Firm match of September 1931, silenced the chanting Rangers fans behind Thomson's goal. Thomson tragically died later in hospital.

Alan Morton himself ranks with 'Meek' in the Ibrox all-time greats, his signing in 1920 a masterstroke on the part of Struth. Morton's wing play, whether for club or country, bamboozled opponents and inspired songs and rhymes that have been passed down the generations. Standing at only 5 foot 4 inches, he actually arranged the studs on his boots so that he might swivel and twist past defenders more easily, while his crossing was as accurate as his ball control was assured. He had the balance of a gymnast. It was all the result, as he himself testified, of endless practice as a boy in the backyard of his home, firing balls at a hole in the cellar door. Archie McKenzie, who watched Morton from the Ibrox terraces in the 1920s, recalled the famous 'Morton Lob' in the book *It's Rangers for Me?*: 'He specialised in lobbing the ball from the left wing into the goalmouth, which gave his forwards extra time to get into the penalty area and a great many goals were created in that way.'

Astonishingly, Morton continued his day job as a mining engineer during his time as a Rangers player, training with the club in the evenings. He wore a bowler and carried a brief-case to work and was given the sobriquet of 'The Wee Society Man' to go alongside that of 'The Wee Blue Devil' which was coined by an English journalist after Scotland's famous 5–1 win at Wembley in 1928. Archie McKenzie remembered the fans' parody of the popular song 'Red, Red, Robin': 'When the Wee Blue Devil goes bob, bob, bobbing along'. Every great team needs a truly extraordinary player, and Morton was that player during his 13 years at Ibrox. His service to Rangers continued on into the boardroom after he stopped playing, and a celebrated oil painting of him still hangs in the famous hallway at Ibrox.

If Morton terrorised opposing full backs, the sturdy frame of his inside left partner, Bob McPhail, caused havoc in the penalty box. McPhail, signed from Airdrie in 1927, was to score 281 goals for Rangers, including the club's 3,000th league goal in 1930. McPhail had big boots to fill; the man he replaced, Tommy Cairns, had played over 500 games for the club. It was a tribute to McPhail that the fans did not dwell on Cairns's departure. However, 'Greetin Boab', so called on account of his moaning on the pitch, benefited hugely from the physical presence of first Jimmy Fleming and then Jimmy Smith, both fearless centre forwards who made ample openings for McPhail as well as scoring plenty of goals themselves. In defence Ulsterman Billy 'Bucksy' McCandless, signed from Linfield in 1920, was a polished full back, while in 1923 Struth brought goalkeeper Tom Hamilton to Ibrox. Hamilton was to prove a redoubtable last line of defence, and he wrote himself into the history books with his stunning point-blank save from Celtic's Paddy Connolly in the 1928 Scottish Cup final to keep the game at 0–0 and inspire Rangers to Cup glory.

Football fans are never completely satisfied and there were many critical voices among the Rangers support during the Struth years even although titles and honours were being accumulated. One poor season, in 1925–26, saw the pressure mount on the manager to dispense with players some fans deemed to have reached 'the sare and yellow stage', as the boss put it in his contribution to the handbook for the following season. However, Struth knew that 'a blight of injuries' had taken its toll that previous season and that, restored to fitness, his boys still had much to offer. This was characteristic of his loyalty to his players and his ability to push them to achieve more when perhaps they themselves were beginning to believe their critics. The following season's league title vindicated Struth, and underlined the wisdom of his practice of blooding young players such as James Marshall and Dougie Gray while retaining a core of experience in the team. Gray would go on to make a record number of appearances for Rangers by the time he finally hung up his boots in 1947.

By 1929 Rangers were playing in front of Archibald Leitch's magnificent new grandstand and seeing off all comers for the title once more. However, it was the feats of season 1929–30 that truly befitted the newly developed Ibrox – a 'phenomenal' year in the retrospective view of Struth, and an historic one to this day. The 'Grand Slam Team', as they were dubbed at the time, has a strong claim to be the greatest ever in the club's colours. They won the league and cup Double for the second time in three seasons and added the Glasgow and Charity Cups to the Ibrox Trophy Room. Eight Rangers players were capped by Scotland that season: Morton, Fleming, Craig, Meiklejohn, Gray, Buchanan, Muirhead and Archibald, while McCandless and McDonald were picked for Ireland.

In the early 1930s Motherwell were the team that served the strongest challenge to Rangers, and the 'Steelmen' grabbed the title in 1931–32. Celtic were rarely in the running, so much so that Struth actually welcomed their 'reincarnation' in 1936 as good for the game. Before that, though, there was to be another Rangers Double in season 1933–34. This achievement was all the more gratifying given that Alan Morton had retired, and Bob McPhail was missing for much of the season through injury. Again, Struth made the changes he had to and trusted in veterans like Meiklejohn.

The side also featured a number of other tremendous players. At the back was the rugged figure of Jimmy Simpson (father of future Celtic goalkeeper Ronnie), supporters could also see the cultured play of George Brown at wing half and up front was the intimidating presence of Jimmy Smith at centre forward. Between the posts stood Jerry Dawson, the 'Prince of Goal-keepers' as he was known, with his commanding style and consistently dependable performances. He was to play 545 games for Rangers before leaving the club in 1945. Like many others the outbreak of war in effect cut short, or at least diluted, a brilliant career.

There was one player missing from the line-up, however, centre forward Sam English having been transferred to Liverpool in the summer of 1933. Dawson had been at the other end of the field in the fateful Old Firm clash at Ibrox in 1931 when his Celtic counterpart, the great John Thomson, dived at the onrushing English's feet and sustained a head injury from which he never recovered. In a sense English did not recover from the tragedy either; it haunted him for the rest of his time at Ibrox and wherever he later played, and he retired from the game five years later aged just 28. In stark contrast he left Ibrox having scored a record 44 league goals the previous season. It would be merely speculation to suggest how good Rangers might have been had he stayed at the club. But in the considered assessment of Bob McPhail, who partnered some legendary greats of the game such as Hughie Gallacher and Jimmy McGrory, English was the best of them all: 'He was lightning. He was fast on his feet and fast in thought ... He seemed to dart away from centre halves. Though he was just 5 foot 7½ inches in height, he was good with his head.' In recent years Rangers fans have made a special effort to commemorate his achievements in the short time he was at Ibrox. Born in Coleraine, English holds a fond place in the pantheon of Ulstermen who have donned the famous jersey, and his image has been captured strikingly in a wall mural in the Ravenhill Road area of Belfast.

The Ibrox team's continual success aroused envy, and there were those who sought to devalue it. In answer to them, the *Sports Dispatch* reflected on the season as follows: 'It has been said that the Rangers were lucky in some of their . . . games. Perhaps they were, but have they been lucky in all their successes through the years? No, neither this season nor in the past have they been indebted to luck for their triumphs. Their record makes any such charge ridiculous. Nor has it been bad luck that has kept other clubs in the background for so long a time.' The paper went on to suggest, perhaps only half-seriously, that the only way there would be a truly competitive league would be to have a handicap system in place.

Titles in 1934–35, 1936–37 and 1938–39 completed a remark-able decade for Rangers. As the Meiklejohns and McPhails hung up their boots, young talent like winger Willie Waddell, known as 'Deedle', who made his debut in 1938 in a friendly against Arsenal at the age of 17 and scored the winner, inside forward Jimmy Duncanson, wing half Scot Symon and centre half Willie Woodburn stepped forward. Success bred success. Struth showed faith in his players and they repaid it. Youth and experience blended felicitously as with all winning teams. If there was the occasional disappointment it tended to be high-lighted precisely because it was an aberration. One such incident, the failure to win the Empire Exhibition Cup in 1938, rankled on account of Ibrox being the venue for the tournament and where the exhibition was formally opened by King George VI and Queen Elizabeth, and the fact that Celtic were the ultimate winners.

As the rivalry between the two Glasgow clubs developed Rangers were to exact plenty of revenge in the immediate post-war years. This started in the 1946 Victory Cup semi-final replay at Hampden Park. Rangers won the match 2–0 but Celtic fans were in uproar as they had two players sent off and two others carried off. Two years later, in a league match at Ibrox, even the presence of former Irish Taoiseach and veteran of the Easter Rising, Eamon de Valera, failed to inspire the 'Bhoys'; Rangers prevailed 2–1 in front of 105,000 spectators. Celtic fans boycotted the 1949 New Year's league match at Ibrox, ostensibly over the referee's decision in the previous match not to send off Rangers' left half Sammy Cox for kicking out at Celtic's crowd-pleasing winger Charlie Tully. The suspicion remains that they feared their team would be soundly beaten anyway, which they were, 4–0.

On the pitch, Rangers' main rivals during these years were Hibernian, the two clubs winning the championship three times each between 1946–47 and 1951–52. Rangers' success in this period, most notably the Treble of 1948–49 (league, Scottish Cup and the League Cup, a follow-on from the wartime Southern League Cup), was built on the famous 'Iron Curtain' defence and this part of the team played together with rarely a break. In fact the Brown, Young and Shaw, McColl, Woodburn and Cox line-up, Scottish internationalists all, tripped off the tongue as easily as the later 1960s side, even if the attacking options were more often permutated. Up front, however, Rangers were blessed with the Waddell-Thornton routine: the winger would use his great pace to outstrip the full back and without looking up he would know in his mind's eye where to find Thornton with the deadly cross swung in on the run – it would be met with extraordinary frequency by the head or the boot of this predatory centre forward.

As the league title race went to the wire in April 1949, Dundee looked like pipping the Gers for the title. The final day saw Dundee needing a point away at Falkirk to ensure that Rangers' trip to Albion Rovers was a wasted one. In the event, Dundee went down 4–1 at Brockville Park, while a Thornton hat-trick inspired Rangers to win by the same scoreline and secure the third and last part of their historic Treble. Willie Thornton's goals underlined the worth to Rangers of this most modest of men. 'I never troubled how they went in – so long as they went in for Rangers,' he once said. The following year the worth of the famous Rangers rearguard was never better showcased than in the crucial league tussle with Hibs at Ibrox, when 101,000 saw Rangers salvage an all-important point in a goalless game. The following week's 2–2 draw against Third Lanark was enough to give Rangers the flag once more.

Two defensive stalwarts above all demand to be saluted: Willie Woodburn and George Young. Both were centre halves, but such were the claims of Woodburn after the war for the pivot's role, that Young moved to right back to accommodate him, replacing the long-serving Dougie Gray. Young would revert to centre half when Woodburn was forced out of the game by a 'sine die' suspension decreed by the Scottish Football authorities after a fourth sending-off in 1954. The ban was lifted two years later but by then Woodburn was 37 and out of sorts with the game. This sad coda to his career should not, however, overshadow the command of the defensive arts that Woodburn consistently displayed for club and country. He was a fierce and uncompromising competitor – the late Jimmy Reid, Scottish trade unionist, politician and Rangers fan, once remarked that Woodburn 'thought that it was against God's express wishes that Rangers should ever be beaten. When they were in any danger Willie became the Almighty's avenging sword' – but it was his temper and not dirty play which got him into trouble with officialdom. In his obituary of Woodburn the late Bob Crampsey, one of Scottish football's most authoritative historians, commented that 'almost all of his tackles were models of technique'. Nor was he a 'lump it up the park' man pure and simple; he could clear the ball intelligently, pass it accurately and read the game with perspicacity. There was, in fact, much of the modern playmaker about his style, even if it is his combativeness and steel which have remained longer in the memories of those who saw him. His nickname, 'Big Ben', was acquired after a challenge match in Lisbon against local side Benfica. At the after-match banquet Woodburn, clearly having wined bountifully on the local plonk, indulged in repeated toasts of 'Viva Benfica!' The 'sine die' verdict today seems ludicrously draconian when set against the disciplinary records of many contemporary players. Then again, players in the 1940s and 1950s were seldom cautioned and still more rarely sent off.

George 'Corky' Young was another player, like Meiklejohn, Greig, Shaw, Shearer and others, who typified Rangers. The *Rangers Historian* described him in telling detail: 'At 6 foot 2 inches and 15 stone, George Young certainly stood out on the field of play – but his stature in the game owed as much to his ability as to his build. True, with an angular, top-heavy physique, George was not quite poetry in motion, but nevertheless his aura, his presence and his talent were immense. Powerful in the air, his positional sense, anticipation and ability to read the game were second to none, more than compensating for any lack of mobility because of his size.' Like Woodburn, Young could strike long accurate passes out of defence and put Rangers suddenly into dangerous attacking positions. Like Davie Meiklejohn, he assumed penalty-taking responsibilities at pressurised moments. Moreover, such was his loyalty to Rangers that he turned down lucrative offers from England and accepted the Ibrox club's relatively meagre wages as simply a fact of life, something that went with the privilege of being a Ranger. Few others have been prepared to put club first as often as big George. In over 700 games for club and country he was booked just once, and that for speaking up for a teammate who had incurred the wrath of the referee. Willie Ormond, left winger in Hibernian's Famous Five forward line and later Scotland manager, paid the following tribute: 'George Young of Glasgow Rangers was the most natural captain, the most instinctive leader of men, that I ever encountered in football.' Young stopped playing in 1957 and it is interesting to speculate if he might have one day become Rangers manager. Instead, a bad experience of management at doomed-to-extinction Third Lanark alienated this most sportsmanlike and generous of gentlemen from the game he served so magnificently.

Although Rangers won another championship and Scottish Cup in 1952–53, speculation was rife about Struth standing down and criticism of the team's performances grew persistent. Rangers fans watched in dismay as their exhausted team exited the Coronation Cup, played at the end of the season, and Celtic lifted another 'Royal' trophy. When the team hit a slump during the early months of the 1953–54 campaign this critical chorus reached a crescendo. It even entered the letters page of the Glasgow Herald, a newspaper that then seldom condescended to give football significant coverage. Rangers fans wrote to complain about falling standards, alleging that the management was old-fashioned and incapable of the required degree of modernisation. One fan stated that the club was not the property of managers and directors but of 'decent working men without whose solid backing neither management nor players could exist'. This fan went on to say: 'The hardcore of supporting loyalty which has kept the club at their high financial level, despite the deflation in quality, does not expect a team who cannot be beaten: on the contrary the supporter yearns for a restoration of playing quality and dignity, the capacity to take a defeat in good spirit, and a return to the position where his team – in opposition to the best in other countries – produced that little bit extra which was once so characteristic of Rangers throughout the club's great history.' A shareholder wrote to criticise the management for spending money on floodlights rather than on new and young players, although quite how this tallied with observations about the need for modernisation is not clear.

Much of the criticism was arguably unfair, but parts of it were probably justified. Struth was still signing good players and spotting young talent; centre forward Billy Simpson and South African winger Johnny Hubbard would duly enter the club's Hall of Fame, while he gave a coltish Eric Caldow, a future club captain, his break. Several of Struth's players would still be around for the league title triumphs later in the decade. On the other hand, Struth had hung on longer than was good for the club and for himself. He simply could not face the end even although the health problems from which he was suffering were obvious to everyone around him. Following the boardroom drama that saw him installed as director in 1947 there was nobody prepared to tell him to go. It took a poor season – 1953–54 – with Rangers finishing fourth in the league, for the man himself to hand over the reins. There is a suggestion that he was hanging on to pass the torch to George Young but the latter still had a few years left in his legs. Maybe Struth was determined to wait till someone he thought was truly worthy of the honour was available, and this may have been the case with the man who eventually took over, Scot Symon. Regardless of this, it would all have been more appropriate had Struth retired a year earlier, having steered the team to yet more glory. In the light of his wonderful record the sniping at the end of his tenure seems churlish. Yet it is a good reminder of the game's old adage that you are only as good as your last result. At no club was this truer than Rangers.

5
THE BLUE RIBAND

Few episodes in Rangers' history have been recalled as vividly and as fondly as Scottish Cup triumphs, particularly the winning of the cup in 1928. This victory, by an ultimately resounding 4–0 margin over Celtic, ended a 25-year wait for glory in the competition. This quarter century seemed to last so long and Rangers' luck appeared so wretched, that it had become common to refer to it as a 'hoodoo' which had the club under a kind of malign spell. That the hoodoo was broken in such style in 1928, before a record Hampden Park crowd of 118,115, has ensured that this match is remembered as a milestone in the club's progress.

The match has assumed such significance because at the time the Scottish Cup was the Blue Riband of the sport. While connoisseurs would vouch for the league championship as the true test of a team's mettle over the whole season, there was no doubt about which competition truly captivated the ordinary fan. The cut-throat nature of the knockout format, combined with the final being played at the season's end in the national stadium, attracted greater attendances and a more feverish press than the league.

If eyebrows had been raised before the First World War about Rangers' relative lack of success in the tournament, then the post-war decade before the 1928 final saw ever-increasing bewilderment and intensive scrutiny of the team's supposed failings, not to mention plenty of jokes and digs at the club's expense. It was as if Rangers' dominance of the league championship in this decade only rendered all the more glaring their failures in the cup. For those of a supernatural bent, it had to be a jinx, a mocking hand of fate. For those more inclined to rational explanations, a theory grew about the supposed brittleness of the Ibrox men in such nerve-shredding jousts as one-off cup ties as opposed to the humdrum league fixtures. In contemporary parlance, it was alleged, quite simply, that the team did not have the 'bottle' for the cup. On the face of it this was absurd: the Rangers team of the 1920s was stuffed full of strong characters such as Meiklejohn, McCandless, Muirhead, Cunningham, McPhail and others. There were several inter-nationalists and, of course, the skills of such players as Alan Morton were beyond question. In addition manager Bill Struth had created a remarkable team spirit and an aura of excellence and ambition around the entire club.

Yet even Struth betrayed his exasperation about the team's puzzling Scottish Cup form. In his contributions to the club handbooks of the 1920s, he was to refer to disappointments and frustrations and attempted to reassure the fans that the ill fortune could not continue much longer. It may indeed have been the case that even such a talented, experienced, proud and redoubtable bunch of players had started to entertain doubts, if only subconsciously, at decisive moments in con-secutive seasons, that they had allowed the buzz of speculation, the mischievous press coverage and the supporters' fervent hopes and expectations to weigh them down. Maybe, as on the occasion of the 1922 final against Morton, the odds of playing with ten men for most of the match were simply too much to overcome, or, as in the 1925 semi-final, they just froze at the penultimate hurdle against a Celtic team they had coped with comfortably in the league. It was as if desperation was taking possession of the players and preventing them from playing their normal game.

On 14 April 1928 the stage was set for another titanic struggle. It was the 50th Scottish Cup final, between league leaders Rangers and cup-holders Celtic. The score at half-time was 0–0, thanks only to a wonder save by Rangers keeper Tom Hamilton who denied Celtic right winger Paddy Connolly a certain goal. Ten minutes after half-time the Rangers fans had ample cause to wonder if the hoodoo was again sending evil vibrations. At that moment, a goalbound shot from Rangers centre forward Jimmy Fleming was fisted out by Celtic defender Willie McStay. It appeared that the ball had actually crossed the line but the referee gave a penalty. In his often quoted words, first recorded by club historian John Allan in his book *Eleven Great Years*, the Gers skipper Davie Meiklejohn, entrusted with the responsibility of dispatching the kick, recalled the weight of history on his shoulders: 'I saw, in a flash, the whole picture of our striving to win the Cup. I saw all the dire flicks of fortune which had beaten us when we should have won. That ball should have been in the net. It was on the penalty spot instead. If I scored we would win; if I failed, we could be beaten. It was a moment of agony.'

At 4.01 p.m. the Rangers captain lashed the ball home to a deafening roar of both joy and relief. As he later confessed: 'For ten minutes afterwards I was in a trance. I have only a hazy idea of that period, and now I feel that if Celtic had realised my condition and had played on to me, I would have been clay in their hands.' Fortunately, the rest of the players seemed to feel liberated from the supposed hoodoo and proceeded to play with verve and ebullience. Three more goals were rattled in without reply. First McPhail, then winger Sandy Archibald with two late shots of pinpoint accuracy completed the tally. Celtic had no answer. In addition to scoring the vital penalty, Meiklejohn, despite his ten-minute 'trance', policed Celtic's danger man, Jimmy McGrory, expertly. It was, too, the culmination of a wonderful fortnight for the winger Alan Morton who had played such a big part in the 'Wembley Wizards' of Scotland's 5–1 hammering of the 'Auld Enemy' at the end of the previous month.

The celebrations at Hampden began long before full-time when the Rangers support serenaded their heroes with the lilting ballad 'The Bonnie Wells o'Wearie'. Post-match, the team were cheered all the way to the city centre, and the trophy later displayed to the audience at the Princess Theatre where the then resident comedian George West had to admit that his running joke about Rangers' failure in the tournament had now lost its currency.

Defeat in the 1929 final against Kilmarnock might have got the nerves jangling again were it not for the fact that this period witnessed the further development of one of the finest Rangers teams in the club's history. Season 1929–30 saw the team sweep the board, including the Scottish Cup after a replay against Partick Thistle. This was a hard-fought success, achieved with only ten men for all but 15 minutes of the match. Alan Morton was forced to go off with the recurrence of an injury suffered 11 days earlier playing for Scotland at Wembley. In his absence the Gers dug deep and took the cup with a winning goal from 'Tully' Craig. Around half a million people had watched Rangers during the cup games that season, a tribute to the drawing power of this great team and to the continuing glamour of the tournament itself.

Two years later Rangers again required a replay to win the trophy. A plucky Kilmarnock had been denied on the Saturday only by a goalkeeping error that had allowed Bob McPhail's 30-yard shot to creep in. Rangers upped a gear in the replay and won comfortably 3–0 with goals from Fleming, McPhail and the record goalscorer of the season, Sam English.

By then Rangers fans were finding it hard to remember the torture the cup had visited upon them in the past. Between 1934 and 1936 all the 'hoodoo' memories were banished completely as the team brought home the cup in all three seasons and emphasised their pre-eminent status in the Scottish game. In 1933–34 the first round saw a club record win of 14–2 against Blairgowrie at Ibrox. In contrast, Rangers had to work hard to progress in the later rounds. Hardest of all was a 2–1 victory over Hearts at a packed to overflowing Tynecastle in the third round replay. Rangers eventually met St Mirren in the final at Hampden Park. However, the team from Paisley, who had accounted for Celtic and the high-flying Motherwell en route to the final, were no match for the unstoppable Gers. This was Rangers in their pomp with Meiklejohn still commanding at the back, and McPhail still deadly up front even though he was actually carrying an injury. On the left wing Billy Nicholson's two-goal display stopped the fans from missing Morton too much. In their history of the Scottish Cup, Kevin McCarra and Hugh Keevins refer to this team as 'an awesome blend of youth and experience buttressed by a depth of reserve strength unsurpassed anywhere else in the country'.

The 1934–35 cup-winning campaign was a notable personal success for the club's top scorer and centre forward Jimmy Smith. He scored both goals in a 2–0 second round win against Third Lanark, all four in a 4–1 triumph in the quarter-final tie with Motherwell at Fir Park and twice in the final as Rangers ground out a 2–1 win against Hamilton Academical. Smith, after his playing days were over, went on to serve Rangers first as trainer then chief scout, and was the first to receive a pension from the club when he retired.

Rangers completed the hat-trick of cup final triumphs the following year with a 1–0 win over mid-table Third Lanark, whose Cathkin Park ground lay in the shadow of the national stadium. A Bob McPhail goal in the second minute of the match proved to be the difference. It was indeed to be McPhail's cup swansong, while the occasion was also the last of its kind experienced by the inspirational Meiklejohn, who lifted his last trophy for the club before his retirement at the end of the season.

Were it not for the intervention of the Second World War in 1939 Rangers would most likely have been back at Hampden for a Scottish Cup final before they eventually returned nine years later. However, Rangers had great success in the various competitions arranged in Scotland during the years of the conflict, winning at least three trophies in each of the seven seasons. Football had been reorganised at the onset of war and the normal competitions suspended. There were crowd restrictions, and a plethora of guest players depending on who was stationed in Scotland at any given time. Thus Rangers were able on occasion to field Stanley Matthews, the magical and elegant outside right from Stoke City among other star players. Matthews, however, turned out for other Scottish sides as well, one of them being Airdrie who were beaten, despite his presence, by Dundee United in the semi-final in of the Emergency War Cup 1940. In the final Rangers beat United 1–0 courtesy of a Jimmy Smith goal before 90,000 at Hampden.

When football returned to a semblance of normality in 1947–48, the Labour government, which had been elected in 1945, had nationalised several industries and were introducing a welfare state and a National Health Service in its quest for a 'New Jerusalem'. However, Hampden remained the Promised Land for the Scottish football fan. It was indeed an era of exceptional crowds, the ordeals of wartime forgotten in the throng and the continuing privations of peace in a ravaged and bankrupt Britain transcended at least for 90 minutes each week.

It was also a time when a force rose in the East, not Stalin's Russia, rather a Hibernian team that would enjoy the unprecedented success of winning the league championship in this particular year, and follow it up with further titles in the early 1950s. Matches between Rangers and Hibs in these years caught the public imagination like no other. If there was a simplistic tendency to characterise them as struggles between Rangers' 'Iron Curtain' defence and Hibernian's 'Famous Five' attack, this was still a glowing testimony to the compelling spectacle which meetings between them habitually provided. In any case Rangers would not have worried too much about their defenders receiving all the attention if it meant that Hibs neglected to prepare as sufficiently for the threat posed by the wing play of Willie Waddell and the lethal finishing of Willie Thornton. Both had forced their way into the Rangers team as callow youths before the war, and they established themselves in peacetime as a seasoned double-act probably without parallel in Rangers' history.

It was in fact their combination that undid Hibs in the 1947–48 Scottish Cup semi-final before an astonishing 143,570 at Hampden, the national ground now being employed for the penultimate as well as final stage of the competition. In the final Rangers needed a replay to defeat a gallant Morton side with a Billy Williamson goal. Williamson's appearances in a blue shirt had been rare, and his inclusion had involved shifting Thornton to inside forward. However, it was not the first time that a bold stroke pulled by Struth, belying his image as a stickler for solid dependability, had been well rewarded, and it would not be the last.

The following year a Rangers side on its way to a historic Treble of trophies – the League Cup had been introduced after the war – defeated East Fife, managed by future Gers boss and former player Scot Symon, in the semi-final. Thornton registered a hat-trick in this match. In fact, as McCarra and Keevins point out, he had not missed a match since being discharged from the army – he served with great distinction in the war – in September 1946. Over 108,000 watched Rangers vanquish Clyde 4–1 in the final, two of the victors' goals coming from the penalty spot courtesy of George Young. Young had become a cornerstone of the famed Ibrox defence, which also boasted the formidable figures of Jock 'Tiger' Shaw at left back and Willie 'Big Ben' Woodburn at centre half. Another of the Gers' goals came from that man Williamson who, bizarrely, was playing in only his second Scottish Cup game for the team.

His strike against Clyde meant that he had scored in each game – both cup finals.

Another Treble, this time of consecutive Scottish Cups, was completed the following year when East Fife, enjoying a halcyon period under Symon, provided the opposition at Hampden. A first-minute goal by Bob Findlay settled any Rangers nerves, and Thornton went on to add two more. The 'Iron Curtain' did not give a sniff to the men from Fife. In *The Rangers: A Complete History of Scotland's Greatest Football Club* author John Fairgrieve writes of the team's style in this period: 'Frequently, the other team battered furiously at the Rangers defence for long spells. It seemed, even, that the frenzied attackers were sometimes on top. Of course they were nothing of the sort. They were allowed to break their hearts . . . Picking the right moments, there would be a stabbing pass from Ian McColl or Sammy Cox to, say, Willie Waddell, only too eager to accept. And in perhaps three moves, the ball would be safely in the back of the other net . . . Lucky Rangers, cried those critics. But there was nothing lucky about it. Rangers scored goals methodically, just as they prevented goals methodically. They were essentially a team.'

Rangers quite simply played to their exceptional defensive strengths, secure in the knowledge that such unbending resistance would demoralise opponents. It was also as if the team were perfecting a style of play which would become known much later as 'hitting on the break'. It helped too, of course, that Rangers had talented offensive players and were able to master the art of turning defence instantaneously into attack.

Three years were to pass, however, before the Ibrox men again displayed their method of winning the cup. Bill Struth was now suffering severe ill health yet he struggled on in charge of the club he loved. The 1952–53 Scottish Cup was to be his tenth and last. Rangers faced Aberdeen in the final and a tense match finished 1–1. After only eight minutes Rangers lost keeper George Niven with a head injury and Young took over in goal until Niven, against medical advice, returned after half-time wearing a leather helmet. The wounded goalie still managed to prevent Aberdeen snatching the cup with some dramatic late saves. For the replay the ailing Struth contrived to pull off another of his inspired cup final changes – Ulsterman Billy Simpson was drafted in up front and he notched the all-important goal to send the great majority of the 112,000 crowd home delirious.

The 'Iron Curtain' years were drawing to a close, and Struth would retire in 1954. Rangers would not make the Scottish Cup final again till 1960 when they emerged victors over Kilmarnock. By now under the stewardship of Scot Symon, the club were entering another remarkable era and while the Scottish Cup would retain its prestige for years to come, arguably its heyday had coincided with that of Struth.

6
ALL THE WAY TO AMERICA

The Rangers players' reward for smashing the Scottish Cup 'hoodoo' in 1928 was a close season tour to the USA and Canada. This was the first club tour of these parts though it would be followed by an even more extensive visit two years later. These trips were certainly not holidays. The reputation and honour of Rangers and Scotland were at stake, and there was also the matter of boosting the popularity of 'soccer' in that continent.

Bill Struth relished the challenge of spreading the word about Rangers and the 'beautiful game'. He had organised tours abroad already in his management period, most notably to Denmark in 1921. He was in a football sense a classic 'New Frontiersman' and where better than America to venture in the cause of what he himself referred to as a 'missionary' endeavour. The fans at home also looked with interest on such exploits; reading about their heroes' victories across the ocean was a pleasant way of filling in the time before the start of another domestic season.

The Rangers party was given a rousing send-off on 19 May

1928. As the Anchor Line ship *California* made its way down the Clyde past the shipyards, large crowds gathered to wave. Besides the 16 players in the party there was Struth, two directors and the trainer. All were resplendent in the club blazers complete with new silk ties and souvenir badges specially struck for the trip.

On arrival in New York the Rangers party was met by hordes of expatriate Scots and the Clan Maclean Pipe Band. The tour kicked off in Philadelphia with an 8–2 hammering of a National League Select XI, and proceeded to Brooklyn where a healthy crowd of 15,000 saw a 4–0 victory over the Wanderers. The next opponents, Fall River Marksmen, included several players with experience of the Scottish league and they forced a scoreless draw. However, Rangers, who had to play a day after the previous match, were not best pleased by the rough-house tactics of the Fall River team, nor by the state of the Massachusetts pitch. In one of his reports back home player Andy Cunningham called it a 'travesty' of a football field: 'It was simply a rolled out mud patch; certainly absolutely level and smooth, but like concrete. There was not a single blade of grass anywhere.' The match was played in the most hostile atmosphere that the Ibrox men would experience on the tour, and the result in the circumstances was more than creditable. Rangers also had to play the game, which took place on a Sunday, without McPhail. The player, whose father was a church elder, did not wish to play on the Sabbath. Like the famous Scottish runner Eric Liddle, who had trained at Ibrox and had strong connections with the club, McPhail held to his personal convictions, at least on this occasion. Later on he was prevailed upon to play in another Sunday match when injured and tired players had to be rested.

A stop in Pittsburgh saw Rangers taken care of by the Clan Grant Society and given a formal banquet and reception. Cunningham commented on the distances travelled by exiled Scots to see the team play a local Select and win resoundingly by 9–0. He said that a number admitted to homesickness at seeing 'the once familiar blue jerseys'. A 1–1 draw in Detroit followed, with a Press Association report commenting that, 'The Scottish champions outplayed their rivals in every phase of the game, and the sensational work of the Detroit goalkeeper alone prevented them from rolling up a big tally.' Another unnamed correspondent made the following assessment of the visitors: 'They offered conclusive evidence as to why they are champions in this universal sport. To the uninitiated, as well as the average soccer fan, the skill displayed by the ensemble from the banks of the Clyde was a revelation, a concrete example of the great heights that can be reached in the realms of soccer development, and a wonderful lesson in the science of co-ordination of mind and muscle by a team of experts.' And all this for a drawn match and a rapidly tiring set of players.

It was on to Toronto next, and a tumultuous welcome from the many exiled Scots in that city. Almost 20,000 turned out for the match against Ulster United, which ended in a comfortable 7–0 victory for a revitalised Rangers clearly very much at home among their 'ain folk'. This was a record crowd for a soccer match in Canada. However, after the game the ranks of the squad were depleted with the return home of the team's two part-time players, Jimmy Fleming and Alan Morton, who had to resume their jobs. Another impressive display in a 5–1 win in Montreal followed, then it was back to the States and a 2–2 draw in Boston where a former Partick Thistle player, Johnny Ballantyne, netted both goals for the home side. Some welcome heavy rain accompanied a 4–1 win against Illinois All Stars in Chicago, before the tour concluded with a 6–0 win back in Brooklyn over another Select side.

It cannot be said that the American and Canadian press did not appreciate the efforts of Rangers and the high levels of skill and entertainment they brought. Before the Boston match the local paper the *Globe* referred to the Ibrox team as 'perhaps the world's foremost exponents of the fast and flashing game of soccer', going on to note admiringly that 'they move in perfect patterns on the field and their mastery of the ball is as exact and as scientific as that of a skilled billiard player.' Following the match in Montreal, the local paper the *Star* observed that Rangers played in 'a truly scientific style' and advised Canadians to 'emulate their coolness, quickness and precision in passing the ball' in order to advance the game in their country.

Rangers had come through undefeated and gladdened the hearts of the exiles. At the end of the tour the players relaxed by taking in a baseball match featuring the legendary 'Babe' Ruth of the New York Yankees. It was a visit that helped them realise the grip the sport had on the American public and the difficulties of promoting soccer as a popular alternative. Andy Cunningham seemed ambivalent about the sport's future in the USA, and was not impressed by either the condition of the pitches or the high admission prices. Yet clearly the club thought the adventure well worthwhile for preparations were soon made for another one.

The 1930 trip came at the close of an even more successful domestic season. The 1929–30 season had, quite simply, been the best year in the club's history when every competition entered had been won. Rangers' departure for Canada, where the tour was to commence this time, followed hard on the heels of the club's victory, albeit on the toss of a coin, over Celtic at Hampden in the Charity Cup final, the last trophy secured by what became known as the 'Grand Slam Team'. A large crowd of jubilant fans gathered at St Enoch's station and carried the players shoulder high to the train. 'Barriers had been erected to keep all out but ticket holders from the platform,' commented the *Glasgow Herald*, 'but the obstructions were swept aside, and the crowd swarmed round the reserved compartments. Round after round of cheers was given, and the last minutes of the wait were whiled away by singing of the followers team songs – "We Will Follow Rangers" etc.' The scenes at Greenock, where the party embarked for their voyage on the ocean liner *Andania*, were similarly raucous. The Rangers contingent were entertained on the way by the piano playing skills of their new wing half, George Brown, a graduate of Glasgow University.

The voyage itself was not without incident and there was a scare when the ship passed close by an iceberg.

But all was well and the ship berthed safely in Canada on schedule. On arrival in Toronto on 20 May the visitors were given another Scottish welcome, this time by the Old Times Club, a Govan organisation. The first match against Ulster United saw the Gers come from behind to win narrowly by 4–3, but the next encounter, with Hamilton Thistle, ended in a more comfortable 3–0 success. Hamilton, like Toronto, boasted a big Scottish colony, and they turned out in force. It was also the former hometown of Rangers' Belfast-born 'Whitey' MacDonald who was made captain for the day in recognition of the fact. Then it was over the border and down to New York and another tight 5–4 win over the New York Nationals after being 3–1 down. Some 20,000 were in attendance for the match, and the *Evening Times* reported that 'Blue caps and handkerchiefs were prominent all round.' Once again exiled Scots travelled in some cases hundreds of miles to be there. This game was quickly followed by a reunion with 1928 adversaries Fall River, a 'needle' match which saw Rangers narrowly prevail by 3–2 before a 10,000 crowd.

A return to Canada for the next leg of the tour involved matches in Montreal, Winnipeg, Vancouver, Edmonton, Victoria and Calgary, which were all won for the most part emphatically. In Calgary, during the pre-match preliminaries, Rangers chairman Duncan Graham accepted a magnificent buffalo head some two feet in length and weighing 110 pounds, a donation from the local St Andrews society. Then it was back to America and sterling displays in matches in Chicago, Detroit and Cleveland, the latter two taking place under floodlights, which was a novel experience for the players.

A 6–1 triumph in New York against Fall River concluded the tour most satisfactorily. In this last game Jimmy Smith scored a personal triumph with four brilliantly executed goals, while there was another 'first' for the club when manager Bill Struth substituted Morton with Nicholson after the winger had been hacked down in the first minute. Struth, who did not like the practice of using substitutes and hoped it would never enter the game back home, felt constrained to compromise his principles on this occasion. Morton had clearly been injured as part of a cynical ploy to weaken Rangers in this final chance for the Americans to best their visitors but Rangers were just as keen to maintain their hundred per cent record for the tour. Following the match Rangers offered terms to Fall River defender and ex-pat Scot Bob McAuley, who did not need to be asked twice. He became a Rangers player, and a Scottish inter-nationalist, the following season. McAuley indeed went on to be a scout for Rangers in the Edinburgh area in his later years and was the man who signed up both John Greig and Sandy Jardine.

So the tour ended with Rangers having played 14 matches and won all of them, a remarkable achievement after such a long domestic season. It certainly capped the record-breaking exploits of season 1929–30 in the finest of styles, and offered further proof, in the circumstances of the time, that the club was one of the best in the world. The team, looking 'very fit and bronzed', returned at the beginning of July to an appreciative reception from a large crowd of fans at Glasgow Central Station. They were back just in time for pre-season training.

In his message to the fans through the club handbook for 1930–31 Struth summed up the tour in these words: 'The western continent was traversed from shore to shore, and although the heavy programme of matches and the arduous travelling imposed a heavy strain on the players, they worthily upheld the prestige of the club and of Scottish football. It is safe to say that no more popular club has ever visited Canada and America. Everywhere the party went there were manifest-ations of welcome and reminders that the name and fame of the club are known far beyond the confines of Scotland.'

7
RULING BRITANNIA

As the country reeled from the economic woes of the 'Hungry Thirties' and observers nervously eyed the rise to power in Germany of Adolf Hitler and his Nazi Party, football fans in Britain had another matter of national importance to ponder. In September 1933, the champions of Scotland and England, Rangers and Arsenal, were to play a two-legged tie for the right to claim the title of Britain's Best.

Arsenal were managed by the colourful figure of Herbert Chapman, the Special One of his day who was applying the approach of Barnum and Bailey to the world of football. Chapman was ahead of his time in his promotion of floodlit football and his big money moves on the transfer market. He had transformed Arsenal from also-rans to champions and he thirsted for more accolades. He recognised in Rangers and their manager Bill Struth a club and a manager with similar ambition.

The scene was set for two epic encounters, which in the absence of European and other supra-national club competition would confer great honour and prestige to the victors. Appetites were whetted in Glasgow by the appearance of Scotsman Alex James, in many ways the focal point of the Arsenal side. James, a flamboyant and supremely confident player in the typical Scottish 'wee barra' mould – he stood at only five foot five inches tall – had been one of the 'Wembley Wizards' of five years before when Scotland had hammered England 5–1. The Gunners' attack, moreover, boasted internationalists like Cliff Bastin and David Jack, and their defence the experienced Eddie Hapgood.

Before the first match at Ibrox it appeared that James was getting his excuses in first. 'If the Rangers win', he said, 'it will not prove that they are the better side. Besides the advantage of playing before their own crowd, they will find Arsenal not at full strength.' In fact, Arsenal fielded a strong side in both legs with all their big names included in the line-ups. At Ibrox in front of 37,000 they were soundly beaten, the 2–0 scoreline hardly a reflection of Rangers' superiority. Goals by Jimmy Smith and Bob McPhail were the difference but the margin would have been much greater if it not been for the goalkeeping heroics of Arsenal's Frank Moss. The *Evening Times* reporter claimed that it all proved that 'our best can equal England's best'. As for James, he had by his standards a quiet match, although the reporter enjoyed his 'mannerisms'. Bob McPhail, a rival to James for the Scotland inside-forward position, recalled in his memoirs that James quizzed him after the match about his goal: 'He had a very active, inquiring mind and was always seeking opinions, ideas and thoughts from opponents or teammates.' James himself had to admit that his team were 'outclassed'. He commented: 'The crowd were crying out, "Gie Wee Alec a kick at the ball," but either Davie Meiklejohn, their right half, and Alec Stevenson, the inside right, did not hear, or else they were selfish, for I can tell you that I played no great part in the game.' He added generously that Rangers players like Brown, McPhail and Nicholson would walk into any side.

A week later during which time, amazingly, Rangers had

played both Celtic and Dundee, the return leg took place at Highbury. It was a day of joy for the many London-based Scots in attendance as Rangers romped to a 3–1 triumph and laid claim to the mantle of Champions of Britain. The jokes circulated about Chapman getting ready to buy half the Rangers team, and he probably would have taken out the cheque-book if there had been a realistic chance of Struth entertaining the prospect. As it transpired one of the Rangers scorers at Highbury, James Marshall, did eventually move to Arsenal a year later. All in all, this was another almighty shock to the English fans and journalists who had just about got the 1928 Wembley humiliation out of their system.

Before a crowd of 46,000 Arsenal took the lead through Lambert and Rangers were pressed back. The turning point came five minutes from before the interval when 'Doc' Marshall brought the Ibrox men level with a wonderful goal. The *Evening Times* reporter described it thus: 'Not for a moment did anyone think that when Brown took the ball about midfield and raced out to the left with it that a goal would result. The half back sent in a lightning cross to Marshall, who, running full tilt, took the pass just inside the penalty area. He seemed to drag the ball and at the same time fire in a terrific shot which beat Moss all the way. Arsenal players stood dumbfounded. They have seldom seen a counter like it.'

In the second half two Jimmy Fleming goals decided the match and even the London paper *Sporting Life* acknowledged that Arsenal were given 'an object lesson' in the art of teamwork. James was again a figure of frustration as the wily Meiklejohn shadowed him effectively. 'A London Scot' was moved to exclaim: 'Not since the memorable international at Wembley has Scotland displayed such footballing prowess. We who live in London are sick and tired of hearing that soccer in the north is third-rate. We needed an exhibition like last night's to point to when we next hear this undeserved criticism of football in the Old Country. Good old Rangers, and thanks very much!' McPhail recalled an Arsenal director coming into the dressing room to congratulate the Rangers team after the game and stating that on such form they would beat the England team.

A proud Struth later reflected in the club handbook: 'I doubt if any victory gave, or should have afforded, deeper satisfaction than the two splendid sporting wins against Arsenal at Ibrox and at Highbury.' He recalled how the London Scots had 'thronged' the Highbury ground and made a 'gala night' of their victory.

Rangers had scored a notable triumph for Scotland and Scottish football, as they would do in later competitive matches with Wolves and Leeds and in several friendly matches through the years. Games against English opposition were always spicy affairs with more at stake than just the reputations of the clubs involved. There would in the future be more titanic struggles, with Arsenal in particular, and the historic and close relationship between the clubs was recognised in 1973 when Rangers asked the Gunners to do them the honour of providing the opposition for the occasion of the club's centenary celebrations. Over 71,000 filled Ibrox on a night of great nostalgia. At half-time there was a parade of Ibrox legends including Bob McPhail, a hero of those memorable matches in 1933 when the outcome suggested that Rangers were Britain's best and a match for anyone the world over.

8

WAR AND A VISIT FROM THE DYNAMOS

There was plenty of football played in Scotland during the Second World War, and a real sense of competitiveness was maintained. It is important to stress this, since it has often been assumed that the war years constitute a virtual blank space in the history of the game in this country. In helping to keep up public morale during the crisis, football played a not insignificant part in the war effort.

Rangers especially deserve credit for their contribution. Bill Struth strove to field strong line-ups, including guest players on occasion, as was the case with other clubs during this period. The most famous such guest was English winger Stanley Matthews who played twice for the Gers. With the league split along regional lines to minimise travel, Rangers actually had a presence in both, fielding a second team in the North-Eastern League, a championship they actually won in 1941–42. The first team, moreover, won 25 out of the 34 competitions played during the course of the war, maintaining a high level of entertainment for the public. Rangers' attitude to their wartime responsibilities stood in stark contrast to that of their rivals across the city whose commitment has been described as 'tepid' by football historian Bob Crampsey.

Rangers also had several players serving in the armed forces, including Willie Thornton who did not play for the club for two years, and future trainer Davie Kinnear. Thornton was to win a medal for his bravery in combat. Other players were found work in reserved occupations, mostly in nearby Clydeside work-shops, manufacturing munitions. The club also played many matches for war charities and army funds. When hostilities finally ceased in 1945, Struth reflected on the club's contrib-ution to the wartime football scene and commented: 'We on the home front, charged with a duty to maintain the morale of the workers in the factories, shipyards and other branches of industry, can claim to have played our part in the victorious end of the German war, and as far as football is concerned it may be truly said that no request made to the clubs for any war object was left unanswered.'

The standard of football varied during the war and there were some bizarre results. Rangers found themselves on the end of an 8–1 hammering by Hibs in Edinburgh in 1941, but blitzed Celtic by the same score at Ibrox on New Year's Day 1943, still a record score for an Old Firm match. This latter game was watched by around 30,000 and featured the usual controversies. Indiscipline and harassment of the referee resulted in Celtic having two players sent off following George Young's spectacular 50-yard free kick that gave Rangers a 4–1 lead in the second half. From that point on it was a question of how many. However, this match may not have taken place if the authorities had followed through on a threat to ban Old Firm encounters while the war lasted. This threat was aired in 1941 in the wake of rioting on the part of Celtic fans at Ibrox, and the Parkhead club had their ground closed for a month as punishment. It is fair to say that old antagonisms between the supporters of an Irish political nature were not helped in wartime and in the early post-war years, first by the neutrality of Eire in the war, and then by her withdrawal from the British Commonwealth amid a feverish Irish unity campaign in the late 1940s.

While Rangers' record during the war was commendable, it was still an unwelcome interruption, or in some cases an unfortunate ending, to brilliant careers. Less appreciated has been the loss of young players to the armed forces who never resumed football to a serious level. Even in the 1946–47 club handbook Bill Struth commented regretfully on the many youngsters who were still being called up to deal with the frequent conflicts that arose in the uncertain times of the war's aftermath.

When the elation of the war's victorious ending had evaporated, Britain faced a long period of austerity with shortages and the persistence of rationing. A practically bankrupt country was forced to seek aid from its wartime ally, the USA. In November 1945 the visit to Britain of a football team from another allied country, the Soviet Union, fired the imagination of a long-suffering populace.

Moscow Dynamo's four-match British tour has gone into folklore. Huge crowds turned out to see them play Chelsea and Arsenal in London and Cardiff City in Wales. A 3–3 draw in the first match was followed by a thrilling 4–3 win in the second before Cardiff were swamped to the tune of 10–1. Although many other English clubs had petitioned to play the Russians, it was clearly felt that a game in Scotland would be appropriate. There was only one club the Dynamos could play. As Glasgow Lord Provost Hector McNeill said in his welcome to the visitors, it was only right that they should come to 'the centre of sport and industry to play that other great team, Glasgow Rangers'. He added that it was 'one of the greatest things which had ever happened in Scottish sport'.

It seemed that everyone in Scotland wanted to see the game. The long queues for tickets when they went on sale in Glasgow virtually brought the city centre to a halt, and when thousands were left disappointed fights broke out. The press fed the public every morsel of news they could find about the Russians and in particular their outstanding players such as goalkeeper Alexei

'Tiger' Khomich, club captain Mikhail Semichastny and forward Konstantin Archangelski. There was also pre-match controversy when the Russians refused to allow Rangers to field Jimmy Caskie whose transfer from Everton was in the process of being completed, on the grounds that his name was not on the original list of Rangers players they had demanded in advance. Dynamo believed they had been tricked by Arsenal fielding several 'guests' in their match in London and were determined not to let the same thing happen again.

Officially, 90,000 attended the match on the afternoon of 28 November but the true figure was probably some 10,000 more. Tickets were bought on the 'black market' for up to ten times their face value. Many thousands simply downed tools at work or 'plonked' school. Given the massive interest aroused by the visitors this could never be a mere 'friendly'. From the start Rangers were 'up for it' but it was the Dynamos who struck first from a free-kick inside two minutes. Rangers' full-throttle response earned them a penalty when Williamson was brought down but Khomich saved Waddell's spot kick. Regaining the initiative the Russians then doubled their lead with a goal of distinction resulting from a spellbinding set of passes which even the stunned crowd had to applaud. For a short while it seemed that Rangers were going to be overwhelmed, but they dug deep and a scrambled Jimmy Smith goal five minutes before half-time got the fans roaring again.

The second half was memorable for the continuous Rangers pressure, the heroics of Khomich, and farcical incidents such as when Torry Gillick and Jock Shaw noticed that the Russians had 12 men on the pitch at one brief point in the match. This was probably the outcome of the Russians' use of substitutes, something considered devious and 'foreign' from a British football perspective, and something with which Rangers again struggled during their Russian tour 17 years later (see chapter 10). The Dynamos were as resilient in defence as they were incisive in attack, but 12 minutes from time Williamson was adjudged – by a Scottish linesman – to have been impeded in the box and a penalty was awarded. As the vast Ibrox throng held its collective breath, George Young took over the spot-kick duties and lashed his shot into the net. The remainder of the match saw the Gers press for the winner and almost get it when Watkins's drive cannoned off a post. However, few would have quibbled with the 2–2 final score.

As David Downing put it in *Passovotchka*, his book on the Russians' British visit: 'Rangers had upheld British pride against the foreigner and Scottish pride against the English; Dynamo were bloodied but had retained their unbeaten record. The Russians could have put the game beyond reach long before half-time; Rangers had looked the likeliest winners at the end.' Praising the Rangers' fightback, Scotland's foremost football journalist of the day Rex Kingsley wrote: 'I do not honestly believe that any other club side in Britain could have done it. Certainly none has. For no match in the history of the game has been so tense with patriotic fervour and fever.'

The tensions evaporated with the final whistle and comradeship was much on display at the post-match banquet, in some contrast to the pre-match squabbles and the keenly contested game itself. In his autobiography George Young recalled the chumminess between the players in spite of the obvious language barrier, but acknowledges that the Rangers players could not prevail upon their Russian counterparts to partake of a dram of whisky albeit that 'Tiger' Khomich's eyes kept straying to the bottle. In his address at the banquet Rangers' chairman James Bowie remarked that people had wanted to attend the match not just for the football but also 'to pay tribute to their Russian allies in the war'.

So began a relationship with the Moscow Dynamo club that would be renewed with another challenge match at Ibrox on the 25th anniversary of the original game. Rangers won this by the only goal of the game. Rangers were also to prevail two years later in an altogether more momentous encounter in Barcelona (see chapter 19), sealing the historic relationship that had developed between the clubs.

9

'RITCHIE, SHEARER, CALDOW . . .'

They inspired hero-worship unprecedented even by the standards of Rangers teams of the past. They were celebrated in
songs, books, playground ditties and father-to-son anecdotes.
They possessed a player who perhaps more than anyone
else became emblematic of the arrogant allure and thwarted
dreams of the Scottish game. They wrote a chapter in Rangers
history which still produces the warmest glow among supporters.

'They' are the Rangers teams of the first half of the 1960s.
'It's Ritchie, Shearer, Provan, John Greig, MacKinnon too; It's
Baxter, Henderson, George McLean they proudly wear the blue;
there's Millar, Brand and Wilson what better could you want?'
So ran one song of the time: 'R-A-N-G-E-R-S', the flip-side of
Bluenose comedian Lex MacLean's more famous 'Every Other
Saturday', which is still a fans' favourite today. The players
listed in that song were the mainstays of the Treble-winning
side of 1963–64, in effect the culmination of a remarkable, if
tragically brief, era. For many older fans the team line-up
would read: Ritchie, Shearer, Caldow, Greig, MacKinnon,

Baxter, Henderson, MacMillan, Millar, Brand and Wilson. On paper this is probably the strongest Ibrox line-up of the early 1960s, and it is the team taken as the template of author Bob McCallum's contention in his book *The Best of the Blues* that it is the finest Scottish club side of all time.

The snag here is that McCallum's side only actually played together on five occasions, a fact pointed out by Robert McElroy, editor of the *Rangers Historian*. It is true that they were undefeated in those five matches, but it remains too flimsy a basis for firm judgements. Nevertheless, there was a consistency of selection of Rangers' teams in this period – as there had been in earlier times such as the post-war years of the famous 'Iron Curtain' defence. In common with other great sides a pattern was established and developed in these seasons with new players carefully chosen to fit into it. There were no upheavals; changes were made sparingly. This was an era well before the prevalence of what we now call 'squads' and tactical ploys such as 'rotation'.

Yet this truly was a distinctive period in Rangers' history. In May 1962 when Uruguay arrived to play Scotland at Hampden, the visitors' first outing was to see a virtual reserve Rangers side play: 'We have heard so much about your Glasgow Rangers,' commented the Uruguay spokesman, 'we decided we couldn't miss the chance to study them. We know they will not have a full team, but nevertheless to go back to Uruguay without seeing them play would be entirely wrong.'

Although much has been made over the years of the robust playing style of Rangers teams, and journalists and commentators have long been fond of characterising Rangers – sometimes favourably, sometimes critically – in militaristic terms, the early 1960s saw much more than a physical style of play. However much the club's supporters chose to celebrate the hard and dour indomitability of defenders Harold Davis and John Greig, the teams of this period gave them many reasons to celebrate skill, artistry, and – indeed – genius as well. If, in the past, the ball skills of an Alan Morton or a Torry Gillick had not received the popular acclaim quite equal to the reverence accorded to the courage and strength of a Woodburn or a 'Tiger' Shaw, then, for at least a few seasons, the fans could not but salute above all the luminous craft of Jim Baxter, the precision passing of Ian MacMillan, the scintillating wing play of Willie Henderson and Davie Wilson, and the art of the goal poacher in Ralph Brand or Jim Forrest.

The phenomenon of Rangers in the early 1960s confounds the lazy stereotypes so beloved of sportswriters: in particular, the physical and dour Rangers continuing to play in the image of their poker-faced and authoritarian maker Bill Struth, contrasted with the happy-go-lucky Celts from across the city forever mirrored in characters like 'Cheeky' Charlie Tully or 'Jinky' Johnstone. The truth is, of course, always more complex. Perhaps, too, Rangers supporters need to be more appreciative of the contributions made year by year by skilful players of the highest order, and ensure that they are not overshadowed in the folklore of the club.

The bountiful years of the 1960s were the product of the club's slow but sure progress under the management of Struth's successor, Scot Symon. Following some initial transitional hiccups, Rangers secured the League championship in 1955–56, 1956–57 and 1958–59. These were crucial achievements, for they permitted the club entry to the new European Cup, the premier competition, and Rangers' early experiences in this tournament were often memorable (see chapter 18) and went a long way in strengthening the club's reputation both at home and abroad. However, there was no Scottish Cup success between 1952–53 and 1959–60, and this competition enthralled and enthused the fans at this time like no other. Moreover, there were no League Cup successes either, and Rangers' sole appearance in the final during the 1950s was probably the darkest day in their history, the 7–1 reverse to Celtic, a result that cast a shadow over even the most creditable results of the next couple of seasons. The Rangers teams of the second half of the 1950s boasted some entertainers such as the South

African striker, Don Kichenbrand, nicknamed 'The Rhino' on account of his burly physique and rumbustious style, and his compatriot, pint-sized winger Johnny Hubbard. Hubbard's scoring record for penalty kicks – 54 out of 57 – still stands for the club today. Nonetheless, those teams lacked a certain spark that their 1960s successors possessed.

Between 1959–60 and 1963–64 Rangers lifted the Scottish and League Cups four times each and were champions on three occasions. They racked up these trophies by playing some of the best football in the club's history. It should not be forgotten either that in these years the competition in Scotland was keen: there was not the Old Firm dominance that came to characterise later decades and indeed had been the norm before the Second World War. Hearts were champions in 1959–60; Dundee in 1961–62 and Kilmarnock in 1964–65. Hibs, Aberdeen, Motherwell and Dunfermline all boasted excellent sides. There was not the economic gap between the Old Firm and the other Scottish clubs which later opened up to become a veritable canyon. Players were still paid relatively modest wages, and it was only the winning bonuses which put the Rangers players out in front in terms of higher earnings. The club, indeed, traded off its name: its glamour and prestige attracted players more than the promise of wealth.

This was also an era notable for the impact made by Scottish players in England. Examples of great Scottish players being transferred to the top level of the English League are numerous: Alan Gilzean and Charlie Cooke from Dundee to Spurs and Chelsea; Dave Mackay and Alex Young from Hearts to Spurs and Everton; Ian St John from Motherwell to Liverpool; Ian Ure from Dundee to Arsenal; Pat Crerand from Celtic to Manchester United; and, in 1965, most regrettably of all, Jim Baxter from Rangers to Sunderland. Indeed, the thought arises as to whether Rangers, if they had dispensed with their wage restrictions and seen fit to invest in the transfer market on the lines of the top clubs in England, could have strengthened still further the great teams of this era, and prolonged success during this decade. Might Cooke, for example, have replaced Ian MacMillan and teamed up with Baxter? Although it seems sacrilegious to suggest breaking up the Millar-Brand attacking partnership, it is tempting all the same to imagine the team with St John or Gilzean leading the line.

Hypothetical speculation aside, the Rangers of the early 1960s can certainly advance a claim to the title of Scotland's greatest. Like all outstanding teams they were a felicitous blend: strength and skill; combativeness and trickery; solidity and flair. The mental toughness and the self-confidence were also clearly in evidence.

In Jim Baxter, purchased from Raith Rovers in the close season of 1960, they had a genius: his imperious talents and his 'gallus' demeanour spread confidence and belief through the team and intimidated opponents. In the words of football scribe John Moynihan in his classic 1960s book *The Soccer Syndrome*, Baxter could 'tune a game to his own composition, offering contempt through his long striding runs and shattering passes'. He could also exasperate his own teammates: Davie Wilson recalls having regularly to hold his run while Baxter dribbled around three or four opponents before releasing him with a killer pass. For Baxter, that was what he was there to do: to entertain and inspire and make deposits in the fans' memory banks, not simply to do the functional thing. His teammates may not have fully realised it in the heat of the matches but Baxter's possession play and mickey taking were devastating weapons when it came to demoralising opposing teams. Harold Davis has reflected on the way Scot Symon indulged Baxter like no other player at the club, and he feels that 'Slim Jim' would sometimes not stir himself to do what he was capable of on the pitch. Some of these points may have validity. However, it has to be said that if Symon was over-indulgent he showed perspicacity in doing so. Handling Baxter during the time he was at Ibrox was one of Symon's triumphs as a manager. It would have been futile to try to apply the same rules to a player and a character like Baxter. Had Symon attempted to do so

Baxter would probably have been lost to Rangers earlier and maybe to the game as a whole.

The acquisition of Baxter was the catalyst for the greatness that followed and he transformed Rangers on the field while his cult of personality off it gave the club's broader image a welcome dash of colour and fun. Baxter's massive popularity in Scotland was, of course, partly down to his impish performances for Scotland against England in 1963 and 1967, the latter occasion when he was playing for Nottingham Forest. Nevertheless, he was first and foremost a Ranger and he identified with the club without reservation until he died in 2001.

It may be legitimately observed that this Rangers side of the early 1960s, although they were the first British club to reach a European final – in the Cup-Winners' Cup tournament of 1960–61 – following a semi-final appearance in the European Cup itself the previous year, did not make the breakthrough in this arena. Critics will point to the emphatic defeat over two legs to Tottenham Hotspur in the Cup-Winners' Cup of 1962–63, and to Real Madrid in the European Cup in 1963–64. These setbacks showed how far the team had yet to go to reach the pinnacle of the game. Yet it is also important to remember that the game itself and the level of competition – as well as individual teams – fluctuates in quality. In this respect Rangers were most unfortunate. The era of Ritchie, Shearer, Caldow, Provan et al. coincided with that of the two best European sides of the post-war years. Spurs went on to win the Cup-Winners' Cup that season, and the Real Madrid of Puskas, Di Stefano and Gento were simply without peer. With all due respect to Celtic's later achievement, nobody they faced in 1966–67 on their way to European Cup glory came close, not even Inter Milan, a team that a lame, Baxterless Rangers side came close to eliminating in 1964–65 when Inter were much stronger.

But the question still has to be asked as to whether the Rangers management got the best out of the exceptional bunch of players who formed the great sides of the early 1960s. Scot Symon was undoubtedly highly regarded by many players and considered to be a true gentleman – 'a thoroughbred of a man' in the words of Baxter. Some players seemed to have been comfortable with his conventional approach and his tendency to let the players sort out any problems on the pitch themselves. This after all was a time-honoured practice; Symon and Struth before him had entrusted team captains like George Young and Davie Meiklejohn to take charge.

On the other hand, there are those who, over the passing years, have voiced criticisms ranging from mild to stringent about Symon's style and the way that, in retrospect, he did not tap the players' full potential. Not long after he left Rangers Ian MacMillan squarely blamed Symon for a lack of tactical awareness in vital European ties such as the Eintracht Frankfurt European Cup semi-final of 1959–60. In the first leg of this tie, in West Germany, the score at half-time was 1–1. The situation seemed to call for the team to play it tight and see out the game with the second leg to come at Ibrox. Instead the team continued to play almost as if the opposition was a Scottish club, and the final score was a humiliating 6–1 defeat. The tie in effect was over there and then. By contrast, Jock Stein's Celtic, renowned for their attacking virtues, played the dourly defensive game that was required in the away leg of the European Cup semi-final of 1966–67 against Dukla Prague. Of course, the game had changed somewhat in the interim. Nonetheless, there seemed to be a stubborn refusal on Symon's part to prepare and instruct the team to play a different kind of game. In his book *A Captain's Part* John Greig, while supportive of Symon's overall record, referred to his resistance to new developments in the game even although he had an impressive understanding of them, 'He seemed to prefer the styles he had always known,' said Greig. More recently, in an interview on Rangers TV, Harold Davis also depicted Symon as being too set in his ways and accused him of allowing Rangers to 'slip back'. For Davis, Symon did not learn sufficiently from European experience in relation to possession play, and did not do enough in training to work on technical deficiencies or underdeveloped skills. 'We all realised we had to change but we weren't allowed to,' said Davis. He went on to cite the example of a match at Tynecastle in 1960 when Rangers lost goalkeeper Billy Ritchie to injury early on and the ten remaining players (there were no subs in this era) had to take matters into their own hands. 'Let's play some football,' Davis recalls someone saying, and the team proceeded to play the great stuff of which they were capable but did not often produce. The handicapped Gers team passed a strong Hearts, then reigning champions, off the pitch and won 3–1.

Looking back and viewing the film of the 1963–64 Scottish Cup final victory over Dundee at Hampden also serves to show the heights the team could reach. The quality of this game was exceptional: it was as gripping a match as any in the tournament's long and illustrious history. Dundee played their part in the drama, although it would be more accurate to say that it was their goalkeeper, Bert Slater, who kept them in it with a series of improbable saves. However, Rangers just kept coming as club director and legend Alan Morton later put it: 'Down the years Rangers have shown – as we witnessed again here – that we never give up as long as there is a second left in which we can win. The crowd saw once more what Rangers' tradition and courage could mean. Dundee had lots of spirit and pluck. True, but that very fact enhanced our achievement.' The thrilling sight of the sweeping move up the field which led to Brand's climactic goal in the final seconds was a cameo of the best of an era. 'Hampden aflame with excitement!' roared the one and only Arthur Montford in his television commentary as the classic match concluded.

In fact it was also to be the end of an era. It is certainly true that Baxter's departure at the end of the following season brought the curtain down officially, yet the team had simply not been the same since that glorious day against Dundee. Unrest over wages and speculation about players leaving brought a disastrous start to the 1964–65 season from which the team never really recovered, although the League Cup final win over

Celtic in October, masterminded by Baxter again, appeared to signal business as usual. Another iconic Baxter moment – when as skipper for the day he swaggered around on the pitch after the match tossing the cup high into the air – recalled the sight of him strolling triumphant from the field after the 1963 Cup final replay with the match ball up his shirt. He had tormented Celtic on a night when the gloom left over from the League Cup final of six years before was finally dispelled.

If Baxter conducted the orchestra, then Willie Henderson was its magical fiddler. Both were irrepressible mavericks, utterly in tune with the raffish and irreverent mood of the times. As pop stars like the Beatles and the Dennistoun-born Rangers fan Lulu were idolised, so too were footballers like Baxter and Henderson. New concepts of fame and celebrity and popular culture were being fashioned as Britain finally threw off the shackles of cultural conservatism and social deference. Baxter's notoriety indeed foreshadowed that of the Irish football wizard George Best. The difference was that the gambling and the drinking, and the rows with managers schooled in a different era who tried to steady their wayward charges, were less publicised when Baxter was at his peak with Rangers. It was said by his biographer, Ken Gallacher, that Baxter turned the St Enoch's hotel in Glasgow city centre, where Rangers and their fans would then traditionally gather to celebrate trophy wins, into his personal nightclub. Henderson, an avid boxing fan, palled up with Muhammad Ali (then still known as Cassius Clay) when the latter visited Scotland for an exhibition bout. Between them Baxter and Henderson gave Rangers' image a makeover, however ephemerally.

Rangers' troubles on the pitch in 1964–65 were in large part down to Henderson's early season absence with bunion problems and the tragic leg-break suffered by Baxter in Vienna seconds before the end of a consummate personal performance in Rangers' impressive 2–0 win over the local side Rapid in the European Cup. Baxter missed the ensuing quarter-final tie against Inter Milan, returning half-fit shortly afterwards to lead the team to a 2–1 defeat at Hibernian in the Scottish Cup. Henderson too was not quite the devastating winger he had been prior to the bunion operation. A measure of his cult status came when thousands turned up at Ibrox for his return in a reserve match. The roar when Willie, early on, flicked the ball over the left back's head and scampered down the wing was of hope for the resumption of the happy times when he tormented opposing defenders both in the light blue of Rangers and the dark blue of Scotland.

Baxter's transfer to Sunderland – his lifestyle had scared off more eminent English clubs – removed the 'greatness' ingredient from Rangers just at the time when Jock Stein was implanting it – in his own way – at Celtic. Without Baxter even talented stars like Henderson were diminished. The times ahead would be trying indeed.

But the proper note to end a chapter on the Rangers of the early 1960s is not a sombre one. Better to focus again on the glory days, the so 'Easy, Easy' outclassing of Celtic that it became simply routine. In season 1963–64, for example, Rangers beat Celtic five times out of five, scoring eleven goals with the loss of one. Or on the night when an injury-ravaged Rangers were reduced to ten men after 30 minutes yet drove themselves on to victory over Hibs to virtually ensure the 1960–61 league title. Or the silverware that graced the shrine to historic laurels that was the new Ibrox Trophy Room. Or on the stunning blow struck for Scotland on the Russian tour of 1962 and the rapturous welcome home on the part of those fans who, in their blue scarves, flat bunnets and woolly 'tammies', packed the terraces of Ibrox and Hampden and other grounds the length and breadth of the country.

On the way to becoming the first British club to reach a major European final in 1960–61, Rangers had to eliminate Wolverhampton Wanderers, a powerful side who had recently been English champions. An injury-hit Rangers endured the further handicap of Harold Davis pulling up after seven minutes and having to hobble out the rest of the match on the wing.

After repelling Wolves pressure, Rangers struck through Alex Scott, and late in the game Ralph Brand added a second. The novelist Alan Spence, born and raised a Bluenose in Govan, recalls Davis dragging himself through on 'willpower alone, while the whole 80,000 crowd sang "Follow Follow" like I'd never heard before, the noise vibrating in the soles of my feet and right up my spine, overwhelming.' In the second leg, with some 15,000 Rangers fans having journeyed south, the team again dug deep, Billy Ritchie pulled off a wonder save early on, and a 1–1 draw was ultimately secured. The fans invaded the pitch at the end and carried the players off shoulder-high. The citizens of Wolverhampton had never seen anything like it, 'The scenes, as dozens of banners, Union Jacks and Lion Rampant flags were paraded through the city centre by the singing and cheering multitude, resembled nothing less than a cross between Glasgow on Hogmanay and VE night', penned the correspondent of the Glasgow *Evening Times*, going on to say that the celebrations continued through the night and choruses of 'We Will Follow On' greeted the dawn.

Even today 'When the Rangers Came to Wolverhampton Town' is sung in tribute: a tribute to a glorious era; to a generation of fans who passed on their passion for an extra-ordinary club; to teams brushed with greatness that might even have been greater.

10
COLD WAR CONQUERORS

The Rangers tour of Russia in June 1962 still claims a special chapter in any history of the club. The team that returned undefeated to a tumultuous heroes' welcome at Renfrew Airport earned a nation's admiration and gratitude.

The episode's significance needs to be considered with due reference to its times. First, there was the political and diplomatic complexity of accepting an invitation to play behind the Iron Curtain at the height of the Cold War. The year before, the Berlin Wall had been erected, and within a few months of the tour the world would hold its breath over the Cuban missile crisis. The image of Russia in the West could not have been more forbidding. Deep in the popular consciousness lay preconceptions about spies, espionage and plots.

The background to the invitation was a European Football Congress in Bulgaria where the secretary of the Scottish FA, Willie Allan, was approached by an official of the Russian FA who asked for a 'top class' Scottish team to visit the Soviet Union. Rangers were subsequently approached and thus became the first Scottish club to undertake such a venture. The reaction to the decision was generally one of surprise and – among the fans – not a little trepidation. Quite apart from the political tensions, the Russian teams were considered to be capable outfits who would be likely to inflict defeats on the Scots so far from home. Memories of the dazzling Moscow Dynamo side that had entranced Ibrox in 1945 were still quite fresh. Although Rangers had emerged on that occasion with a creditable draw, it was broadly agreed that the teams they would have to face in Russia would be all the stronger on their home turf where the honour of the Soviet Union – no less – would be at stake.

Added to this was the fact that Rangers had just finished a long domestic season on a low, having conceded the league championship to Dundee, and that they would be without the player who had become their mercurial talisman, Jim Baxter. Baxter, it now seems bizarre to recall, had to fulfil his National Service duties in the army. Even his customary replacement, Billy Stevenson, could not make the trip. A group of weary players – some in dispute about wages – was to be asked to make the long trip to a culturally strange environment to play three games in ten days against teams that included the current Soviet champions.

It seems that the club decided to go for the experience of playing matches against opposition they were not used to facing, and for the opportunity to spread the fame of Rangers. For manager Scot Symon, who played in the fabled match against Moscow Dynamo, there may have been a personal yearning to reforge the Russian connection. Certainly, there were good football reasons for the trip: European competition was looming larger over the Scottish and British game; critical voices were urging British teams to cast off old habits and learn new ways of approaching and playing the game and continental teams were generally reckoned to have a lot of technical ability from which they could learn. Had the Ibrox management been thinking along such lines they would have reflected on Rangers' progress in European competition since the late 1950s and justifiably felt that a European Cup semi-final in 1959–60, and a European Cup-Winners' Cup final appearance in 1960–61, suggested that finding an extra gear through challenges like the Russian tour could just be enough to see the club make a historic breakthrough and be the first Scottish and perhaps even British side to capture a European honour. The motivation for the Russians certainly seems to have been the chance to gauge their teams' standards with a view to entry into the European tournaments. Rangers, it should be remembered, had had more experience of big-time continental football at this stage than any other club with the exception of Real Madrid.

Sensibly, Rangers took the players on a holiday to Copenhagen prior to flying on to Russia. They journeyed in good spirits but arrived in Moscow to a low-key reception on the part of the Russian FA. Indeed, as the press commented at the time, it was all something of a 'mystery tour'. John Greig reflected not long after the adventure that 'the arrangements at the Russian end had been kept pretty much in the dark, seemingly smothered in red tape somewhere in Moscow.' The players had to adapt quickly to spartan standards of food and accommodation. Davie Wilson recalls the hotel being like 'a youth hostel', and the players being watched and followed by the KGB and warned about who they spoke to. On one occasion in Moscow as the players stood around viewing the sights, a stranger came up to Wilson and pressed a letter with an Austrian address into his hand. Davie pocketed it and duly posted it on his return to Scotland. From the start, however, the players were struck by the friendliness of the ordinary Russians, and – remarkably – the generosity of the welcome extended on match days.

On the field of play Rangers excelled themselves. The first match against Lokomotiv Moscow, who had finished fifth in the Russian League the previous season, ended in a 3–1 victory before a 20,000 crowd and 2,000 Red Army soldiers who took up position near the touchline. The goals came from Brand, MacMillan and Wilson, the latter's strike being hailed by a

Moscow radio commentator as 'the goal of a genius'. Davie Wilson indeed recalls that, despite the rain, he was chaired off the field by some new fans, locals who appreciated the winger's art as both he and Willie Henderson displayed it that day. Henderson, in fact, came on as a substitute for Alex Scott and made an immediate impression in setting up the team's second goal to put them 2–1 up. As John Greig later commented this was Rangers' introduction to the practice of substitutions and it had them baffled for a time. Lokomotiv used four substitutes in contrast to Rangers' one. It was as if the Ibrox club thought there was something not quite proper about it, and felt constrained to make only a token gesture.

As it turned out one was enough, both in the positive sense of Henderson's impact but also, less edifyingly, in relation to the developing rivalry between Henderson and the player he replaced, Alex Scott. By the end of the 1961–62 season the 17-year-old Henderson had edged the established inter-nationalist Scott out of the Rangers side, being preferred, for instance, in the Scottish Cup final win over St Mirren, and had set in train a series of events which would see the highly talented Scott transferred to Everton. The Russian tour only hastened this course of events, although Scot Symon was quick to turn on the travelling pressmen for suggesting that Scott had fallen out with him over the substitution. However, it was clear that Scott's pride was hurt. Somewhat ironically, when Henderson was again brought on during the next match on the tour, he linked up with Scott as a right-sided partnership with devastating results.

This match saw Rangers face Dynamo Tbilisi in Georgia in searing 90-degree heat in front of 30,000. For many of the journalists covering the tour this was Rangers' finest hour. Jack Harkness thought it 'possibly the greatest ever in Rangers' history', while Hugh Taylor commented that, 'never was I more proud to be a Scot. Never did Rangers do a better job for the club.' It was an against-the-odds triumph in which goalkeeper Billy Ritchie performed heroics, youngsters Ronnie McKinnon, at centre half, and John Greig, filling Baxter's left-half berth, took major steps to becoming cornerstones of the team. Henderson continued to mesmerise the locals, scoring the only goal of the game and then executing a cartwheel that would have graced the Russian gymnastic team.

Henderson's eagerness to relay the news later to his girl-friend Mary Bell back in Scotland involved him making a telephone call to the call box at the end of her street in the hope that a neighbour would answer it. A local boy did so and, after initially refusing to believe he was talking to Willie Henderson of the Rangers, duly fetched Mary to come to the phone.

By now word was spreading about Rangers in Russia and pride was swelling back home. The final match took place in the Ukraine against Russian champions Dynamo Kiev and drew an audience of 60,000. A measure of the good spirits the team were in came at the close of a training session before the game when the players burst into a chorus of 'Auld Lang Syne' to the delight of the locals. The game itself was notable as perhaps the finest match played by the redoubtable Harold Davis who laid on the goal scored by Ralph Brand. It looked like being the winner until only minutes from time when Kiev equalised. Rangers were thus deprived of a hundred per cent record and were furious about the award of the free kick-which resulted in the equaliser. The travelling journalists also lambasted some farcical refereeing and there was more than a suspicion that forces were at work to preserve the home team from sullying the honour of the country.

Nonetheless, Rangers had emerged undefeated and covered in glory. Some of the players earned even more admiration and praise from the locals when they dived into the Black Sea to rescue a drowning man during the last day of the trip. Writing in the immediate aftermath of the tour the renowned sports journalist Rex Kingsley observed: 'This terrific one-club achievement has done more for Scotland's soccer prestige than all the SFA-inspired tours since the last war.' For Kingsley these matches had drawn out of the players the skills and

The end of the 'Hoodoo': action from the 1928 Cup final when Rangers defeated Celtic 4–0

Top row: G. Gillespie, W. McNeil, P. Campbell, J. Watt
Middle row: W. Dunlop, D. Hill, T. Vallance, S. Ricketts, M. McNeil
Front row: J. Watson, A Marshall

The 'Gallant Pioneers'. Skipper Tom Vallance is in the centre of the middle row and Moses McNeill on the extreme right

GLASGOW RANGERS F.C.   Season 1911-1912.

The Rangers line-up season 1911–12

Top left: Alan Morton is framed by the lifebelt as the Rangers party prepares to sail for North America in 1928

Above: A European Night at Ibrox in the late 1950s

Fans celebrate another trophy at St Enoch's Square, the traditional gathering place after cup finals in the 1950s and 60s

The remarkable welcome home at Abbotsinch Airport from the Russian tour, 1962

Rangers players celebrate the 3–0 Cup final replay triumph over Celtic in 1963

Action from the drawn first match, 1963

John Greig waves his bowler as the team prepare for a European jaunt c.1963

The team go for a half-time break, c.1960

The pre-match rituals: Rangers v Moscow Dynamo, 1945

This pre-season (1964–5) photo features many of the legendary figures of the early 1960s glory era

'Slim Jim' Baxter

The heartbreak of Nuremberg: the extra-time goal which sunk Rangers in the 1967 European Cup-Winners' Cup final

John Greig lets fly at Parkhead in 1968

Bobby Russell – a skilful ball-player in the Baxter mould

John Greig celebrates clinching the treble with Jock Wallace, 1976

Willie Johnston scores the third goal in the European Cup-Winners' Cup final of 1972

The team that made history in Barcelona

Chief Executive
David Holmes, 1986

Above: The new
management
team: Souness and
Smith, 1990

Right: The late,
great Davie Cooper

Ray Wilkins and Graeme Souness lead
the players in pre-season training, 1988

Ally McCoist and Mo Johnston
relaxing pre-season, 1989

The Rangers squad celebrate clinching nine-in-a-row following the 1–0 win over Dundee United at Tannadice

Right: Mark Hateley in action against Marseille in 1992

Far right: Richard Gough – captain of the team that won nine league titles in a row

Below: Dave McPherson in action against Leeds in the 1992 Battle of Britain

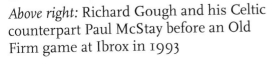

Above right: Richard Gough and his Celtic counterpart Paul McStay before an Old Firm game at Ibrox in 1993

Right: The scintillatingly skilful Brian Laudrup

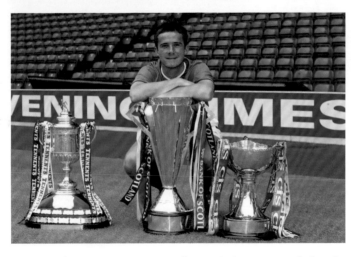

'True Blue' Barry Ferguson poses with all three major honours after the amazing 2002–03 season

Sir David Murray   The training ground that bears his name

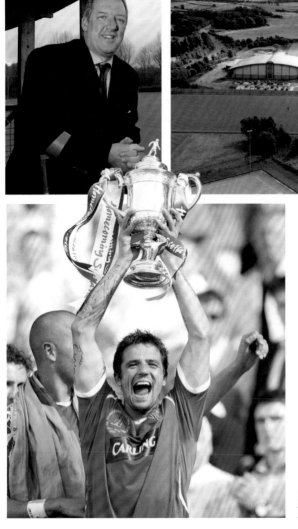

Fans' favourite Nacho Novo lifts the Scottish Cup in 2009

reserves of strength perhaps even they were unaware they possessed. It was a challenge that demanded they find new peaks of form. It was the form they would have to reach again if European success was to be achieved. Testimonies from the players suggested that they too believed the tour had developed their abilities.

Hugh Taylor remarked of the Kiev match that Rangers paced the game beautifully: they slowed it down and speeded it up when appropriate. This seemed to bode well for future European competition. Taylor also singled out the contribution of Jimmy Millar and his calming influence when he dropped back from centre forward to half back in a bid to protect the defence. Millar's ability to hold the ball and play this deeper role should have been tactically exploited by Rangers in European ties to come when the club was playing away from home. That it never seems to have been used in such games indicates that not all the positive aspects of the trip were properly adopted for the full benefit of the team in the European arena. Millar himself observed in an article for the *Rangers Supporters' Annual* previous to the Russian trip that the fans would not stand for the continental style of play at home, and anyone advocating a more sophisticated style would come up against an engrained conservatism encompassing managers, players, fans and administrators. The season following the Russian tour Rangers were to crash out of the European Cup-Winners' Cup to an admittedly brilliant Tottenham Hotspur side. Yet, the 5–2 defeat in the first leg at White Hart Lane betrayed the same tactical naivety, conventional approach and inept defending at set pieces that had resulted in previous calamities such as the European Cup semi-final loss to Eintracht Frankfurt in 1959–60. It was as if the transcendent displays of the team in Russia in the summer of 1962 had never happened.

Reflecting on the Russian tour, John Greig made the point about the Russians being convinced that Rangers performed so well because they had a game plan. Greig insisted that there was no such plan and no special tactics. This is in accord with what other players remember of this era as a whole. Davie Wilson recalls Scot Symon tending just to leave it to the players to sort matters out on the park. Nevertheless, the matches in Russia proved that the players could adapt to situations and play the game intelligently and effectively, conserving resources when necessary and springing attacks that made the best use the team's capabilities. Whether direction was coming from the management or from the experienced players on the pitch, Rangers showed in Russia that they could cut it at the top level and could rise above the 'hurry-burry' of the game at home. It is a cause of great regret that they did not do so more often, and that the shining achievements of the Russian tour were in a playing sense contained and sealed in that remarkable ten days.

However, the tour was about more than just the football. Rangers gave the whole of Scotland a boost. How much the club's feat was appreciated was expressed in the astonishing welcome given to the team on their return to Renfrew Airport. This homecoming entered the folklore of the club and more widely that of Scottish sport. The journalist W.G. Stewart of the *Evening Times* proclaimed that 'No conquering army ever received a more vociferous homecoming', while James Sanderson of the *Scottish Daily Express* called it 'the greatest homecoming of any sportsmen to Scotland – bar none!'

On approaching the runway, Sanderson wrote, 'the bellow of triumph seemed to make the frail shell of our aircraft quiver'. The fans indeed had swarmed onto the tarmac and the pilot – obviously taken aback – had to abort his first landing. When the plane eventually touched down the cheering supporters surrounded it and the players were only with the greatest difficulty shepherded onto waiting buses.

Estimates of the crowd at the airport varied from 10,000 to 15,000. Supporters' clubs had arranged coaches to transport fans, while many went by car or simply walked. Many who started out intending to get to the airport were prevented from doing so by traffic congestion. For airport officials it was

Armageddon: they could only watch in fear as the many fans who were smoking lunged close to the aircraft. The police were helpless. Eventually, as John Fairgrieve chronicled in his book *The Rangers: Scotland's Greatest Football Team*, flares were shot above the crowd, which incidentally contained many women and children. The road leading to Glasgow was jammed, and the fans refused to leave the airport for some time after the team's arrival, entertained by accordion bands that had been assembled to serenade the players with 'Follow Follow'.

Sporting success in such a daunting place as Soviet Russia served to copper-fasten the identification of Rangers with Scotland itself. W.G. Stewart made the point about so many Scots looking to Rangers to boost – and in many ways salvage – national pride. He argued that Rangers' success in contra-distinction to the national football team's less distinguished forays abroad in World Cups and playing tours, helped to explain why so many instilled 'a patriotic fervour into their support of the Light Blues'. The previous year, following the 9–3 calamity at Wembley on the part of the national team, it had been Rangers, a few days later, who had restored Scottish pride by beating Wolverhampton Wanderers to become the first British side to reach a major European final. For Stewart and other commentators Rangers became a surrogate for Scotland as a whole when they faced continental opposition. James Sanderson echoed these sentiments: 'Yes, let the English talk about Spurs, Arsenal and Manchester United!' he wrote defiantly, happy to point to Rangers as the Scottish reply. He even praised the supporters' welcome home as an exercise in casting off 'our traditional dourness' and indulging in justified celebration.

The only sour note was struck by the *Glasgow Herald*, bastion of those middle-class denizens of the leafier parts of the West of Scotland who snootishly held football in disdain. The *Herald* excoriated the jubilant fans for the danger they had posed to safety and said that the team's achievements in Russia had been 'magnified out of proportion to its real importance'. It was

probably no accident that the paper's regular football correspondent was the spiteful and tediously anti-Rangers Cyril
Horne.

Olympian sniping from the *Herald* aside, this was probably
the high point of Rangers' popularity throughout Scotland.
The club, its accomplishments and its image and reputation
all were admired in the nation as never before or since.
Hugh Taylor considered the club 'wonderful ambassadors for
Scotland' and in his book, *We Will Follow Rangers*, wrote in
military metaphors about their deeds on foreign soil for the
glory of the country. Taylor also touched on the social demo-
graphics of the club's support of the time – its appeal in
particular to 'the Clydeside shipyard worker' type of craftsman;
yet he also noted the club's appeal far beyond 'the purlieus of
Govan' to the towns and villages of the Highlands and Lowlands.

This was the era before the gap between the big clubs – in
effect the Old Firm – and smaller clubs in Scotland became
increasingly widened in monetary terms, and before the Old
Firm's grip on domestic honours became so vice-like. Moreover,
it was also still an era in which Rangers could appear comfortably part of a broader Scottish patriotism, and indeed stand
as a symbol of Scottish qualities and characteristics.

11
DARK DOMESTIC DECADE

Towards the end of season 1964–65 Rangers faced Dundee United at Ibrox before a meagre attendance of 15,000. It was to be Jim Baxter's valedictory appearance before his transfer to England. Rangers, out of all cup competitions, were heading for fifth place, the second-lowest finish in their league championship history. At one point during a listless match Baxter attempted to find winger Davie Wilson with a trademark slide-rule pass inside the full back. He uncharacteristically over-hit it while Wilson, equally unusually, had failed to read his intentions anyway. It was a cameo of the unravelling of the glory days of the previous seasons.

Rangers' troubles coincided with Jock Stein's revival of Celtic. Stein brought to the club's historic rivals fresh ideas and a wily capacity for getting the best out of his players. Within months an underperforming team had lifted the Scottish Cup and posted a warning about the challenge they would present in the future. Besides the track-suited and media-savvy Stein, Scot Symon looked already out of step with the times before their respective teams truly locked horns.

It was clear that Baxter could not be replaced and, at first, Rangers did not look for another big name player; rather they trusted to the ones who remained to dig deeper and redouble their commitment to the cause. No player answered the call more resolutely than new team captain John Greig. From 1965 Greig became the mainstay of the team on the park and the image of the club off it: his wholeheartedness, his determination and his courage inspired all around him. The club was about to enter a dark domestic decade in terms of playing fortunes, criticism and adverse publicity, but no one did more, over this decade, to salvage the honour and dignity of the club, and to will the team to the successes they did manage, including, of course, the club's first European triumph in 1972.

Despite these dark days, Rangers pushed Celtic very close. In the first three full seasons of Jock Stein's management the points gap in the league was two, three and two respectively. All of these championships went virtually to the last kick of the season. Indeed, in 1967–68 Rangers went through the league campaign undefeated until the final day. Honours were even in terms of the league matches between the Old Firm clubs. Even in season 1968–69, when Rangers finished five points behind their great rivals, the Ibrox team took the spoils in both derbies. In terms of cups, narrow League Cup final defeats to Celtic in 1964–65 and 1965–66 were balanced by the dramatic Scottish Cup final replay victory in 1965-66 when Rangers' Danish right back, Kai Johansen, wrote himself into the history books with a thunderous 70th-minute winner at the Mount Florida 'Rangers end' of Hampden. The huge celebrations following that match, culminating in the traditional gathering at St Enoch's Square in Glasgow city centre, were savoured all the more for the way Rangers had been written off before the final by most journalists and commentators. The team found new depths of resilience that night, and veterans of the better years, like Jimmy Millar and Davie Wilson, seemed to instil the spirit for which the club was renowned. Despite Celtic's formidable form in these years, Rangers did not buckle.

Yet this was a frustrating period in Rangers' history. Although the margin between success and failure was slim indeed, the overwhelming emotion felt by all connected to the club was bitter disappointment. So near to holding off the challenge of a resurgent Celtic; so near to European glory; so near to re-creating the dominance of the early 1960s. But, ultimately, it was not enough. As Celtic became stronger and captured the European Cup in 1966–67 the pressure on Rangers grew. The fans could not accept a situation where the club was in its rivals' shadow. The weight of expectation and the intensity of the fans' demands that the team retrieve their pre-eminent position, resulted in unstable and anxiety-ridden performances and panic measures to bring change. The atmosphere surrounding the club was febrile.

A crisis point arrived with a humiliating defeat to Second Division club Berwick Rangers in the first round of the Scottish Cup on 27 January 1967. This remains perhaps the blackest day in the club's history in terms of matters on the field of play. To the events of this day much in the club's subsequent fortunes can be traced. The 1–0 defeat literally shocked the football world. Even on BBC's *Grandstand* commentator David Coleman eschewed developments in the English league to keep viewers updated on the astonishing happenings at Shielfield Park. In retrospect, it was simply 'one of those days' when Rangers did everything but score, and came up against a goalkeeper, Jock Wallace, who was playing out of his skin. Had the fans known what Wallace would later do for Rangers their gloom may have been lightened, but as the final whistle sounded it felt like an earthquake had laid waste to their world. The fans' anger was echoed in the boardroom and among the management team. Somebody or some people would have to take the blame.

The club acted swiftly – perhaps too swiftly. The striking partnership of the day of Jim Forrest and George McLean was singled out for special condemnation and neither player was to kick a ball for the first team again. In the space of a few weeks both players were transferred. Ultimately, this was manager Scot Symon's decision, but there is no doubt that pressure from 'upstairs' to send out a signal that the club would not tolerate a repeat performance led him to sacrifice these players. In retrospect the harshness of the treatment meted out to Forrest and Mclean seems staggering: dropping them from the side for a spell would have been a more appropriate course of action, particularly in view of the fact that Rangers remained in contention for the league title and the European Cup-Winners' Cup. In relation to Forrest, in particular, the sense of injustice is deepened in view of his goalscoring achievements up until then. In 1964–65, when Rangers struggled to finish fifth in the table, Forrest set a post-war record of 51 goals. He scored home and away in the European Cup against Inter Milan, following crucial strikes in the earlier rounds. Later in 1965 he scored twice against Portuguese giants Benfica in a challenge match at Ibrox. His scoring record against Celtic was also highly impressive. He was nimble, sharp and pacy and snapped up chances crisply and economically. In 1967, at the time of the Berwick debacle, he was just 22 years of age.

McLean too had reason to feel aggrieved. Converted into a centre forward from an inside right, he took up the challenge of a role which did not come naturally. 'Dandy' scored a more than respectable number of goals, notwithstanding his frequent bouts of clumsiness and some farcical misses. He was the butt of many fans' gallows humour and colourful abuse but he bore it stoically. Such was his phlegmatic character and his capacity to laugh along with his detractors that the criticism simply washed off him. A typical 'Dandyism' came after the Cup final replay of 1965–66 when he insisted that he had 'dummied' Willie Johnston's cross so that Johansen could score. In fact it had been a glaring miss, a 'fresh air' shot which, had the move not culminated in Kai's wonder strike, would have constituted better grounds for his expulsion than Berwick.

After Berwick, Symon placed the goalscoring burden on the

slim shoulders of Alex Willoughby, another player who was more naturally a playmaking inside forward. Willoughby, ironically a cousin of Forrest, rose to the task superbly, scoring no fewer than 17 times, including the winner at Kilmarnock in a match watched by Russian Prime Minister Alexei Kosygin. In such ways was Rangers by now historic relationship with Russia strengthened further, with the fans' tumultuous greetings for the visitor unparalleled even in Red Square. A pre-match photograph indeed captured Kosygin presciently handing the match ball to Willoughby.

Then, with a crucial Old Firm match and a Cup-Winners' Cup semi-final looming near the season's end, Symon appeared to take the view that Willoughby was too lightweight for these occasions. Instead he promoted a jobbing defender, Roger Hynd, to the striking position. Hynd – a relative of Liverpool boss Bill Shankly – was an honest toiler and certainly provided 'presence'; moreover, he scored in the 2–2 draw with Celtic and Rangers negotiated the Cup-Winners' Cup semi-final with him in attack. However, the big man's offensive shortcomings were cruelly exposed in the Cup-Winners' Cup final in Nuremberg where Forrest, McLean or Willoughby would have been likely to have made better use of the opportunities which came his way. If ever Rangers suffered from a self-inflicted wound it was that fateful night, the eventual extra-time defeat to Bayern Munich depriving them of matching Celtic's success in Lisbon of the previous week.

That Symon's job was under threat seemed to be made evident even before the final in Germany when chairman John Lawrence complained that there were too many 'half backs' in the forward line. This viewpoint was expressed in an article for a Scottish newspaper, and it was only afterwards that the players received news of it. Sandy Jardine recalls them being 'incensed' in the light of how well the team had played – Rangers were the superior side in a top-quality match – and felt that credit was not being given where it was due.

Lawrence's intervention may have been all the more galling

for Symon in the light of the board's insistence that certain players be made accountable for the shame of Berwick. If Lawrence and the directors had urged that Forrest and McLean be the specific targets then Lawrence's criticisms prior to the final would have been better directed at himself. If it was left to Symon to select players for the chop then the manager was put in an invidious position.

Despite all this, the Ibrox board seemed to accept some measure of blame and gave Symon another chance before the start of the 1967–68 campaign, providing funds to refashion the team. To get the goals they secured Alex Ferguson from Dunfermline for a fee of £65,000, and further substantial outlays brought Swedish winger Orjan Persson, Danish goalkeeper Erik Sorensen and inside forward Andy Penman to Ibrox. This transfer activity came on top of the significant investments made in Dave Smith and Alex Smith (two of the 'half backs' in the forward line in Nuremberg) at the beginning of the previous season.

In the space of two seasons Rangers had jettisoned the cautious style of piecemeal adjustments to the team that had been such a feature of the past. They were now accused of panic buying, and there was an understandable element of urgency about the club's dealings in this period. Quite simply, Celtic had laid down the gauntlet both at home and abroad. It was an unprecedented situation for Rangers, and it has to be remembered that the demands of their worldwide fan base were at an all-time peak. Nor was it a case of empty 'Wha's like us' posturing to believe that the club could quickly emulate Celtic. Scottish football's standing was high: the presence of the Old Firm clubs in two European finals and Kilmarnock's semi-final appearance in the third competition, the Inter-Cities Fairs Cup, in the same season is ample proof of this. It was not unrealistic for Rangers to think that the right signings could lift them above their rivals and prepare them for an assault on Europe. On the other hand, these new players were going to have to bear a daunting weight of expectations, and the media attention surrounding them concealed a troubling feature of the Ibrox set-up, namely the paucity of promising young players coming through the ranks. Fans who focused on the latest big names to don the famous royal blue shirt might have been better advised to ask if the club's scouting and youth development operations were working in the way they should have been. To take one example, why was Rangers-daft youngster Kenny Dalglish not snapped up? In his autobiography Dalglish says that the 'apathy' of Rangers let in Celtic. The rest is painful history.

Another notable acquisition during the close season of 1967 was David White, then manager of Clyde, to assist Symon. The youthful White was a modern thinker who believed in more contact with the players. In his book *Rangers: The Managers* club historian David Mason contends that White's appointment was with a view to his being 'groomed' for the manager's job after a transition period of a few years. If Symon felt he was being forced into an arrangement of which he was suspicious he certainly did not show it.

In retrospect though it seems that Symon was on borrowed time and needed to turn the tide in relation to Celtic without delay. He got the chance to do this right at the start of the season when the Old Firm were brought together in the same League Cup section. The first of the two meetings between the teams ended in a 1–1 draw at Ibrox, a match in which Andy Penman first missed a penalty then equalised with a free-kick. The return at Parkhead was 'make or break'. Rangers took an early lead and were awarded a penalty with quarter of an hour to go. Johansen, assuming the penalty duty from Penman, crashed his shot against the underside of the bar. The ball may even have bounced over the line – it certainly was a case for 'goal-line technology' – but as it came out a simple opportunity to net the rebound presented itself for the alert Penman. Although he screamed at Johansen to leave it to him, Penman could only watch as the Dane instinctively headed it and conceded a free-kick in so doing. As if in a nightmare the stunned Rangers support then looked on as a galvanised Celtic steamrollered through their traumatised team to end up 3–1 winners. The drama and suspense of this match led Jock Stein to claim it as the greatest Old Firm victory for his club, a piece of hyperbole doubtless designed to heap further pressure on Rangers. Nevertheless, the significance of the match turned out to be profound. It meant the elimination of Rangers from the League Cup, and although the team began the league campaign well and actually defeated Celtic at Ibrox in September with a wonder goal from Orjan Persson, the sense of desperation grew stronger.

On 28 October 1967 Rangers were held to a 0–0 draw at home to Dunfermline. Near the end Symon substituted Penman for Alex Willoughby. This was greeted with boos from the crowd, and the dissatisfaction and frustration built to the final whistle when much of it was communicated to the manager and the directors. The team were still top of the league, but Celtic had a game in hand owing to their trip to South America to play in the World Club Championship. Such matters clearly concentrated minds in the Ibrox boardroom.

The termination of Scot Symon's 13 years as manager took place in the middle of the following week. It was handled clumsily and ineptly and the news was issued via the press. The undignified manner of a clearly bitter Symon's departure was to haunt the club for some time. In effect, it was the first time that the club had publicly sacked a manager, and players and fans alike were stunned, whatever their thoughts on his management. Symon was in a sense a victim of tactical changes in the game with which he was not comfortable, and it should not be forgotten that he had been much more than just team manager: he had in effect run the whole club. White was immediately promoted to Symon's position, and coach Bobby Seith, who had been appointed back in late 1966, resigned in disgust at Symon's treatment. The chairman, John Lawrence, and the directors were grossly remiss in not dismissing Symon face-to-face with a proper explanation. The deed was done indirectly and statements issued to the press added to the puzzlement. Lawrence tried to explain events as follows: 'We wanted a young man with experience in modern football. We spent considerable sums of money buying players, at Mr Symon's request, but the results were not forthcoming and it could not go on indefinitely. The board were not satisfied with the results, which can be seen in the league tables.'

The obvious point to be made about this statement is that it reads bizarrely given that Rangers were top of the league. Clearly, the elimination from the League Cup and the manner of the capitulation to Celtic at Parkhead had set at least some board members against the manager. Yet it should be kept in mind that had Johansen's penalty gone in – and perhaps it actually did – Rangers would have been likely to have seen out the match and progressed to lift the trophy. With an honour secured by late October – the League Cup final was held on the 28th – it would have been very difficult for Symon to be removed. The board also seemed to take the view that it was only a matter of time before Rangers dropped more vital points, like the one at home to Dunfermline, if a change was not made. Moreover, the team was not a free-scoring one. Alex Ferguson had managed a few but he was not looking like the clinical striker the club so needed. In a way an unfair burden had been placed on Ferguson above all the other signings; his goalscoring exploits with his previous teams had come from the inside left position and he was not a 'target man' centre forward. However, the nature of the game was changing and centre forwards were now often finding themselves having to forage without the support of attacking inside forwards. Ferguson was given a role in which he was not comfortable. Much later, towards the end of season 1968–69, Ferguson was briefly paired with that quintessential centre forward Colin Stein who had been bought to replace him. The goals flooded in and fans were given a glimpse of what might have been.

Symon departed on a wave of sympathy. For some who had been well disposed to Rangers if not fervent fans this was a turning point. The club lost respect. For the more football-minded there was probably acknowledgement that his patrician management style was out of date. Perhaps significantly he could not retrieve his reputation during his subsequent years as boss of Partick Thistle. Moreover, there was the irony that his decision to substitute Willoughby turned out to be the 'trigger' factor in his dismissal. Conceivably, his decision to drop Willoughby coming on top of his ruthless disposal of Forrest and McLean had cost Rangers the Cup-Winners' Cup the previous season. In hindsight, Symon was not able to afford the defeat in Nuremberg and the failure to capture a European prize to put alongside Celtic's.

Hindsight would also prompt the verdict that the manager's job came too early for David White. In contrast to Symon, White went on to show his managerial prowess after leaving Ibrox. Nevertheless, the two years he was in charge were the most notable of his career, and it is to his credit that he kept Rangers at the top of the league and undefeated until the final day of the season in 1967–68. Against anyone but a Jock Stein-led Celtic, Rangers would have coasted to the championship. White also drew from the team some exciting attacking football, with the conversion of Willie Johnston from left winger into an attacking inside left a particularly effective ploy. In the space of four consecutive league matches, before a battling 2–2 draw at Parkhead on 2 January, Rangers scored a staggering 23 goals, including a 10–2 victory over Raith Rovers at Ibrox. But the pressure got to the team in the run-in and their cause was not helped by energy-sapping and emotionally draining exits from the Inter-Cities Fairs Cup at the hands of Leeds United, and the Scottish Cup after a replay against Hearts. Johnston's loss of form following a substandard display in the Scotland-England international in February helps to explain these losses, and it should be remembered that Celtic by this stage in the season had only the league to worry about having been eliminated from both the European Cup and the Scottish Cup in the first round.

The following season began for White much as Symon's last season had done: defeat to Celtic and elimination from the

League Cup, followed by an Old Firm victory in the league, this time a 4–2 triumph at Parkhead in which Willie Johnston's speed and finishing were memorable. However, White was not content with the attack and secured the backing of the board to splash out for Scotland's first £100,000 player, striker Colin Stein. At the same time Alex MacDonald, Kinning Park born and raised, joined his boyhood heroes from St Johnstone for half that sum. Both were to play vital roles in the European triumph of 1971–72.

Stein, a dashing centre forward who captivated the fans, made an explosive start to his Rangers career with two successive hat-tricks, including one against his former club Hibs, and a double at Dundalk in the Fairs Cup. Alex Ferguson was now out in the cold. Stein's combative style gave Rangers a new threat, but his short fuse on the pitch resulted in cautions, sending-offs and suspensions. Fatally for Rangers he was suspended for the 1968–69 Scottish Cup final and the team, with Ferguson restored to lead the line, fell to a hapless 4–0 defeat. 'I seek no alibi' wrote White in the club handbook, 'blunders were made for which we had to pay heavily.' The three first-half goals were all the result of glaring defensive errors, while chances at the other end were scorned. The loss came on top of a late slump in the championship allowing Celtic once more to prevail.

But the season's agony was still not at an end. Rangers then crashed out of the Fairs Cup at the semi-final stage to an ordinary Newcastle United side amid scenes of crowd chaos at St James' Park. The public standing of the club in the close season of 1969 was probably at its lowest point. Criticism flowed over hooliganism, the club's unwritten policy of discriminating over the acquisition of players on religious grounds and the failure to come up to the standards of the club's past on and off the field. By the end of the 1960s values and attitudes in society had shifted in ways that made institutions like Rangers appear hidebound and vulnerable. Increasingly, the club was being called to account as never before, and the defensive reactions of those in charge of it were unconvincing and inadequate.

When Rangers re-signed Jim Baxter in the summer of 1969 it was almost as if the club was taking refuge in nostalgia. It was clear that Baxter was unfit and had lost the edge of his earlier playing days at Ibrox, yet he remained a powerful talisman, a reminder of the how it used to be. Fans hoped against logic that Baxter's mere presence could be the catalyst for a new glorious era. In retrospect Baxter's return was White's last card.

The early signs were that it just could be an ace. Once more Rangers and Celtic were put together in the same League Cup section. At Ibrox in the first match Baxter defied the ravages of his lifestyle to orchestrate a joyous 2–1 victory. His free-kick onto the head of Greig who transferred the ball to Johnston to nod the winner was a moment of sublime artistry. But Baxter then was forced to miss the return at Parkhead through injury and the match was lost. Other dropped points saw Rangers fail to qualify for the latter stages of the trophy. Moreover, the challenge in the league stuttered early on. The looming crisis duly enveloped the club when Gornik of Poland eliminated Rangers from the European Cup-Winners' Cup on a foggy November night, Baxter's superb early strike countered by three killer second-half goals to leave the fans voicing their disgust.

White was sacked the following day. His gamble on Baxter had not paid off; indeed an incident in the lead-up to the Gornik match, when Baxter and Henderson had missed training, led to speculation about a lack of discipline and falling standards. White's assistant for over a year, Ibrox legend Willie Thornton, took the team for the following league match when the fans vented their rage in personal terms against chairman John Lawrence. The very mystique of the institution appeared to be evaporating. White had not enjoyed the best of luck and the team had played some good football during his stewardship but at this juncture Rangers were drifting. It is unlikely that White could have arrested the slide.

The club then turned to another of its folk heroes, Willie Waddell, to restore its standing and bring back the pride in its name. Waddell was by now working as a sports journalist, and he had been pursuing White for what he believed were the young manager's inadequacies for the task of steering Rangers. Waddell's attacks were cruel, not least a damning piece published prior to the Gornik match with the headline 'The Boy David'. Waddell took over in the spirit of the boss he had served under, the man who was still held as the epitome of what the club should stand for: Bill Struth. Waddell stormed back to Ibrox determined to weed out those who did not measure up to his standards and expectations. Predictably, one of the first casualties was Baxter who was given a free transfer. Within weeks there was no doubt that Waddell was Rangers in the manner of Struth. The chairman and directors along with everyone else were simply in awe of him.

The old Waddell-Thornton partnership was revived on paper, but in reality Waddell called all the shots. He was concerned with the players' fitness and, in a general backroom shake-up towards the end of the 1969–70 season, he brought in Jock Wallace, the Berwick goalkeeper of that fateful day, as trainer and coach. Wallace's intensive methods and his strong personality were to have an immediate impact and Rangers strung together an impressive run of results. But the season unravelled following defeat at Parkhead in a rowdy Scottish Cup quarter final.

Rangers had in fact approached Waddell on at least two previous occasions before he took the job in December 1969. 'I would never have returned for any club but Rangers,' he said, 'the players must have pride in themselves, in their character and in their public image.' However, his career switch since leading Kilmarnock to that club's one and only league championship in 1964–65 was arguably inimical to his chances of being the managerial success story Rangers craved. Perhaps if he had gone to Ibrox in 1965 at a point when Rangers were in transition, Waddell's advanced thinking about the game could have been fruitfully implemented. At the very least it is intriguing to speculate on the battle of wits that would have ensued between him and Jock Stein, both of whom had studied the methods of Inter Milan coach Helenio Herrera. Several years in journalism may also have built up personal enmities, which would shackle him at Ibrox and render certain working relationships difficult.

As well as his formidable drive to put the club back where it belonged, Waddell exhibited a flinty stubbornness. His arrival, if anything, confirmed the board in its conservatism. It was one thing to try to restore the best traditions for which the club stood; it was another to stand against the changes that had to be made sooner or later, particularly in relation to the Protestant exclusivity that chained Rangers to the past. Like those before him, Waddell simply took the view that the club's internal affairs were nobody else's business. However, football clubs do not exist in a bubble, and notwithstanding the inward-looking culture of the game in general, the outbreak of the Troubles in Northern Ireland from 1969 should have alerted the club to its wider responsibility to avoid anything that exacerbated sectarian divisions. After all, the echoes of Ulster were being heard on the terraces. The religious obsession was perceived by Alex Ferguson to have been a problem for him at the club on account of his marriage; furthermore, it was to lead to the resignation of director David Hope, the man who had masterminded the expansion of the Rangers Pools operation in the late 1960s and early 1970s. The evidence suggests that Waddell, apparently along with the chairman and directors, was not in favour of the club making a change to its selection policy, at least not until it and the fans were better prepared for such a move. Interviewed for a German documentary film, *The Big Clubs*, in 1973 he states emphatically that he hopes the club's traditions never would change, leaving little doubt that this was one of the 'traditions'. On the other hand, Waddell weighed in energetically against the increasing hooligan problem (see chapter 22) from which he separated the sectarian matter in defiance of media opinion. Whatever way the question is approached and examined, Rangers were to pay a heavy price for fidelity to a 'tradition' that had begun to develop in the decades after the First World War.

Waddell's first season ended without a trophy, but the following campaign, 1970–71, began brightly with the League Cup won in highly romantic fashion against Celtic when 16-year-old Derek Johnstone headed a sensational winner for a Rangers side severely weakened by the loss to injury of captain John Greig. However, it was to be another false dawn. The league challenge was effectively over before Christmas. Then, on 2 January matters off the field eclipsed those on it when the second Ibrox Disaster, following that day's Old Firm game, took the lives of 66 fans and stunned the club and its followers the world over (see chapter 21). In the weeks afterwards Waddell rose magnificently to the challenge of organising the club's representation at the funerals, dealing with the world's media, and generally coping with a catastrophe on an unprecedented scale. In sports broadcaster Archie Macpherson's words he 'faced the world full square' and his every interview 'carried strength and understanding'. For this the club will always be in Willie Waddell's debt. In the aftermath the team battled bravely, reaching the Scottish Cup final, but they succumbed to Celtic after a replay, leaving behind a period of grief and recrimination. The following season was hardly a month old before Rangers had suffered three Old Firm defeats and had in effect put themselves out of contention for two prizes. But while domestic form was patchy at best, the team did rise to the occasion in Europe. Rangers' eventual capture of the European Cup-Winners' Cup (see chapter 19) on an unforgettable night in Barcelona was a fitting achievement in the club's true centenary year. At the time, following the error made by previous club historians such as John Allan, it was still believed that 1873 marked the foundation, and the centenary celebrations duly took place in 1973 with glamour matches against Ajax and Arsenal.

Barcelona was the pay-off for the long years of striving towards European success, and a personal vindication for Waddell and his revival of the pride, ambition and resolution of earlier days. On the playing side his purchase of the highly skilled right winger Tommy McLean, and his introduction of the talented youngster Alfie Conn, paid dividends. More generally, his strength of character in 1971-72 saw the club emerge from its darkest hour of disaster to claim a place in the elite roster of Europe's finest. His handling of the fallout from the scenes of crowd disorder in Barcelona was also masterly.

Having secured a European trophy and to great surprise, Waddell stood aside in the close season of 1972, taking a role as general manager and handing control of the team to Jock Wallace. It was a strange move and one that saw an uneasy relationship develop between the two men. Waddell continued to be the real power at the club, conducting the buying and selling of players and speaking with more authority than anyone else. In 1973 Matt Taylor took over from John Lawrence as chairman (another event that did the club no credit) but even the new chairman stood behind Waddell in the pecking order. Waddell's service to the club after the Ibrox Disaster, combined with his successful campaign to reduce the ban from European competitions after Barcelona, in effect put him in an untouchable position. It was Waddell too who decided that Ibrox Stadium should be redeveloped following the Disaster, and that the future for spectators would be an all-seated one. In this he was prescient and visionary, if as usual autocratic.

Jock Wallace, however, was also a strong-minded individual. Whatever the disagreements that ensued, he put his stamp on the team. Season 1972–73 was initially problematic with the loss of Barcelona goalscorers Stein and Johnston. Both in effect left over Rangers' refusal to meet their wage demands and the knowledge that they could cash in on their high profile and enhanced reputation in the English league. Derek Parlane was then converted from midfielder to striker and developed an effective partnership with the flamboyant Conn, while winger

Quinton Young was signed from Coventry as part of the deal for Stein, and the steely defender Tom Forsyth bought from Motherwell. As the season progressed the team grew in confidence and Wallace's fitness regime, which featured the infamous slogs over the Gullane sands, reaped its rewards. A spirited challenge to Celtic in the league came up just short on the last day, but revenge was sweetly exacted the following week in the Scottish Cup final.

A pulsating encounter saw fortunes ebb and flow till Forsyth famously tapped in a rebound from a post to give Rangers the winner in an epic 3–2 struggle in front of over 122,000 supporters. A disappointing season in 1973–74 doused the raised expectations of the Rangers support. Celtic completed nine titles in a row, and there seemed to be no end in sight to their dominance. Wallace came under severe pressure as a decade was clocked up without a championship. A good start in 1974–75 was imperative and to the fans' relief it materialised. A victory at Parkhead in September instilled belief. With new goalkeeper Stewart Kennedy in the form of his life, and Sandy Jardine by now recognised as a world-class right back, the team slugged it out at the top with their Old Firm rivals till a 3–0 mauling of Celtic at Ibrox tipped the balance. After this Celtic folded and Rangers were able to claim the title before the end of March with a 1–1 draw at Easter Road. The goalscorer in that match against Hibs with a bullet header was none other than Colin Stein, re-signed a few weeks before. On the last day of the season 60,000 partied as skipper John Greig rode a chariot around the Ibrox track. The match, which ended in a 1–0 defeat, was happily incidental. Rangers had finally emerged from a decade of domestic tribulations.

12
TREBLE KINGS

When Jock Wallace's side followed up their title success of 1975 by winning the domestic Treble the following season, Bobby Russell was a slightly-built midfielder resuming his career at Shettleston Juniors after a spell as an apprentice at Sunderland had failed to work out.

When Wallace captured his second Treble just two seasons later, Russell was one of the main men in the Ibrox side. 'I had just turned 19 when I was approached by Rangers in 1976,' Russell recalls. 'I played in a trial match against Dundee United reserves one night and was invited in to Ibrox the next day to sign. It was agreed that I was to be called up once Shettleston were out of the Scottish Cup but fortunately, or unfortunately, we got to the semi-final so that was the season all but over and I went in for pre-season at Ibrox in the summer of 1977. I think Shettleston got a minimal fee. It was exciting more than anything else going from junior football to senior football at Rangers. I wouldn't have classed myself as even a semi-professional at Shettleston. We trained two nights a week.

During the day I worked in a whisky bond, often working on a Saturday morning. Once it had been agreed I was going to Rangers I went to Ibrox on a Tuesday night to train. The Albion [the club's training ground, situated across the road from the stadium] had no floodlights so we trained in the area under the enclosure. I heard years later that big Jock didn't want to sign me because I didn't meet his criteria. I wasn't big, strong and physical. I think it was scout Willie Thornton, a Rangers legend, who persuaded him to sign me, as there were other clubs interested, but I am not sure if that was a hundred per cent correct. Before pre-season started I was befriended by the late Bobby McKean. We trained together, running up the hills and doing weights so when I reported for pre-season training I was two or three weeks ahead of everyone else. But I was in awe because all of a sudden I was in the dressing room with guys like Alex MacDonald and John Greig, people I used to go and watch when they won the Treble two years previously.'

But Russell's time at Ibrox had yet to come when Rangers comfortably won the first and newly formed Premier Division in 1975–76, six points ahead of Celtic who were followed by Hibernian and Motherwell. The side that won the title that year was a strong one. Peter McCloy and Stewart Kennedy fought for the goalkeeping position with a robust and steady defence picked from Sandy Jardine, Colin Jackson, Tom Forsyth, Greig and Alex Miller. In centre midfield there was MacDonald and Johnny Hamilton, bolstered by wingers Tommy McLean and Bobby McKean, and in attack the prolific Derek Johnstone was supported by Derek Parlane and Martin Henderson.

Although they secured the League Cup with a 1–0 win over Celtic in October, it was in the second part of the season that Rangers really showed their mettle, going unbeaten from 6 December, when they lost 1–0 at Aberdeen, right through to the end of the campaign. The run extended to 21 league games, 26 in total including the Scottish Cup, which was secured with a 3–1 victory over Hearts in the Hampden final. Johnstone, who had scored after 22 seconds to clinch the title at Dundee United the previous week, put Rangers ahead within a minute before scoring another along with MacDonald, whose goal had given the Light Blues their League Cup triumph.

Despite their domestic joy, Rangers continued to fail on the European stage, losing 4–1 on aggregate in the second round to eventual finalists St Etienne after beating Irish club Bohemians in the first round.

After the feast came the famine. In 1976–77 Rangers won nothing, finishing nine points behind champions Celtic and losing the Scottish Cup final to their Old Firm rivals with a disputed penalty. The League Cup saw a 5–1 thrashing by Aberdeen in the semi-final at Hampden and there was more disappointment in Europe as Rangers were knocked out of the first round of the European Cup by FC Zurich 2–1 on aggregate. It had been an inexplicably disappointing season but three new signings in the summer of 1977 were instrumental in a significant Rangers revival. Clydebank's exciting young winger Davie Cooper, who the previous year had tormented Rangers in their epic League Cup quarter-final tie against the Kilbowie side which stretched to four games before the Light Blues eventually won through, was recruited by Wallace for £100,000. Another winger, Gordon Smith, arrived for £65,000 from Kilmarnock. The third recruit, Russell, arrived with less of a fanfare. It was not unusual for senior clubs to recruit from junior football and indeed it had been a long-established practice for players to be farmed out to junior sides to 'toughen them up'. But few made as instant an impact as the playmaker who was signed from Shettleston Juniors. Three months in to his senior career he was heralded as the best player in Scottish football by then Aberdeen boss Billy McNeill after a 3–1 win for Rangers at Ibrox.

Russell says: 'I believe in the old saying about first impressions being important. We went on a Highland tour in pre-season and I was included in the squad although when I saw my name on the list I thought I was just going up there to fetch and carry the kit. But I was on the bench for the first game against Ross

County where Cooper made his debut. I made my debut against Nairn County and scored in a 3–2 win. But a lot of attention was on Coop that summer, and to a lesser extent Gordon, and that was confirmed the following week when I made my Ibrox debut against Southampton in the Tennent Caledonian tournament. I was going up the marble staircase for my pre-match meal and coming down was Willie Waddell, the main man at Ibrox at that time, who stopped me and said, "Where are you going son?" I told him I was going up for my pre-match meal and he looked at me for a while and then said, "Okay, on you go." I'm not sure he knew who I was. Neither did the fans. It was the old-style Ibrox with terraces behind each goal. My girlfriend was standing with her brother and nephew and when I came running out people around her were saying, "Who is that No. 8?" But I got off to a good start at Rangers. My league debut was against Aberdeen at Pittodrie and I scored, although we lost 3–1.'

Battles with the Dons, of which there were seven in all, became a feature of that season. However, amid a whirlwind start to his senior career, Russell was to experience his first Old Firm game just over a month after he had made his debut, on 9 September, when Celtic visited Govan. 'I enjoyed Old Firm games, they were fantastic but the atmosphere for my first game against Celtic was the best ever,' he said. 'It was incredible. We had lost to Aberdeen and Hibs in our first two league games before beating Partick Thistle but then we were two goals down at half-time to our big rivals. I think it was Edvaldsson who had scored both for them but we weren't playing that badly and Celtic had scored against the run of play. However, I remember walking into the dressing room and thinking, with Jock's reputation, that there were going to be things flying around. But he told us all to sit down and have a cup of tea and very calmly said that if we continued to play the way we were playing then we would come back into the game. And sure enough, we got an early goal and the fans could sense something special was happening. The atmosphere was great, you could hear the supporters stamping their feet in the Main Stand as we came back to win 3–2 and that got our season going.'

After that Old Firm win Rangers lost only one of their next 23 games with Russell more than holding his own. He insists the players around him made the transition from junior to senior football almost seamless. 'None of the players were envious towards me coming straight into the team,' he said. 'No disrespect to the Shettleston boys but I went into a team laced with seasoned professionals and internationals so it made my job a lot easier. My football knowledge wasn't great, I just wanted to play, but the older players pulled me through. We had Tommy McLean, Sandy Jardine, Smith and Cooper, guys who liked to play football but also guys like Colin Jackson who was an unsung hero. I watch old games on television and big Colin was magnificent for us. He wasn't a silky player but he did his job week-in, week-out. You also had Alex MacDonald, Tom Forsyth and Greigy and they could all battle but as I say there was football there as well.'

Despite apparent initial misgivings, Wallace became a great fan of Russell and that respect was reciprocated. 'Jock was a man's man, a motivator and if you went about your business he would treat you accordingly,' says Russell. 'He wasn't the most tactically gifted manager, he was sergeant major material and as everyone knows he had been in the war. But when you played for Rangers or Celtic in those days, apart from playing against Aberdeen or in the Old Firm games, where you had to be aware of the opponent's danger, the thinking was "Let them worry about us." And I think Jock was right. Fitness is the most important thing and you find that out very quickly. You can have all the talent in the world but if you go into games unprepared then you are not the same player.

'We went to Gullane Sands for pre-season and it wasn't too bad for me because I didn't have a lot of weight. After a session of running up and down the dunes you would finish on Murder Hill and go up and down that until you were sick. The older guys would go first to make the steps in the sand, which would give you a foothold, and youngsters like myself would be well warned not to go outside them. Afterwards, we would get washed in the sea and then go for a fish supper. Different days. Greigy took the players to Gullane when he became manager, as did Alex MacDonald when he was at Hearts, and the proof of its benefits is the number of players from that time who played into their mid-30s.

'Murray Park [the club's new training ground, opened in 2001] was a godsend for Rangers when that was built, not only for the youth development but also for the first team. We trained at the Albion, which had a grass pitch and an all-weather pitch that was basically red ash. Once Gordon Smith took a shot that went over the wall and towards the nearby flats. Jock sent him looking for it but by the time he ran round the ball wasn't there. Someone told him a wee boy had run into the flats with it and Gordon was chapping doors asking for the ball back. Also, the players and youths get fresh training kit every day. Our training gear didn't even get washed. We put it on a hanger after training and the young kids would put it in the drying room overnight. By the Friday morning the tops were like cardboard. Contrast that with Murray Park which has wonderful pitches, a gym, individual showers, Jacuzzi, saunas, everything that players need and more.'

Russell's competitive debut at Pittodrie had ended in defeat and Aberdeen would prove to be a thorn in the side of the Govan club all season. However, he insists Rangers' most impressive performance of the Treble-winning season was in the first leg of their League Cup third-round tie on 5 October when the Dons were thrashed 6–1 at Ibrox. Smith scored a hat-trick with further goals from Johnstone, Alex Miller and MacDonald. 'That was by far the best game I have ever played in for Rangers, in terms of the whole team playing well,' Russell said. 'It was a good Aberdeen side at that time but that particular night everybody in our team played to their full potential. The game is easy when you have three or four options for a pass and every time you had the ball that night, you had options. The game is hard when you get the ball and all you see are backsides. Big Jock criticised me after the game though because I didn't shoot enough. I had two or three chances to score and I ended up passing the ball to someone else. He told me to be more selfish. Everybody loves scoring and I was no different. I just wish I had scored more during my career. People ask me how many goals I scored against Celtic and I say "not enough".'

Rangers and Aberdeen met again on 22 October at Ibrox on league business and the Gers won 3–1, after which Russell received that special accolade from Dons' boss McNeill. Four days later, in the second leg of their League Cup clash, Aberdeen won at Pittodrie by the same scoreline, which Russell recalls was something of a let-off for the Ibrox men. 'We scored very early on to make it 7–1 on aggregate but lost 3–1 – and it was going on six or seven for them.' The Granite City club would beat Rangers 4–0 at Pittodrie in December and then win 3–0 at Ibrox in March. Despite this reverse March was the turning point of the season for Rangers. They clinched the first part of the Treble on the 18th by beating Celtic 2–1 in the League Cup final at Hampden with new boys Cooper and Smith grabbing the goals in the extra-time win. Then, after losing 2–0 at Parkhead on the 25th they began an unbeaten run which secured the second part on 29 April when a 2–0 win over Motherwell at Ibrox made sure of the league title. They finished two points ahead of Aberdeen with Celtic eventually finishing fifth, 19 points behind the Gers.

Part three arrived the following week when Wallace's side confirmed their superiority over Aberdeen with a 2–1 win in the Scottish Cup final thanks to goals from MacDonald and Johnstone. But on a sunny Hampden afternoon in front of over 61,000 fans it was Russell who stole the show and was deservedly named man of the match.

Once more, despite their domestic dominance, Rangers failed in Europe. After getting past Young Boys of Berne in the first round of the Cup-Winners' Cup, Rangers were knocked out by FC Twente Enschede, 3–0 on aggregate after drawing

0–0 at Ibrox in the first leg. Russell, described as the 'find of the year' in that season's *Scottish Football Book (No. 24)*, is clear as to why he and his Ibrox teammates struggled at times in Europe. 'Football was a bit regimented at that time,' he says. 'If you were on the right side you ran up and down the right side and my first experience of players interchanging was against Twente Enschede. I couldn't believe their movement, they were changing position all the time and I didn't know whether to follow my man or not. That was definitely something that I had never seen before and was a steep part of my learning curve.'

However, despite the painful European lesson, Russell presumed domestic success would continue. He said: 'I had won a Treble in my first season. It was fantastic and I thought when we turned up for the next season we were going to do the same again. Then we got hit by the bombshell that big Jock had resigned and Greigy had taken over. It was a shock because you don't imagine a manager will resign after winning a Treble. I still don't know to this day why he did although the speculation remains that he wasn't given enough money.' Wallace had sensationally quit the Ibrox club on 23 May 1978, a couple of weeks after his side had won the Scottish Cup to complete the clean sweep. Greig was immediately installed as boss and called a halt to his playing career. But the Ibrox legend had a difficult time during his five-year spell in the hot-seat – although Russell believes it could have been so different with a little bit of luck in his first season, which started encouragingly.

Rangers won the League Cup in March 1979 with a 2–1 win over Aberdeen at Hampden with goals from MacDonald and Jackson. And the Light Blues would go on to secure a cup Double by beating Hibernian after three games in the Scottish Cup final at the end of the season. But in between the first and second replays, on 21 May, they needed only to draw against Celtic at Parkhead to all but ensure another Treble. MacDonald opened the scoring for Rangers who led at half-time but, despite having Johnny Doyle sent off, goals from Roy Aitken and George McCluskey had turned the game in favour of the home side. When Russell equalised with around 14 minutes remaining it looked like Greig would win the title at the first time of asking. However, Rangers could not hold out and lost to a Colin Jackson own goal and a late strike by Murdo MacLeod.

'To be fair to Greigy, we very nearly won the Treble again in his first season,' said Russell. 'He wasn't a bad manager; he was just a wee bit unlucky. I tell people that we were just minutes away from immortality in that 4–2 defeat against Celtic. My goal came from a corner. I didn't catch the ball great but it went through a lot of bodies and in at the far post. Had the score stayed 2–2 it would have gone down on record that I scored the goal that had more or less won the league. We still had a couple of games to go but if we had avoided defeat we had a great chance of winning the title again. That would have meant back-to-back Trebles and would have changed John Greig's managerial career. The perception is that John was a failure but that was because he didn't win the league. He won the Scottish Cup a couple of times and the League Cup.'

While stressing that Greig was unlucky, particularly in his first season as boss, Russell believes the removal of Johnstone from the front line and Smith from Ibrox altogether was the main reason behind the club's failure to win the title during Greig's tenure. He said: 'I was fine with Greigy but it was the older guys in the team who found it hard, as he did with them. When he took over he thought it was still Jock's team so I think he was too quick to get rid of some players. Big Derek was a fantastic striker and the previous season, 1977–78, he and Gordon Smith had scored more than 50 goals between them. Gordon was sold to Brighton a couple of years later and Derek was moved back to centre half. Derek wanted to go back and he did well but where do you get 50-odd goals from? To me that was a major mistake on Greigy's part. We would have won leagues by a country mile if those two had kept playing together. A blind man could see that. No disrespect to Mark Hateley, he was a great player at Ibrox, but I can't believe Derek is not in the best ever Rangers team. Derek was a penalty box predator who could turn bad crosses into good ones. When he went back into defence it was like Celtic losing Henrik Larsson. You win games by scoring goals. Derek Parlane could score but not as prolifically and Greigy signed Billy Urquhart, a great guy, but he is not going to score you 25 goals. And when we lost MacDonald and Jardine we didn't replace them with players who had the same winning mentality which is crucial at the Old Firm.'

Ironically, while Wallace could not make a mark in Europe despite attaining domestic success, Greig's first continental foray as a manager was relatively successful. In their European Cup campaign that year Rangers overcame Italian giants Juventus and the classy Dutch side, PSV Eindhoven, the then UEFA Cup holders, before going out to German side Cologne. Russell's winning goal in the 3–2 second-leg win against PSV Eindhoven in Holland, following a goalless draw at Ibrox, would prove to be his Light Blues legacy. 'People still remember me most for my goal against PSV,' he admits. 'I get asked about it all the time. I've occasionally done hospitality at Ibrox and Alex MacDonald, who is one of the regular hosts, jokes to the fans that if I hadn't scored that goal against PSV then people wouldn't know me. I remember the goal clearly. No one gave us a chance over there and those doubts looked to be confirmed when they scored in the first minute. We managed to peg it back to 1–1, then it was 2–1 for them and then we came back to make it 2–2. We were through to the next round on that score and Greigy must have been having kittens when I went on a run after Derek Johnstone had headed the ball down to Gordon Smith who then transferred it to Tommy McLean. Before you decide to make runs you look at the guy in possession of the ball. If it had been Colin Jackson then I wouldn't have made the run because he couldn't have played the pass but wee Tam could and did. It was a great and famous win because PSV hadn't ever been beaten at home in Europe but as a youngster you are not aware of what you have achieved at the time.

'In the previous round against Juventus, the Italian press and my teammates were praising me for my performance in the first game in Turin when we lost 1–0. Juventus were a right good side with players like Zoff, Bettega, Cabrini, Causio and Tardelli, and so the second game at Ibrox, when we won 2–0 to go through on aggregate, was a special night. It was the first time that Rangers had recovered from a first-leg defeat to win a two-legged European tie.'

Greig's failure to win the league title ultimately saw him depart the club in October 1983. Jock Wallace left Motherwell for a second spell in charge but that move didn't work out, leading to the sensational arrival in 1986 of player-manager Graeme Souness, which in many ways revolutionised Rangers and Scottish football – but signalled the end of Russell's time at Ibrox.

'Souness's arrival was good for Rangers but it wasn't good for me and I was there for one more season,' said Russell. 'He played in my position and there was no way I was going to get in ahead of him. He wanted me to play wide right and if there is one regret it is that I rebelled against that. I should never have done that. I should have buckled down and given it my best shot but I didn't. I could have been at Rangers for another three or four seasons and might have been there for the nine-in-a-row. But you can't turn the clock back. I moved to Motherwell and was in time joined by Coop and had a great time there. I played against Souness for Motherwell and felt I had a point to make. I nutmegged him and shouted "nuts" and he shouted to me, "What's your bank balance like son?" I also scored the winning goal for Motherwell against Rangers at Fir Park after being put in by Coop at the edge of the box. I was one of the first into the tearoom after the game and Derek Ferguson came out and told me Souness was still in the dressing room ranting and raving. Apparently he wasn't caring about getting beat, it was about me scoring the goal. But that doesn't take away anything from my time at Rangers. I won one league title, three Scottish Cups and four League Cups, not bad for ten years. I might be wrong but I think I am the only player to have started in six consecutive

Scottish Cup finals, from 1978 to 1983. I won three and lost three.'

Recalling a fulfilling career, Russell believes his first season at Ibrox was his best. He said: 'I still believe to this day that I should have been with Scotland at the 1978 World Cup in Argentina. Without a doubt. The Scotland manager [Ally MacLeod] took all the same type of midfield players, he never looked at youth. What a lot of people don't know is that in my second season I tore my cruciate ligament. In those days you couldn't do anything for that injury, they just cleaned it up and I was back playing but I was never right again. After that, although I was fit to play club football, I was nowhere near fit enough to play international football. If I hadn't got injured then who knows?'

13
PERMANENT REVOLUTION

In his first league match in charge of Rangers in 1986–87 Graeme Souness was ordered off. He was ordered off again in the match that clinched the championship that season. The scorer of the Rangers goal that secured that title was English internationalist Terry Butcher, who would be one of four players up in court following an Old Firm match the following season. Butcher would depart in 1990, as had several others by that time, after a massive row with Souness. Souness himself continued to clash regularly with the Scottish football authorities and to engage in protracted warfare with the Scottish media. As Rangers headed for a nail-biting league title climax in 1991 Souness suddenly quit the club. In between all this Souness was instrumental in bringing about a change in the ownership and control of Rangers, and crashed through the infamous 'barrier' to the signing of Catholic players with the audacious capture of former Celtic hero Mo Johnston in the summer of 1989, an event which has taken its place in the history of 20th century Scotland along with wars, home rule and the discovery of North Sea oil.

The sheer non-stop turbulence of the five-year Souness era has to be underlined and fully appreciated. This was not merely a revolution that overturned an 'old guard' and put in place a new order. It was a revolution that permanently rumbled through Ibrox during the manager's time in charge. There was little in the way of order; just constant change, ever-present controversy, and the restless insatiability of a man who rescued the club from near oblivion and turned it again towards the stars; yet whose departure probably conferred an equal blessing and permitted a welcome period of settled direction and considerable achievement.

It is hard now to recall the depths to which Rangers had slumped in the first half of the 1980s. Following the Treble-winning joys of the late 1970s, the routine nature of the team's faltering title challenge before the season was half over in the era both of John Greig's management and Jock Wallace's second spell in charge, plunged fans into despair. Greig's appointment – in the close season of 1978 following Wallace's resignation and subsequent decision to take up the job at Leicester City – came much too soon for someone who had just decided to stop playing. Nevertheless, the nucleus of the side that had enjoyed such success in the mid-1970s was still there, and it saw the team come agonisingly close to another Treble in the singular season of 1978–79 when a fearsome winter led to a fixture pile-up. With Rangers still battling it out in the European Cup in March, the demands and pressures simply told on the players.

John Greig wheeled and dealed but his signings could not lift the team to play to its potential. Indeed Rangers were left behind by the 'New Firm' of Aberdeen (bossed by former Ranger Alex Ferguson) and Dundee United (managed shrewdly by Jim McLean) as well as old rivals Celtic. The entertainment for Rangers fans in those years was often supplied solely by the brilliance of winger Davie Cooper, although he too seemed to lapse into baffling ineffectiveness at frequent intervals. Attend-ances at the new ultra-modern Ibrox stadium, transformed into a 44,000 capacity ground with some 36,000 seats by 1981, fell on several occasions below five figures. In his memoirs, sports broadcaster Archie Macpherson relates the story of new director David Holmes's introduction to the other directors' pre-match sweepstake ritual of guessing the crowd on the morning of a match, and the way he was mocked for suggesting that it would be close to capacity; the winner, chairman John Paton, had suggested a remarkably accurate 13,000.

This anecdote suggests that a certain complacency and small-mindedness, even cynicism, had come to pervade the top echelons of the club. In fairness, it has to be kept in mind that the costs of rebuilding Ibrox, a project for which the club neither sought nor received financial aid from outside bodies, undoubtedly hampered the task of rebuilding the team; and that the club felt constrained to insist on a rigid and modest wage structure for even its most valuable playing assets like Cooper. It was galling in the extreme for Rangers fans to watch as club captain and Northern Ireland internationalist John McLelland left for the better-remunerated terms offered by Watford in 1984. It should also be said that the Rangers board could be excused for taking the view that Greig, a club legend after all, had to be given a proper chance. When it was decided, after another bad start in season 1983-84 and in view of the fans' demonstrations, that he had to go, the two best young managers in the game in Scotland at the time, Ferguson and McLean, were approached in turn to take over. Both refused, but McLean at least has stressed on record that the directors made clear that he would be free to sign any player he chose. This suggests that at boardroom level it was accepted there had to be radical change.

The shock of being rejected not once but twice seems to have propelled the board into attempting to relive past glories by entrusting the task of a 'quick fix' to former boss Jock Wallace. Certainly, there were few other likely contenders around, and it was a popular choice among supporters who had to be attracted back as a matter of urgency. The price of such a move, however, would be to put on hold any necessary departure from Rangers tradition as interpreted by the still intimidating figure of Wallace. Big Jock, in fact, relayed the news to Archie Macpherson in the form of a 'party song' over the telephone.

He made a promising start by leading the team to a League Cup triumph over Celtic, but Wallace could not recreate the chemistry of his winning teams of the 1970s. There was nobody with quite the spirit of Alex MacDonald or indeed John Greig, and Derek Johnstone was a shadow of his former self by the time he was brought back from Chelsea in 1985. Cooper continued to entrance, and young talent such as Ian Durrant, Derek Ferguson and Robert Fleck were blooded. Such players would flourish under Souness, as would the irrepressible Ally McCoist, originally signed by Greig in 1983 but not a first choice striker until Wallace's arrival. McCoist played a prominent part in a remarkable Old Firm match of fluctuating fortunes in March 1986, which ended in a 4–4 draw. Rangers celebrated the result like a win whereas Celtic could only view it as points dropped in the title race with a then rampant Hearts side. It was a state of affairs that demeaned Rangers; a fact made worse as that point ultimately proved crucial to Celtic's ultimate success in the championship.

By this time, therefore, it was apparent that Wallace was no longer capable of working the magic. Off the field, moreover, matters were taking shape with significant purpose. Lawrence Marlborough, grandson of John Lawrence and inheritor of the latter's building empire, manoeuvred himself into position as the majority shareholder and installed director David Holmes as chief executive with full control of the running of the club. In the spring of 1986 Holmes secured the agreement of Souness to return to Scotland from Sampdoria in Italy, where he was still playing, to take on the role of player-manager. Following defeat to Tottenham in a friendly match, arranged because Rangers had been eliminated from the Scottish Cup, Wallace's reign ended. Souness was promised money to rebuild – money that had not been made available to Wallace – and the freedom to sign anyone.

The move electrified the Scottish game, and indeed the wider society. Fans simply wanted the existing season to finish and the new one to begin. At first the focus was on Souness himself gracing the Rangers midfield, then on whether he would immediately sign a Catholic player. In the latter respect he almost did, in the person of Scotsman Ally Dick of Tottenham, but such was the tawdry coverage of the matter in the tabloids (one paper published a mocked-up photo of Dick with a cross around his neck) that it was considered advisable to drop the idea. During his first season, Souness's attempt to acquire Ray Houghton ran into the difficulties of persuading the player – a Glaswegian who played for the Republic of Ireland international team – to defy the hostility among his co-religionists to such a move. Over the years Rangers had been guilty of allowing this matter to become a weapon in the hands of their critics and antagonists. Such people in turn were very reluctant to relinquish the weapon and the Rangers-bashing to which they believed it entitled them.

The issue in any case came to be somewhat overshadowed in Souness's early days by his coup in bringing English internationalists Terry Butcher and Chris Woods to Ibrox. They would be followed during 1986–87 by Graham Roberts, thus setting a pattern which would continue through the seasons and see such distinguished English players as Ray Wilkins, Trevor Francis, Trevor Steven, Mark Hateley and Mark Walters don the famous shirt. During Souness's time in charge 20 out of the 37 players he brought to the club were English.

This in itself was a revolution unprecedented in Scottish football history. Virtually overnight Souness reversed the customary flow of talent from north of the border to the south, and made the English media and football world take proper notice of Scotland. It was certainly true that he was helped by the ban on English clubs participating in European competitions after the Heysel stadium disaster; yet there was such a long history of English condescension to the Scottish game that only Souness's personal standing in the football world and the drive of his personality could have effected such a transformation. Rangers fans were at first bewildered then increasingly gratified by the English influx and, because success came quickly, were not disposed to question the longer term implications of this policy. In his book, *The Final Whistle?*, which inquired into the condition of the national game in 2005, journalist Harry Reid made the pertinent point that Souness's reliance on buying established English and other non-Scottish talent meant that Rangers and eventually Celtic had less incentive to develop their own young players. 'And when they did sign promising young players from other Scottish teams,' wrote Reid, 'they tended to languish in the reserves, bereft of first-team football.' Rangers fans were disinclined to acknowledge it at the time, but in a way Souness's approach only compounded a long-running cause for concern at Ibrox regarding the relative scarcity of youngsters coming through the ranks, a state of affairs which dated back to at least the 1960s, although some credit is due to John Greig in his time as manager in this respect. When, later on, the money for transfers would not be so plentiful the fans would have cause to reflect on this matter more ruefully.

On the coaching side, in contrast to the playing pitch, Souness chose a Scot to assist him – Rangers fan Walter Smith – who had been assistant to Jim McLean at Dundee United. Smith's profound knowledge of the Scottish game would prove crucial to Souness, as would his ability to calm the manager down in moments of stress and defuse at least some of the confrontations that arose. In the first season, after a calamitous start that saw Souness dismissed from the field at Easter Road, the team settled down to play some fine football. The League Cup was won in dramatic fashion against Celtic with Durrant and Cooper on target. The same two players had combined memorably in the Old Firm league match earlier in the season to give Rangers victory in that as well. In Europe only desperate ill-luck prevented Rangers from getting past a strong Borussia Mönchengladbach side. The turning point in the title race probably came in the matches over the Christmas and New Year holiday period when successive victories at Ibrox over Dundee United and Celtic instilled the genuine belief that the title was coming home.

In his foreword to journalist Chick Young's record of this remarkable season, *Rebirth of the Blues*, cult hero Jim Baxter's explanation of the Rangers' revival was that they had 'gone for class'. 'The biggest compliment I can give them is that they look a lot more like the Glasgow Rangers I used to play for,' he wrote. Baxter went on to draw the comparison between himself and Souness, noting the arrogance which was a feature of both their games. At no time was this more starkly in evidence than the cauldron of the New Year Old Firm game at Ibrox when Souness imperiously put his foot on the ball, swung one way, sold a dummy to one Celtic player, and swung the other way to release Davie Cooper. It could have been Baxter 20-odd years before. And, in hindsight ironically, the Celtic player momentarily shown up by Souness's class and his arrogance was Mo Johnston.

Rangers clinched the title on an emotional day at Aberdeen and then celebrated in front of a packed Ibrox the following week. The rehabilitation of the club seemed to have been triumphantly completed in double-quick time, at least on the playing side. However, football being the game it is and the Old Firm phenomenon being what it is, the following season saw a rejuvenated Celtic, under new manager Billy McNeill, register a league and cup Double in their centenary year while Rangers could capture only the League Cup. A 1–0 reverse at Celtic Park in August saw Souness sent off and then later clash with the referee. It was as close as he came to walking away from Rangers and from Scottish football up to that point.

Rangers did make a credible showing in the European Cup but were severely hampered with injuries when they faltered in the quarter-final. Injuries in fact were central to the story of this frustrating season: in October, Terry Butcher broke his leg, while after the New Year McCoist had to undergo a cartilage operation. The loss of both at vital times was incalculable: Butcher, in Souness's opinion, had been the catalyst for the club's re-emergence and the rock on which its success had been built.

Yet the manager could be said to have made crucial errors of judgement. Not long into the season he sold striker Robert Fleck to Norwich, and allowed new striker Mark Falco to return to England after barely three months at Ibrox. This left the team woefully short in attack and Durrant was temporarily moved up from midfield. Although he performed well his contribution to the midfield was sorely missed. When McCoist was out injured Souness brought in Ian Ferguson from St Mirren, a Rangers diehard who would have played anywhere for the cause but who was also a midfielder. The comings and goings of players had indeed reached farcical levels, and the effects were unsettling. The constant transfer activity was later likened to a 'revolving door' by Richard Gough who had also joined in 1987–88. Towards the end of this season a spectacular fall-out between Souness and Graham Roberts saw the man who had become a fans' favourite transferred to Chelsea. The season ended in bitter recrimination.

On a more positive note, another of season 1987–88's sign-ings, Mark Walters, proved like Gough to be an excellent investment. The black winger from Aston Villa produced some breathtaking skills, but more significantly his recruitment sent out the message that racist attitudes would not be tolerated. The player in fact was given an outstandingly supportive welcome at Ibrox and this helped him over some initial hard times when he was subjected to racial abuse, most notably on his debut at Parkhead when the Celtic supporters threw bananas and made so-called 'monkey noises'. The Scottish media's reluctance to draw attention to this incident was, to say the least, puzzling. Most commentators seemed more exercised by what were tendentiously viewed as the supposedly 'un-Scottish' and 'Thatcherite' qualities of Souness. In this Souness was simply a few steps ahead in a game which was becoming increasingly commercialised and business-oriented. Equally, Souness's open contempt for many journalists simply guaranteed him a hostile press.

Souness certainly had contacts in the world of business, and one in particular became a close personal friend. David Murray was one of Scotland's outstanding entrepreneurs having made his fortune from steel and overcome the personal hardships of losing both legs in a car accident and his wife tragically to cancer. In 1988 Souness persuaded him to buy a controlling interest in Rangers. Souness himself invested a considerable sum of his own and became a director as well as team manager. It appeared to be a signal that Souness was in for the long haul, and the Souness–Murray partnership was clearly bent on piloting Rangers into a European elite. More and more there was talk of a European Super League, and Rangers were now getting ready for it. Further expansion and improvements were made to the stadium, and the club led the way in providing executive boxes, hospitality and business facilities.

On the field season 1988–89 was a satisfying one overall. An early routing of Celtic – 5–1 at Ibrox – set the tone, and the team looked formidable. No Rangers fan who was at Ibrox on 27 August 1988 will ever forget it. Other decisive victories over the club's fiercest rivals have followed, including a 4–1 win that same season, but the delirium of this particular day has not been surpassed. And it began grimly. Shortly after kick-off as the rain cascaded down, Frank McAvennie shot Celtic ahead. Memories of the previous season's trials came to mind. The team, though, shrugged the blow off and began to press. The sun came out. Ally swept home the equaliser. There was only one team in it. Just before half-time Ray Wilkins connected with a Gary Stevens' throw-in and sent the sweetest of volleys whistling into the corner of the net. In its controlled execution this was as fine a goal as has ever been seen in an Old Firm game. The remaining nerves in the stands and the East Enclosure were calmed a few minutes after the interval when Celtic keeper Ian Andrews allowed McCoist's looping header to drop over him into the net. Celtic were now tottering. The fourth goal knocked them flat. A piece of sublime trickery on the right by Walters was followed by an inviting cross which Kevin Drinkell converted with a diving header. The ball simply soared into the top corner. Incredibly, two minutes later, Walters himself added a fifth after the Celtic defence had got into a spectacular fankle. Ibrox was jumping, the fans bug-eyed with joy. There were still 30 minutes to go and some fans now regret that the team eased up, that no more goals were scored, and that the chance to wipe out the calamity of the 7–1 defeat of 1957 was not taken. That, however, could only have been a minor consideration at the time as the fans piled out of the stadium exultant, and the car horns blared in triumph along the red, white and blue carnival of Paisley Road West.

Then, a couple of months further on, disaster struck when midfield maestro Ian Durrant was crippled at Aberdeen by a savage tackle from Neil Simpson. Durrant was to be out for over a year while his knee was in effect rebuilt. A gloriously creative flame had been brutally snuffed out. Inside the club and across the vast support base this incident and others saw the start of a defensive and embattled mentality. It was all too clear that Rangers' success, their willingness to spend big and the aspiration to join a European elite evoked sheer hostility, envy and often hatred in a broad section of Scottish opinion, well beyond traditional rivalries. The limited degree of sympathy for Durrant and the apparent tolerance of the perverted responses of some Aberdeen supporters confirmed many involved with Rangers in the view that the club could expect little in the way of backing for their ambition. Relations between the club and the Scottish FA nosedived. Among the 'Tartan Army' – the term coined for supporters of the Scottish national team – there was no obvious regret, as there ought to have been, that the chances of Scotland producing another world-class player in the mould of Dalglish or Souness had gone with Durrant's injury.

But Rangers marched on. They secured the League Cup in a thrilling final against Aberdeen and then processed straight-forwardly to the title. Celtic lay in wait in the Scottish Cup final. In a poor match a Celtic goal, scored from a throw-in which had been awarded to Rangers yet taken opportunistically by Celtic skipper Roy Aitken, was enough to deny the Ibrox club's Treble hopes. Terry Butcher also had a late, headed goal mysteriously chalked off. Souness raged in the dressing room about the injustice but also muttered cryptically that their opponents that day had a shock coming to them.

So had the country. On 10 July 1989 Rangers unveiled new signing Maurice Johnston, a matter of weeks since the inter-national striker had apparently pledged to return to Celtic after a spell in France. He had even been photographed prior to the Scottish Cup final in a Celtic strip. For Souness and Murray this was the greatest gamble of all. Not only was Johnston Catholic, he was an ex-Celt whose conduct at Old Firm games had out-raged Rangers fans. The supporters in general were prepared for change but were they prepared for their world to turn upside down?

Before long the answer to that was an affirmative on the part of the great majority. Packed houses welcomed Johnston, and any misgivings evaporated in November when he struck a sensational winning goal against Celtic at Ibrox. This was not, in fact, his Old Firm debut: that was at Parkhead in August when he actually spurned two good opportunities in a 1–1 draw, a match played in what journalist Jack Webster, no fan of Rangers, described as a 'cauldron of hate' whipped up by the Celtic fans. It certainly assisted Johnston's acceptance that the transfer had struck Celtic such a demoralising blow.

However, perhaps the crucial factor was Glasgow and west of Scotland humour. The Johnston affair was a veritable factory of jokes and wind-ups; the bitterness of some fans on both sides was eclipsed by the other side to the Old Firm rivalry, the often less heralded day-to-day banter and the social adhesiveness of the popular culture surrounding it. That said, Rangers had discarded the albatross around the club's neck that the religious issue had become, and there were those in Scotland – Celtic fans mainly but not exclusively – who resented being deprived of the justification for what was often in any case a phoney sense of moral superiority. In much of the English coverage of the affair there was another kind of superior attitude, something along the lines of the 'barbaric' Scots and their 'Calvinist' obsessions. Rangers indeed were depicted almost as the sporting wing of the 'Wee Free' fundamentalists.

Nevertheless, Scottish media comment was positive. 'It is a significant move in the right direction and a breakthrough for Scottish society as a whole', concluded the editorial of the *Scotsman*, while the *Glasgow Herald* admonished the Catholic Church spokesman who described the move as 'a purely financial one'. The *Herald* leader, like that of the *Scotsman*, did, however, allude to the part played by Rangers' Super League ambitions and the risk of 'an outdated club policy' rendering them ineligible. This was a valid point but when all was said and done the decision was ultimately that of Souness, a man who had made it plain from the beginning that he would make such a change. His was a forward-looking, restlessly ambitious and decidedly unparochial spirit. The doyen of sportswriters, Hugh McIlvanney, observed at the time that Rangers fans tended to venerate their 'hard men' – the Woodburns, Greigs and 'Tiger' Shaws. He added that they had another one in Souness and that their world would never be the same. True, but the world of these fans remained the Rangers.

Johnston joined Rangers the same year the Berlin Wall came down and the world moved beyond the Cold War. Maybe there was just something in the air. He was in fact the 16th known Catholic to have played for the club, as the *Rangers Historian* publication chronicled at the time. Others, largely from the pre-First World War era, included Archie Kyle, the son of Irish immigrants who was born in the shadow of Celtic Park, and

Willie Kivlichan, a qualified doctor. The *Historian* brought to light the equally little-known fact that there had also been 14 previous players who had turned out for both clubs.

The acquisition of Johnston paid dividends on the field as Rangers widened the gap between them and Celtic and captured another title. Europe, however, brought only further disappointment. It was Rangers' misfortune to be paired early on with Bayern Munich. Even though the club's profile now suggested the heights of the game, there were still serious shortcomings on the playing side. At this time the rules of European competition stated that only two (later raised to three) non-Scottish players could be fielded.

Souness's frustrations around this matter deepened the following season when Rangers again crashed out early, this time to a scintillating Red Star Belgrade. He vented his anger at journalists and began to wonder if he had taken the club as far as he could. The stark truth was that the Scottish game was in decline, with fewer truly gifted home-grown players to work with. The level of competition in Scotland simply did not compare with countries like Italy, Germany, Spain and indeed England, whose clubs were readmitted to European competition in 1990.

Suddenly, early in 1991, the Liverpool job became vacant with the resignation of Kenny Dalglish. Souness's recollections make it clear that an accumulation of problems in Scotland – some undoubtedly of his own making, particularly in his relations with players – and the constant aggravation he was subjected to from opposition fans made him decide to move when Liverpool offered him the post. In his book *The Management Years* he refers to an undignified confrontation at Perth with Aggie, the St Johnstone tea lady, over the state in which the Rangers players had left their changing room, as the final straw. Perhaps too the scabrous abuse he had to endure at Parkhead from the well-heeled Celtic supporters in the main stand, as Rangers slumped to a 2–0 defeat in the Scottish Cup, played a significant part in his decision. Scotland in many ways was quite comfortable with bigotry, or with scapegoating one club for it. That day Rangers did not just lose, they imploded: the team lost its discipline and had three players ordered off. In a sense this indicated that Rangers needed to move on from Souness as much as the other way round. It was time for a new management style.

Murray was aghast at his friend's departure and told him he would come to regret it. The parting was indeed badly handled, and there was a palpable sense of betrayal. In time, however, this was forgotten and forgiven by the overwhelming majority of Rangers fans who knew that Souness had performed something like the kiss of life on the club, and that his legacy was keenly felt through the rest of a remarkable decade in Rangers' history.

14
NINE-IN-A-ROW

There can have been few occasions during the Old Firm's long rivalry when the skipper of one of the Glasgow giants would feel sorry for the other, but Rangers legend Richard Gough had exactly those feelings towards his Celtic counterpart during the Light Blues' nine-in-a-row years from 1989 to 1997. The former Scotland skipper was friendly with Paul McStay, captain of the Hoops during most of the 1990s, when Celtic could only watch helplessly as their superior rivals dominated the Scottish scene.

He recalled his feelings at the time in an interview with the *Daily Telegraph* in May 2009: 'During that period I would go out with Paul McStay, whom I knew from playing beside him for Scotland in World Cup games,' Gough said. 'I loved Paul and thought he was the best player Celtic had for years, but I felt sorry for him. I was playing with maybe the best of British at that time and even in the tunnel I would look at him as if to say, "You've got no chance here, pal". And he would look back and you could tell he knew that as well. It was down to the quality of players we had. Okay, it's a derby and anything could happen, but most of the time we would win, which was down to the level of players at both clubs.'

Gough's transfer to Rangers from Spurs in 1987, which made him the first player to be signed for £1 million by a Scottish club, typified the financial disparity between the Glasgow giants at that time. The South African-born defender, who had been overlooked by Rangers as a youngster, moved from Dundee United to Tottenham. He skippered Spurs to an FA Cup final in 1987, before he teamed up with Graeme Souness and Walter Smith at Ibrox, which had changed in all manner of ways since his last visit there.

Souness's arrival as player-manager in 1986 had been a turning point for the club and in many ways for Scottish football. Souness had worked under Smith briefly during the 1986 World Cup in Mexico but it was at the request of the club's chairman, David Holmes, that the two men were reunited in Govan. Souness told the story in an interview for the *Daily Record* in April 2010: 'We were thrown together by David back in 1986 – it was his idea,' Souness said. 'I had worked with Walter when I was a player and he was Jock [Stein] then Alex Ferguson's assistant at the World Cup. I didn't know a great deal about him. But very quickly at Rangers, I lent heavily on Walter. He had been around Jim McLean and saw how he operated. Although I had played at the highest level with Liverpool and I'd won trophies, I was reliant on Walter when coming back to Scotland. None of what I'd seen or done as a player prepared me for management at Rangers and I was totally reliant on him, not just at first but throughout the five years I spent at Ibrox.'

After dramatically winning the league title for the first time in nine years in his first season, Souness watched Celtic snatch it back from Ibrox in the Hoops' centenary year. However, on 13 August 1988, when England international Gary Stevens, a £1 million summer signing from Everton, scored the first goal in a 2–0 win over Hamilton, few inside Douglas Park would have believed Rangers had taken the first step on the road to nine-in-a-row.

Equalling Celtic's league record was still a long way off but there was an opportunity to set another record straight two weeks later. In the Old Firm league meeting at Ibrox the visitors took an early lead but Rangers roared back to win 5–1, a record league win over their old rivals. To this day, many Gers supporters believe that was the perfect chance to avenge Celtic's 7–1 League Cup final win of 1957 as did many of the players in the team who were Rangers fans.

Ian Ferguson, who had achieved a boyhood dream when he signed from St Mirren for a fee of £850,000 in 1986, said. 'Even though I was happy that we had won 5–1, me, Coisty, Bomber [John Brown] and Durranty were raging. We had never had a better opportunity. We had them rattled.'

It was an early indication of the dominance Rangers were beginning to enjoy over the Parkhead men. On 3 January there was an equally convincing 4–1 win over Celtic and then on 1 April Rangers managed their first victory in the East End of Glasgow in nine years when Kevin Drinkell and Ferguson scored in a 2–1 win. The Light Blues went from strength to strength and a runaway championship victory was sealed with a 4–0 win over Hearts at Ibrox. Rangers had won 14 out of their last 16 matches, including a run of nine victories, and finished six points clear of runners-up Aberdeen and ten ahead of Celtic.

The summer of 1989 will be forever remembered for the signing of former Celtic striker Maurice Johnston, the first high-profile Catholic to play for the club in decades. Despite fears to the contrary, the overwhelming majority of Rangers supporters took to the former Nantes striker right away and were repaid in November when he scored a dramatic and famous last-minute winner against Celtic at Ibrox. Johnston was to finish as the club's top scorer that season and helped Rangers to their first New Year Old Firm win at Parkhead since 1964 when Nigel Spackman scored the only goal of the game.

There was a more comfortable 3–0 win over a struggling Celtic side at Ibrox on April Fool's Day and the title was confirmed when Trevor Steven headed the winner in a 1–0 victory over Dundee United at Tannadice with two games to spare. Significantly, it was again Aberdeen who had finished runners-up, seven points behind the champions who were 17 ahead of Celtic who tied on points in fifth place with Motherwell and Hibernian. The balance of power in Glasgow had swung firmly towards Govan but nothing is ever smooth in the world of the Old Firm and despite the positive mood around the club, Rangers would end the following season with a different manager.

Mark Hateley became the next big name to join the club when he was signed from AC Milan for £1 million ahead of the 1990–91 season and, after an indifferent start, he would prove to be a huge success at Ibrox. A strong middle part of the season saw Rangers go on a 15-match unbeaten run until they were beaten 1–0 at Pittodrie by Aberdeen, who again were the closest challengers. The Gers got back on track immediately but the fans were stunned on 16 April, when, weeks after saying he could never leave Rangers, Souness sensationally brought an end to his often turbulent tenure, opting to return to Liverpool to succeed Kenny Dalglish as manager.

The Ibrox club appeared in turmoil but just three days after Souness left Murray brought an end to speculation about a new manager by appointing Smith as his successor. It was something of a surprise even for Smith who, at that time, was a low-profile figure at Ibrox and who had no managerial experience. 'Graeme had already had an opportunity to go to Liverpool and turned it down. When he took it the next time it came up, he asked me and Phil Boersma to go with him but there was staff already there in Ronnie Moran and Roy Evans so I didn't feel there was a place there for me,' said Smith. 'Although I was grateful to Graeme for giving me the opportunity it wouldn't have worked out. I was in limbo a wee bit but Sir David Murray called me and asked me to be caretaker manager to give him some time to think about what he was going to do but after three or four days he said he was going to offer me the job and I was obviously delighted. At that time Sir David could have gone to most clubs in the country and asked for their manager because Rangers were on a par with the top teams in England. The easiest decision was to go and get a far more experienced manager and I would have had to leave, that's the way it was, but it worked out all right and I will always be grateful to him for making that decision. Who knows what would have happened to my career after that? There was always the nagging doubt whether you would be able to handle all the aspects of the job and produce a winning team, which is what Rangers is all about. Fortunately for me, I got my first opportunity (to win a title) in only my fourth match in charge, against Aberdeen at Ibrox, in what was effectively a title decider. It's not often that happens. We won so that gave the support a bit of faith in me.'

The transition from Souness to Smith was seamless but who knows what might have happened if Rangers had lost to the Dons. Following Souness's departure, Smith had engineered victories over St Mirren and Dundee United but a shock 3–0 defeat away to Motherwell meant that on the last day of the season Aberdeen only needed a draw in Govan to take the title.

Super fan Garry Lynch, who followed Rangers all over the globe before he sadly passed away in February 2009, recalled that game as his favourite in terms of atmosphere: 'Everyone was walking around outside Ibrox before that game really charged up. I'm usually fairly optimistic but that day I didn't think we were going to do it. We had a team of walking wounded but their spirit and determination was brilliant and the support that day was just the best it's ever been. The fans at Ibrox are at their best in adversity and I honestly believe they won the game for Rangers. That day every one of them deserved a medal.'

Lynch's thoughts are echoed by Ian Ferguson who recalled the fervour of the supporters as the teams warmed up: 'The atmosphere before the game was incredible,' he said. 'I knew we were not going to get beat.' However, despite Ferguson's confidence there were plenty of nervous moments for Rangers before a Mark Hateley double clinched title number three and confirmed his status as an Ibrox hero.

Smith, helped by new assistant Archie Knox, was up and

running and in the summer of 1991 he began the wheeling and dealing in the transfer market. With success came riches and Rangers were able to compete for some of the best British players available, while others left to make room. Trevor Steven left for Marseille for a fee of £5.58 million while Chris Woods, Mo Johnston and Mark Walters moved to Sheffield Wednesday, Everton and Liverpool respectively. One of Smith's first recruits was goalkeeper Andy Goram from Hibernian for £1 million while Alexei Mikhailichenko, Stuart McCall, David Robertson, Dale Gordon and Paul Rideout also arrived in Govan.

In 1991–92 a fourth successive championship was secured for the first time in over 60 years and the Scottish Cup was won for the first time in 11 years with a 2–1 win over Airdrie at Hampden with Hateley and McCoist – the Millar and Brand of the 1990s – grabbing the goals. McCoist had long since rehabilitated himself in the eyes of the Rangers support after a uncertain start to his Ibrox career – like Hateley – and would end the season as the league's top scorer with 34 goals. Those goals won him the European Golden Boot – the first time a Scot had won the award, and a feat he repeated the following year.

Hearts took over from Aberdeen as the main challengers that season but a McCoist winner at Tynecastle on 1 February kept the Ibrox side on an impressive run which saw them lose just once in 24 matches – to Celtic at Ibrox – before clinching the title with a 4–0 home win over St Mirren. Rangers scored more than a century of goals in the league, finishing nine points ahead of Hearts and ten ahead of Celtic.

In 1992–93 the Rangers team of that era peaked, both domestically and in Europe. It was one of one of the most successful seasons in the club's history and undoubtedly the best European campaign since the Cup-Winners' Cup triumph of 1972. Rangers stampeded their way to a domestic Treble – the fifth in their history – and also went to within one game of the Champions League final.

After beating Stranraer 5–0 away in the League Cup on 19 August, Smith's side went on an unbeaten run in all competitions of 44 games, only ending with a 2–1 league defeat by Celtic at Parkhead on 20 March. The championship was retained with four games to go when Gary McSwegan scored the only goal of the game against Airdrie at Broomfield. Rangers finished nine points ahead of Aberdeen and 13 ahead of an increasingly bedraggled Celtic side. The Scottish Cup was secured with a 2–1 win over the Dons at Celtic Park, to add to the League Cup that had been captured earlier in the season with another 2–1 win over the Pittodrie club at Hampden.

The winning of the Treble allowed Ferguson, born in the shadow of Celtic Park, to fulfil a lifelong ambition. 'I had never been in the Trophy Room before,' he said. 'I had said I would only go in if we win the three trophies. When you think of all the great players of the past, it was brilliant.'

Europe was the one frustration that season. Rangers beat English First Division champions Leeds United home and away in the last qualifier to silence a condescending English media. In the group stage Rangers remained undefeated, winning two matches and drawing four but it was Marseille who topped the section and went on to beat AC Milan in the final. The French side were later found guilty of match fixing in the game that clinched their Ligue 1 title, but that was of little comfort to the Ibrox club. Like many Rangers fans, Walter Smith could only ponder on what might have been that season. 'We had a good dressing room with good characters,' he said. 'The group grew in confidence that year as the tournament went on. If we hadn't lost Mark Hateley for the game in Marseille, after he was sent off against Brugge, we would have got to the final in 1993. We may well have beaten AC Milan in the final. I'm not saying we were a better team but that Milan team had four years of heavy football behind them. By their standards, they were struggling.'

That narrow miss was to be the high-water mark of Rangers' European challenges in the 1990s although domestic success continued. The following season, 1993–94, Smith's side came close to an historic back-to back Treble during an injury-hit campaign. They had secured the services of Duncan Ferguson, who arrived at Ibrox from Dundee United in July for a then British transfer record fee of £4 million, but despite promise and potential the lanky striker's impact was to be minimal. As Rangers stuttered in the early part of the season Gordon Durie signed for £1.2 million from Tottenham in November to give the Ibrox fans a boost. Despite poor form Rangers began to grind results out, starting out on a 17-match unbeaten run with a 4–0 win at St Johnstone on 18 December.

Rangers were helped by the fact that their own injury problems that season were small beer compared to the worries of their Old Firm rivals, who were in tatters. The Parkhead club had already been through several managers in their bid to halt the runaway Ibrox club. Billy McNeill (1987–1991) and Liam Brady (1991–93) were found wanting and Lou Macari was away by the end of the season 1993–94, replaced by Tommy Burns. The former Celtic midfielder was installed by new owner Fergus McCann who had ended a family dynasty at the club in March 1994, while rescuing it from potential bankruptcy.

The Celtic directors must have known their days were numbered on New Year's Day, 1994, when Rangers raced into a three-goal lead at Parkhead with less than half an hour played. Gough believes that game, which the visitors eventually won 4–2, revealed how far Celtic had fallen. 'Even Oleg Kuznetsov scored,' he mused. 'That's how bad it was.' That defeat appeared to be the final straw for some of the Celtic fans who watched their team capitulate to their greatest rivals. There was an almost sinister atmosphere in the ground as Hoops fans in the main stand turned on the club's directors, throwing missiles, including coins, pies and mars bars into the directors' box, where Smith was also sitting. Irate Celtic supporters also invaded the pitch and one had to be bundled to the ground by Gough, John Brown, police and stewards as he ran towards Rangers keeper Ally Maxwell. Thankfully the simmering malevolence remained mostly in check as Rangers ran out comfortable winners. The course of Celtic's history would change just three months later when McCann took over but by then Smith's side were out of sight, seeing off the challenge of Aberdeen and third-placed Motherwell to make it six-in-a-row.

Much had been made of the Ibrox club's team spirit during that period and Brown, whom Souness had bought from Dundee, personified that never-say-die attitude. 'There was a great camaraderie about the squad,' he said. 'Even when we went behind we kept going. Maybe the performances weren't great but the attitude was.' How that team spirit was forged was a contentious issue. Gough coined the phrase, 'The team that drinks together wins together' to sum up the 1992–93 season but Smith believes that oft-repeated maxim has been over-exaggerated by his players over the years. Looking back at the season during an interview in the *Scotsman* in September 2009 he said: 'See that, that's a self-perpetuating thing,' he said. 'They tell everyone what they got up to. But if it was true, what were all the other players from the other teams doing? Were they all out in the pub?'

Earlier in the season, Rangers had won the League Cup against Hibs at Celtic Park in dramatic circumstances. With the game poised at 1–1, McCoist came off the bench for only his fourth appearance since sustaining a broken leg while playing for Scotland the previous April and scored the winner minutes from time with an outrageous overhead kick.

On 21 May 1994 Dundee United stood between Rangers and a back-to-back Treble. The Ibrox side went in to the game firm favourites against a club who had lost their previous six finals at Hampden. However, a mix-up between Rangers defender Dave McPherson and keeper Maxwell gave United striker Craig Brewster the chance to knock the ball into an empty net from a few yards and United emerged shock 1–0 winners. The Treble dream was dead; who knew when another opportunity might crop up?

In the summer of 1994 Smith made another two big-money signings, Basile Boli and Brian Laudrup, for £2.7 million and £2.3 million respectively. Boli, a rugged defender, had scored the winning goal for Marseille against AC Milan in the 1993 European Cup final. However, he struggled to adapt to the Scottish game and his time at Ibrox was disappointing and short-lived. In complete contrast, Laudrup, who had an unhappy time at Fiorentina before Smith brought him to Ibrox, achieved legendary status in his four-year spell in Govan. Many fans consider the Danish striker to be the greatest player ever to have worn the light blue jersey. He was absolutely sensational in his first season at the club and was rightly named Scotland's player of the year as Rangers marched on to title number seven. Laudrup exuded class and style. He seemed to float past defenders and make the game appear easy, the sign of a true great. The only downside to his magisterial performances was the fact that so few of them took place in European competition.

Smith continued to build from a position of strength and the next superstar to join the club was the exciting and excitable Paul Gascoigne. There had never been such a hero's welcome given to a new signing as the one afforded to the English international when he arrived at Ibrox in July, 1995, after his £4.3 million move from Italian side Lazio. There was a predictable media frenzy and, just as at the time of Souness's arrival, the English football journalists were forced to keep in touch with goings-on in Scotland.

Gascoigne was not the only new boy in the Rangers dressing room that summer. Oleg Salenko, who had scored five goals for Russia against Cameroon in the 1994 World Cup finals, Steven Wright from Aberdeen and Gordan Petric from Dundee United were also added to the ever-changing squad, which would be bolstered further later in the season by Derek McInnes (from Morton), and Erik Bo Andersen (Aalborg) while Peter van Vossen (Istanbulspor) would arrive on a swap deal that would see Salenko leave Ibrox.

However, all the attention was on Gazza and a wonderful solo goal against Celtic at Parkhead early in the season endeared the Englishman further to the Light Blue legions. The clinching goal in a 2–0 win turned out to be even more significant than first thought. The Parkhead side were rejuvenated under Tommy Burns and would not lose another league game all season.

But Rangers had Gascoigne and Laudrup, who were head and shoulders above the rest of Scottish football. The Geordie reserved his best performance for the penultimate day of the season against Aberdeen at Ibrox when the title was up for grabs. Gers fans were stunned when Brian Irvine gave Aberdeen the lead but Gascoigne came to life and, in an unforgettable solo performance, he scored a hat-trick to bring the 46th championship to Govan.

A week later in the Scottish Cup final against Hearts at Hampden Gazza was in great form again but even he was over-shadowed by Laudrup. The Great Dane was at his magnificent best, scoring a double and unselfishly helping Gordon Durie to a hat-trick in a 5–1 thumping of the shell-shocked Tynecastle side.

By the close season of 1996, the prospect of equalling Celtic's nine-in-a-row feat was a major topic of conversation in the blue half of Glasgow. Indeed, Rangers fans were expecting the ninth consecutive title to be delivered – anything else would be failure and the players knew that. To that end, Smith refurbished his squad again. Midfield powerhouse Jorg Albertz was bought from Hamburg for £4 million with Swedish international defender Joachim Bjorklund signing from Vicenza in Italy for £2.7 million.

The season started well, but in Europe the strain began to tell. Rangers had failed to build on their European success of 1992–93 and owner David Murray was frustrated. Rangers sustained defeats in their two opening game of the Champions League, against Grasshoppers and Auxerre and needed back-to-back wins against Ajax to rekindle their hopes. Murray was feeling the pressure and explained what he thought was behind it in an interview in the *Daily Record* on 9 October: 'Nine-in-a-row is having a negative effect on us both. Rangers will stand still until it disappears. It's like a monkey on our backs. I've said before I'd rather see success in Europe than nine-in-a-row and I stand by that now. Of course, I'd take satisfaction out of nine-in-a-row – I'd love to see 19-in-a-row – but it's becoming a real strain on us. Celtic are also suffering. I noticed Tommy Burns and the Celtic captain both talking about nine-in-a-row. I can understand why it means so much to so many. They lived through it when Celtic did it. I didn't live through it and I don't agree that it is so vital now. Frankly, I'm becoming tired of it – I'm fed up reading about it. There isn't another country where this would be an issue. For Rangers and Celtic second place has become failure. English clubs start the season looking to win a place in Europe. That is judged as success – but not here. We're so downbeat.'

Despite Murray's words the majority of Rangers fans were thrilled at the possibility of matching Celtic's feat and the two clubs were neck and neck after the first few weeks of the season. Rangers drew first blood in the Old Firm derbies when Gough and Gascoigne scored in a 2–0 win at Ibrox at the end of the September, the Hoops' first defeat in a year.

The Light Blues stuttered before the next Old Firm meeting five games later and were trailing on goal difference to their rivals at the top of the table when they travelled to Celtic Park. However, Rangers again showed their resilience in another remarkable encounter with Laudrup scoring the only goal of a game remembered by many for Peter van Vossen's infamous miss when he blasted the ball over an empty goal. Gascoigne had a penalty saved by Hoops keeper Stewart Kerr and Gers No. 1 Andy Goram, by now on his way to becoming an Ibrox legend, saved a late spot-kick from Celtic's Dutch striker Pierre van Hooijdonk.

Rangers struck another blow when the two sides met again on 2 January at Ibrox. Albertz drove in a trademark free-kick which was cancelled out by Paolo Di Canio before substitute Bo Andersen came on to score twice to keep the points in Govan as television cameras captured the relief and joy on Smith's face as he celebrated the third goal with the fans.

Despite some indifferent performances it was becoming clear as the games were being ticked off that Rangers would not be stopped. Smith's side, who had captured the League Cup earlier in the season with a thrilling 4–3 win over Hearts at Celtic Park, took a giant step on the journey to title number nine on 16 March. A week earlier Celtic had knocked Rangers out of the Scottish Cup at the quarter-final stage but the Light Blues recovered for the final encounter of the season at Parkhead to complete a clean sweep of Old Firm league wins with a scrappy Laudrup goal taking them eight points clear.

A home defeat to Kilmarnock in the next game was not in the script but after wins against Dunfermline and Raith Rovers the Ibrox men were left looking for a home win against Motherwell on 5 May to clinch the title. However, there was another surprising stumble as a 2–0 defeat by the Fir Park side moved the title show up to Tannadice two nights later. Defeat by the Lanarkshire side had served to crank up the tension further and in their desperation to witness what could be an historic night, Rangers fans had secured tickets for every part of the stadium. Smith started with a 3-5-2 line up of Dibble; Petric, McLaren, Bjorklund; Cleland, Moore, Gascoigne, Miller, Robertson; Durie and Laudrup with McInnes, Albertz and McCoist on the bench.

Laudrup's winning goal after 11 minutes is frozen in time. Charlie Miller, a player who promised so much but whose Ibrox career would fizzle out, raced on to a David Robertson throw-in and quickly swung a cross in from the left where Laudrup met the ball to bury a header past United keeper Sieb Dykstra. It was a pulsating game and Rangers should have scored again in the 22nd minute when Laudrup rounded Dykstra but saw his shot blocked by Erik Pedersen, who then thwarted a second effort from Gordon Durie. Gascoigne hit the post in the second half and then Miller crashed the ball off the bar. It was former Rangers players Steven Pressley and Gary McSwegan who came closest for the home side. Pressley had a shot saved by Light Blues keeper Andy Dibble – a stop-gap signing that season – and McSwegan drove inches wide from the edge of the box.

However, Rangers were on a date with destiny and when the final whistle sounded Gascoigne, who had been substituted along with Laudrup to take the acclaim of the Rangers fans allowing McInnes and McCoist to come on, ran immediately to hug Smith and Knox. As the travelling support celebrated Smith went round the park hugging each player individually and Gough, who missed the game through injury, was in tears as he picked up the league trophy in the centre circle.

Smith was overwhelmed as he spoke on television immediately after the game: 'It was a long time coming, that created a lot of tension but we have done it now,' he said. 'I thought we played well and deserved it. This one means we have equalled Celtic – if I hadnae won this I would have been the one person who would have lost nine-in-a-row. There was a lot of pressure during the season.'

The Ibrox celebrations lasted long in to the night with Gazza, still in his strip, leading the singing on the team coach on the way back to Glasgow. It was the early hours of the morning when the players arrived back at Ibrox but the streets around the ground were still packed with celebrating fans.

But the taste of success does not linger long at the Old Firm. The following season Gascoigne would be serenaded with the English rugby anthem, 'Swing low, sweet chariot, Gazza's here for ten-in-a-row' as the Rangers fans anticipated yet another title win. Gough left Ibrox for a new life in America (although he would return in November) and Smith laced his squad with an Italian flavour. Stopper Lorenzo Amoruso came in from Fiorentina, right back Sergio Porrini, an Italian international, was brought in from Juventus and striker Marco Negri arrived from Perugia. In addition, defender Staale Stensaas was brought in from Rosenborg. The Bosman rule had come into play and Sweden international Jonas Thern and young Italian teenager, Rino Gattuso, came from AS Roma and Perugia respectively.

Despite the remarkable early season form of Negri – he

scored in ten consecutive league games to break the top-flight record of eight held by Ally McLeod of Hibs and Frank McDougal of Aberdeen – the campaign was to end in disappointment. After Rangers were knocked out of the Champions League in the qualifying stages by IFK Gothenburg and then eliminated from the UEFA Cup by French side Strasbourg, Smith announced that he would be stepping down at the end of the season. That announcement appeared to have a deflating effect on the Ibrox club. The troubled Gascoigne moved to Middlesbrough in March and Laudrup, who was playing out the last season of his contract, was a shadow of his former self.

Rangers had been knocked out of the League Cup by Dundee United in the quarter-finals in September and although the Ibrox club were more than a match for Celtic in Old Firm games that season – losing only once in five games – they finished two points behind the Parkhead side who reclaimed the title on the final day of the campaign.

There was to be no swansong in the Scottish Cup final against Hearts at Celtic Park a week later. The Light Blues fans were left frustrated at the 2–1 defeat, part inflicted by an early penalty which should never have been awarded, and partly by an all too typical careless mistake by Amoruso. Celtic Park, the scene of so many Rangers triumphs during those nine-in-a-row years, became the graveyard for Smith's squad. Heroes and legends such as Goram, Durrant, McCall, Laudrup, McCoist and Gough would all the leave the club that summer as a new era began under Dick Advocaat. Smith, though, was defiant in defeat, saying: 'The bad news for Scottish football is this is as bad as it gets for Glasgow Rangers.'

Ian Ferguson realised the significance of that afternoon at Celtic Park, yards where he had been brought up dreaming of playing for the team from the other side of the city. 'That was an emotional day,' he said. 'We knew it was the end of an era. It was like part of your family was leaving you. We were all like brothers, we did everything together and we were splitting up.'

Inevitable comparisons are made between the Old Firm's

respective nine-in-a-row feats. Celtic were a European power during their time, winning the European Cup in 1967. Aside from 1992–93 Rangers failed to hit those heights and there were some very disappointing European campaigns. But regardless of that, true-blue Ferguson is fiercely proud of what he helped to achieve during that historic period and still won't give an inch to Celtic. 'Getting the nine, they [Celtic] could never bring that up again,' he said. 'They give it "We got it first" but it doesn't matter. We have equalled it. We've done it and that's what counts. It meant everything to me.'

15
FOREIGN MANAGERS

Rangers have had two foreign managers in their history, Dutchman Dick Advocaat (1998–2001) and Frenchman Paul Le Guen (2006–07). They were two different characters who worked under different financial circumstances and with different expectations placed upon them but who both faced the same problems and pressures experienced by all managers at Ibrox. Neither has much in common but one figure who linked them both is former club captain Barry Ferguson.

One of the first things Advocaat did after taking over from Walter Smith in the summer of 1998 was to hand the then young midfielder a five-year contract. And when it became clear that Italian defender Lorenzo Amoruso, who was Advocaat's first choice as skipper on arriving in Govan, had lost the respect of his teammates, the former Holland coach took the unusual and controversial step of stripping him of the armband and giving it to Ferguson.

By the time Le Guen was appointed almost a decade later, Ferguson had become an influential figure in the Ibrox dressing room. Indeed, some said the man who had progressed to become Scotland captain was too powerful. Certainly, there remains a school of thought that believes Ferguson was central to the downfall of the Frenchman just months after he had taken over from Alex McLeish and days after he had taken the captaincy off the former Ibrox youth player.

However, in the summer of 1998 when Advocaat became the club's first foreign manager Barry Ferguson was still better known as the brother of former Rangers midfielder Derek Ferguson. The capture of the former PSV Eindhoven coach personified the lofty ambitions prevalent at a cash-rich Ibrox at that time. A decade of domestic dominance had seen Celtic's nine-in-a-row feat equalled but one season aside, 1992–93, Rangers had failed to make their mark in Europe. It was hoped that the arrival of the 'Little General' would take the club on to the 'next level', often the most ambiguous of football terms, but which at that time meant the latter stages of the Champions League.

Rangers had chalked up their ninth successive title in 1996–97 but the following season was a bridge too far for a group of players who seemed affected by Smith's declaration that he would step down in the summer. The Light Blue legions salivated over who would be Smith's successor. It was believed that the Ibrox club could attract the best players and managers in the world, and names such as Fabio Capello, Ottmar Hitzfeld, Sven-Göran Eriksson and Marcelo Lippi were being bandied around and discussed in earnest.

Indeed, Alex Anderson, co-author of *Barcelona Here We Come* and *The Advocaat Years*, recalls a sense of anti-climax when he discovered the Dutchman was coming to Govan: 'After all the media speculation about who would replace Walter Smith I have to say I was initially a little underwhelmed,' he said. 'Advocaat was a name I instantly recognised but I'd been given to believe it'd be someone like Fabio Capello, Ottmar Hitzfeld or even Terry Venables – men who had actually taken a club to a European Cup/Champions League final. Walter Smith got us to within a goal of the final in 1992–93 so I thought the only logical replacement was a man who had a proven record of going one stage further. It seems crazy now but in 1998 we really could be that choosy. Within a few days, however, that same media speculation turned to examining Advocaat's past and his reputation. The anecdotal tales of his iron rule, his demand for discipline, seemed to fit the identikit of the classic autocratic Europe-savvy manager. I felt we were leaving Scottish football in our slipstream.'

David Edgar, former spokesman for the Rangers Supporters' Trust and author of *21st Century Blue: Being a Bear in the Modern World*, was impressed with Advocaat's reputation as a disciplinarian. 'His pedigree was solid, if not exciting, and he was very impressive in interviews,' he said. 'His reputation as a tactician went before him and I looked forward to seeing what he could bring in a European sense, because we'd been awful in Europe for a few seasons. Similarly, he had a reputation as a disciplinarian, which I think most fans felt was needed as Walter Smith's first spell was ending chaotically.'

Lifelong Rangers fan Elaine Sommerville also looked forward to an improvement in the European arena: 'I was pleased when it was announced that Advocaat was to be our next manager,' she said. 'I knew a bit about him and thought he could be good for us and maybe help improve our European record. The major disappointment during nine-in-a-row was our European performances and I thought this appointment would help.'

Smith had enjoyed increasingly generous financial backing but Advocaat, who admitted to using the Internet to research his new club, was given almost a blank cheque. He claimed he needed to all but start from scratch in building a side: 'I knew it was Walter's last season but also the last season for a lot of players so I had almost no team,' he said. 'I had only three players: Albertz, Amoruso and Porrini. Craig Moore and Ferguson were also there but they were on the fringes. I had to build almost a whole new team and that was difficult.'

The Ibrox club had never before witnessed such a turnaround in personnel in the summer of 1998. More than a dozen players from the Smith era left Rangers, and fantastic sums of money were spent on their replacements. The most expensive were Dutch stars Arthur Numan and Giovanni van Bronckhorst, who arrived for a combined total of around £10 million from PSV and Feyenoord respectively. Argentinian striker Gabriel Amato (Real Mallorca, £4.2 million), Russian winger Andrei Kanchelskis (Fiorentina, £5.5 million), French goalkeeper Lionel Charbonnier (Auxerre, £1.5 million), English striker Rod Wallace (Bosman) and Scotland skipper Colin Hendry (Blackburn Rovers, £3.5 million) were quickly added to the multi-million-pound squad.

And still they came. France World Cup-winner Stephane Guivarc'h signed for £3.5 million from Newcastle, winger Neil McCann arrived from Hearts for £2 millon, USA international Claudio Reyna signed from Wolfsburg for £1.2 million and keeper Stefan Klos from Borussia Dortmund for £700,000. Such was the money swirling around the game in general and Ibrox in particular that there was little fuss initially made when Romania international Daniel Prodan signed from Atletico Madrid for £2.2 million with a knee injury, which ultimately prevented him ever kicking a ball in anger for the club.

While Rangers fans celebrated their club's largesse, with some wearing it as a badge of honour, editor of the *Rangers Historian* Robert McElroy was almost the lone voice of caution. 'My first concerns arose at the start of the "Souness revolution", when Rangers were paying £750,000 for Terry Butcher and £1.1 million for Richard Gough,' he said. 'I remember asking an old friend, "What on earth are we doing spending that kind of money on players?"'

Many Rangers fans were undoubtedly questioning their new manager's expensive tastes in his first competitive game when Irish side Shelbourne raced into a 3–0 lead in the first leg of their UEFA Cup qualifier at Tranmere's Prenton Park ground. However, embarrassment was saved when the new-look Ibrox side battled back to win 5–3 before finishing the job off in the return game.

In the starting line-up for Advocaat's first league match

against Hearts at Tynecastle on 2 August 1998 the Rangers side showed seven changes to the one which played in the Scottish Cup final defeat to the Jambos at Celtic Park just three months previously. Despite a 2–1 defeat in that first match the Little General's strategy of 'speculate to accumulate' paid off immediately on the domestic front. He spent £36 million that summer and by the next spring had recaptured the championship from Celtic as part of a glorious Treble.

Rangers won the first trophy of the season in November when St Johnstone were beaten in the League Cup final at Celtic Park. Six months later the league title was secured in dramatic and controversial circumstances at the same venue with a 3–0 win over the Hoops. In a poisonous atmosphere in which three players were sent off, two in green, one in blue, referee Hugh Dallas was cut on the forehead when he was struck by a coin thrown by a Celtic fan, several of whom invaded the park to get at the official. A Neil McCann brace and a Jorg Albertz penalty saw Rangers win the title at the home of their greatest rivals for the first time, an achievement that was not appreciated by the home support. The visiting players and management' cowered as they ran up the tunnel following post-match celebrations as they were pelted with coins and other objects. Four weeks later, with the rancour surrounding the Govan club's title win still hanging heavy in the air, Rod Wallace's solitary goal at Hampden against Celtic in the Scottish Cup final clinched a clean sweep of trophies.

However, Advocaat, who was revealing himself to be a distant figure not well disposed to the Scottish media, did not spend the summer reflecting in quiet satisfaction. That close season enough players to make a team left the club while Michael Mols (Utrecht, £4 million), Tugay Kerimoglu (Galatasaray, £1.3 million) and Billy Dodds (Dundee United, £1.3 million) were added to the squad. Again it paid dividends. The 1999-2000 championship was won by 21 points from Celtic and the Double was secured with a 4–0 victory over Aberdeen in the Scottish Cup final, a match that was dubbed the 'Oranje

Final' after the Rangers fans dressed in orange as a tribute to Advocaat and the rest of the Dutch contingent at Ibrox, which by that point numbered half a dozen.

The former Den Haag player's popularity with the Ibrox support was at its peak. He had won five out of six domestic trophies, but perhaps just as importantly, progress was also being made in Europe. Parma had ended Rangers' UEFA Cup hopes in the third round in Advocaat's first season, after good wins over PAOK, Beitar Jerusalem and Bayer Leverkusen. The Govan club, however, had gained revenge with a memorable two-legged win over the star-studded Italian side in the Champions League third qualifier which took them into the group stages to meet Spanish side Valencia, German giants Bayern Munich and Advocaat's former club, PSV Eindhoven.

Rangers were handed a lesson by Valencia in Spain but recovered with two wins over the Dutch side and a draw against Bayern at home, leaving themselves needing only a point from their last two matches to reach the knockout stages. A defeat against a clearly superior Valencia side at Ibrox took it to the last game in Munich. A narrow and undeserved 1–0 defeat in this match is best remembered for the injury to Mols, who had already become a hero to the fans in his short time at the club. His prolific goalscoring, combined with his exquisite twists and turns and deft lay-offs, distinguished him as one of the best front men in Europe, and it was his and Rangers' tragedy that he was never quite the same again after a clash with Bayern goalkeeper Oliver Kahn. The Scottish champions recovered from a shaky start to dominate the match and hit the woodwork three times, but a first-half penalty from Thomas Strunz meant the Ibrox club had to settle for a place in the UEFA Cup, where they suffered a penalty shoot-out defeat to Borussia Dortmund.

But, by and large, Rangers fans were happy with what they were watching under Advocaat. 'The football we were served in his first two seasons was some of the finest I have seen at Ibrox,' said supporter Stevie Clark. 'Advocaat signed some real quality the summer he took over in the likes of Numan and Van

Bronckhorst. He also polished a gem out of a rough diamond in Barry Ferguson who was dominating against some of the world's best midfielders.'

It had not gone unnoticed that Ferguson was one of the few Scots remaining in the Rangers squad, which was refurbished again in the summer of 2000. Paul Ritchie of Hearts and Glaswegian Allan Johnston from Sunderland arrived at Ibrox at the start of June as Bosman signings with the former, who had had a loan spell at Bolton, saying: 'It will be good to be back in the SPL and playing for one of the biggest clubs in Europe in the Champions League as well.'

However, snapping up two Scottish players for free was not an indication that Advocaat was tightening his belt. Fernando Ricksen (£4 million from AZ Alkmaar), Bert Konterman (Feyenoord, £3.5 million), Kenny Miller (Hibs, £2 million), Peter Lovenkrands (AB Copenhagen, £1.5 million) were joined by Dutch superstar Ronald de Boer, the former Ajax player, who signed from Barcelona at the end of August for a reported £4.5 million.

By that time, Advocaat had evidently seen enough of Ritchie to conclude he would not do and had sold the defender to Manchester City for £500,000. It was a bizarre episode, which still puzzles Ritchie to this day. 'I'm still disappointed in the way things worked out,' he said. 'I wanted to play at a top club and Dick took that away from me. Not to have played a competitive game for Rangers is something I will find hard to deal with for the rest of my life.'

While his reputation as a disciplinarian had been confirmed, little was known about Advocaat as a person. Rangers legend John Greig, in his PR role at the club at that time, was assigned to chaperone the Dutchman and keep the media at a distance. The former Rangers manager and captain said: 'He told me right away that all he wanted to do was pre- and post-match interviews. He didn't want to one-to-one interviews because he felt he didn't know the press well enough and he couldn't get over exactly what he wanted to say.'

Fellow bosses fared little better in penetrating the shield

Advocaat had thrown around himself. Scotland boss Craig Levein, then head coach at Hearts, said: 'Dick wasn't the type of guy to come in to your office after matches other than to say hello, I didn't have much dialogue with him at all.' Former Hibs boss Bobby Williamson recalled: 'There are functions at which managers get to meet each other during the season but I didn't meet Dick at any of them, save for the Football Writers' event. We never shook hands before the game and the first I would see him would be just before kick-off. But we shook hands after the game.' Even the Dutch players at the club found Advocaat stand-offish. Mols said: 'I didn't get to know Advocaat any better when I came to Scotland. He kept his distance and only let a few people into his personal life.'

Advocaat's first real domestic challenge came in the 2000–01 season. Celtic had appointed as boss the former Northern Ireland and Nottingham Forest midfielder Martin O'Neill and the Parkhead board backed him with serious money. The pendulum swung dramatically back to the green corner of the city in the first Old Firm game of the season at Celtic Park when Rangers were beaten 6–2.

The Ibrox fans were stunned, but it was a particularly horrific afternoon for new signings Ricksen and Konterman. Ricksen was withdrawn in the first half to end his nightmare at right back against the hitherto ineffective Hoops wide-man Bobby Petta, while centre back Konterman put in the sort of hapless display that would characterise his time in Glasgow. Advocaat would later admit that Konterman had been a huge mistake. 'I understand the criticism of Konterman, definitely,' he said. 'I will hold my hand up and say he didn't do it and I don't know why.' Advocaat remains convinced that 'Ricksen was one of the better players at the club,' but had no sympathy for him that afternoon when he had to embarrass his fellow countryman by taking him off early. Advocaat said: 'I don't care what time in the game it is – if players don't do as they are told I will take them off.' However, there was more to the game than Ricksen's meltdown during a humiliating defeat. In reality it signified the end of Advocaat's dominance over Celtic and things began to quickly unravel at Ibrox.

After Rangers lost three games in a row in October – to Hibernian, St Johnstone and Kilmarnock – Advocaat dumped the erratic Amoruso as captain and replaced him with 22-year-old Ferguson. Gers fans tried to recall the last time such a controversial decision had been made. But it was no big deal to Advocaat: 'It was quite simple,' he said. 'The players didn't accept him [Amoruso] any more as captain and I could feel that by the way they talked about him in the dressing room. If he started talking at half-time they would say: "Okay, okay Lorenzo, we know."'

Unsurprisingly, Amoruso did not accept Advocaat's viewpoint. In his book *LA Confidential: The Autobiography*, the former Fiorentina player, never one to be short of confidence, however misplaced, said: 'When Dick said he was making Barry Ferguson captain I really did think I was living a nightmare – and that is nothing against Barry believe me. I just could not believe he was going to make a boy of Barry's age – he was 22 at the time – the captain of a club like Rangers. Barry was a talented player but he was little more than a kid . . . and being the captain of Rangers is more than just leading the team out and tossing the coin.'

The removal of the armband from Amoruso confirmed that there were dressing room problems, something that had already been the subject of some speculation. Amoruso warmed up on his own before the League Cup game against Dundee United at Ibrox which Rangers won thanks to a Ferguson goal and a strike from Kenny Miller. The relationship between Amoruso and Ferguson subsequently came under scrutiny, but the latter played down the perceived animosity. In his book *Blue: Life and Times of Barry Ferguson*, Ferguson said: 'We were never bosom buddies but he congratulated me on the captaincy. I didn't like his shaved legs – but I rated him as a player.'

However, the leadership issue would soon prove to be the least of Advocaat's concerns. After Rangers had lost 2–1 at St

Johnstone to fall 12 points behind Celtic at the top of the table the Ibrox manager publicly questioned his players' professionalism, branding them 'fat-necks', a derogatory term borrowed from his native land. 'At that time there was complacency from the players,' he later said. 'I could feel it.' Ongoing rumours of a split in the camp were given credence with a training ground fight between Ricksen and Kanchelskis. Only the latter was sent home, which led to further acrimony that Advocaat later acknowledged: 'I made a mistake,' he admitted, 'I should have sent both players home.'

But bigger, costlier mistakes were to follow. On 23 November, days before the second Old Firm game of the season at Ibrox, Rangers set a record by buying Norwegian international striker Tore Andre Flo from Chelsea for £12 million. It was Advocaat's last throw of the dice in his bid to catch Celtic. Flo made a scoring debut in a 5–1 hammering of the Hoops but it was to prove a false dawn. Rangers had cut the gap behind their Old Firm rivals at the top of the table to ten points, but the Parkhead side went on to win the Treble, their first since 1969 and the third in their history.

There was more disappointment for Rangers in Europe. After negotiating two qualifiers to get in the group stages of the Champions League, the Ibrox club were drawn alongside Sturm Graz, Galatasaray and Monaco. Six points from the first two matches, a 5–0 win at home against Sturm Graz and a 1–0 win in Monaco, had revitalised everyone at Ibrox. However, two points from the remaining four games saw Rangers fail to qualify for the knockout stages and consequently they dropped down to the UEFA Cup where they lost over two legs to German side Kaiserslautern.

Although Flo was not the flop he was portrayed to be in some quarters, particularly those who refused to look at his scoring record, in truth he quickly became symbolic of the free-spending era at Rangers, which would in time have lasting implications for the club. David Murray later admitted that the financial gamble he took failed to pay dividends. He said: 'Flo was the pinnacle of our ambition and in hindsight it was wrong. We went for Flo and de Boer to take us to a higher level and it didn't really work.'

Advocaat claims the fee paid for Flo was simply indicative of the problems Rangers had attracting top quality players to Scotland. 'No, I don't regret buying Flo,' he said. 'I hoped he would do it for us but he didn't. The market price for strikers like him or Andy Cole was £10 million upwards and we had to pay that kind of money. We always paid too high a fee and too much salary compared to other countries – or else they wouldn't come.'

After winning five out six trophies in his first two years in Scotland, Advocaat had to lick his wounds after a barren third season. Approaching his fourth campaign at the helm, with the pressure on, the Dutchman reached for the chequebook again. Defender Michael Ball was recruited for a reported £6.5 million from Everton. Midfielder Christian Nerlinger arrived from Borussia Dortmund for £1.8 million. Shota Arveladze, a Georgia international striker, cost £2 million from Ajax. Argentina legend Claudio Caniggia was recruited from Dundee for £900,000 while Russell Latapy was snapped up from Hibs on a Bosman. Added to that, the opening of the new £14 million training facility of Murray Park at Auchenhowie, a brainchild of Advocaat and a long overdue addition to the Ibrox portfolio, was welcomed by Gers fans looking to the future.

The campaign started brightly enough but a 2–0 home defeat to Celtic in September spiked early-season optimism and there was more woe in November when Rangers lost 2–1 at Parkhead – their fifth consecutive Old Firm defeat – to fall ten points behind the Hoops in the title race. Advocaat's loosening grip was exemplified by a verbal joust with Ball as the player made his way up the tunnel after being substituted. The incident was lapped up by Parkhead fans who revelled in the Rangers manager's public humiliation. Advocaat's response to the incident lacked the credibility it might once have had. He said: 'Maybe at a club like Everton you can do that but with a manager of my stature you can't – I don't accept it. I was shocked definitely. It had never happened to me before.'

Lots of things that hadn't happened to Advocaat before were happening but if the domestic season was proving again to be problematic, he did find some solace in Europe. The Govan side had again failed to qualify for the Champions League but Advocaat's last achievement at Gers boss was to keep the club in Europe after Christmas for the first time since 1992–93. Rangers travelled to Paris in December for the second leg of their UEFA Cup clash with Paris St Germain. After a goalless draw at Ibrox and 120 minutes in the French capital, no one had found the net. Ronald de Boer missed a penalty four minutes before the end of extra-time but Rangers proved better in the shoot-out, triumphing 4–3 with Amoruso, Latapy, Numan and Ferguson scoring. In a rare show of emotion Advocaat ran on to the park after victory was secured to throw himself on to a pile of celebrating players. However, no one was surprised – and few upset – when he announced the following morning that he was quitting. 'It was a great night for Rangers and yes, I was so emotional because I knew it was my last game for Rangers,' he said. 'We went through and it was good to stop on a high rather than stop when you lose.'

On returning from France, the Dutchman oversaw a 3–1 win over Hearts at Ibrox on 9 December, his last moment as undisputed boss. Increasing debt would dictate that there would be no more big names at Ibrox. The relatively inexperienced Alex McLeish, who had been boss at Hibernian, was announced as the new Rangers manager and it signified the downsizing of ambition. Advocaat moved into the newly created post as director of football. John McClelland, who had become chairman, was unconvincing when he said: 'We didn't invent a job for Dick. There's an argument for saying every club should have one.' Significantly, when Advocaat eventually left to become manager of Holland on a full-time basis for the second time in 2002, he was not replaced.

Murray defended Advocaat's tenure, saying: 'In Scotland we have a blame culture and everybody has a certain shelf life. Dick won a Treble and then things diminished and people started looking for faults in his make-up.' Arguably, those faults didn't need much finding. By common consensus, Martin O'Neill had simply got the better of Advocaat, which led journalist Hugh Keevins to conclude: 'He was running away from the problems and I don't think you can dress it up any other way.'

Advocaat, though, remains adamant that he was every bit as accomplished as O'Neill – if not better. 'Listen, I have a big reputation and you don't become the manager of Holland twice just because you are a nice man,' he said. 'I'm a well-known manager in Europe, not everyone can say that. I have nothing against Martin O'Neill and I have to be fair and say that he brought in some good players – like Alan Thompson, Neil Lennon, John Hartson and Chris Sutton – and they were never injured. Those players always played so in that way you can say he did better than me in transfers. Because of the luck Celtic had, Larsson played for seven years and was almost never injured. There's no doubt that he was the difference between the two teams because at the other end we were better. O'Neill showed that he is a good manager but I have shown that I am a good manager too.'

The Dutchman admitted the Rangers job had taken its toll on him, saying: 'Four years at Rangers takes a lot out of you. Every game has to be won. A draw is no good and that is hard for a manager. The expectations are so high. If you can manage Rangers and Celtic you can manage any team in the world.'

Advocaat's tenure continues to elicit mixed emotions. David Edgar speaks on behalf of the prosecution. 'Personally I think Advocaat gets an easy ride,' he said. 'His first two seasons were very good, but given the budget he had and the implosion at Celtic – he faced Jo Venglos and John Barnes in those two years – he achieved what I would have expected from a manager of his stature. His sides played some excellent football in the first two seasons, which is what fans remember. However, his third season was a disaster. Faced with the challenge from O'Neill, his team completely fell apart. I think his hubris came back to haunt him. He could ride roughshod over players when things were going for him, but when the going got tough, the players didn't want to go that extra mile for him. He spent unnecessarily and badly in the summer of 2000, then kept throwing money at the problem. I think he did all right as Rangers manager, no better. And I think when he left it was the right decision.'

When asked to evaluate Advocaat's time at Ibrox, Alex Anderson speaks for the defence with his summation: 'European stability, respectability – his final continental tie was that win in Paris over PSG which took us past Christmas in Europe for the first time in nine years – and gave me some of the happiest domestic footballing memories of my life. The 3–0 win at Parkhead on 2 May 1999, winning the league at the home of our greatest rivals, will stay with me until I die. A 5–1 win at Pittodrie was also pretty sweet. He insisted on the building of Murray Park and it's already paid for itself with the sale of Alan Hutton to Spurs. He got rid of the players' drinking culture, which most fans agreed was a no-no for European success, and in knowing when to step aside, who to get in as a replacement and then mentoring Alex McLeish's nascent reign, he enabled us to win titles during a Celtic ascendancy. This averted the kind of nine years in the wilderness we suffered by some knee-jerk decisions when Jock Stein was at Parkhead.'

Somewhere in between is fan Steve Clark: 'I have very mixed views on Advocaat's time at Rangers,' he said. 'The first two years domestically were almost perfect but we still failed to take that step to be in with the big boys of the Champions League. It all started to go very wrong with the arrival of O'Neill at Celtic and he failed to deal with a resurgent Celtic side. He began to blame players publicly for our bad results and he never really recovered from the 6–2 hammering at Parkhead.'

However, it is impossible to discuss Advocaat's time as Rangers boss without taking into account the huge debts which were run up at the club during his tenure, reported to be £70 million by the time he stepped aside. The Dutchman accepted culpability: 'I have some regrets about the debts but as I said at the time every club went into debt because everyone thought that they were going to grow financially.'

Anderson also looks at that issue in context. 'Advocaat represented the money we wanted to spend at the start of the century because he was the man brought in to utilise it,' he said. 'He was a conduit, nothing more. When we won nine-in-a-row, fans were complaining loudly that it meant nothing if we couldn't achieve regularly in Europe. David Murray responded to those demands like a benevolent Croesus and it was only when Celtic gained the upper hand domestically by working a similar trick that the amateur accountants in the Govan Stand began whingeing. Dick Advocaat knew we wanted European success and after our exit on penalties to Borussia Dortmund in the UEFA Cup he said that the difference wasn't luck or tactics – it was simply the quality of players. That he won the UEFA Cup with Zenit in 2008 proved he and Murray knew what they were doing and the fans knew as well as them that it was a plan that required serious cash. We all, collectively, took a gamble – ultimately it didn't work out, but it was well worth trying.'

The debt issue was still being addressed when the next foreign manager came to Ibrox four years later. Paul Le Guen took over from the outgoing Alex McLeish in the summer of 2006, the announcement having been made the previous March. A former France international, Le Guen arrived with a good reputation as a modern coach. He had led Olympique Lyonnais to three consecutive league titles and reached the UEFA Champions League quarter-final.

There were few dissenters and Edgar, like most Rangers fans, was buoyed: 'I was incredibly excited,' he said. 'Given his reputation and standing in Europe at that time, it seemed unbelievable that we'd managed to get him. It seemed a real coup and I couldn't wait to watch his teams play.' Anderson too could only see good things ahead for Rangers. 'I was delighted, excited and thoroughly proud,' he said. 'I felt David Murray had done it again. When the fans demanded domestic success he'd given us nine-in-a-row, our greatest ever league run. When they demanded European success on top of that, he took us to within a goal of the Champions League final and when the fans demanded we do that more often, Murray brought in Advocaat to spend big and properly. When the fans then demanded we be just as successful on both fronts, but on the cheap, the chairman brought in the most exciting young coach in Europe to overhaul the entire club to that end.'

But if Advocaat had started his career at Ibrox impressively before fading badly, Le Guen's fall from grace was almost immediate. He was in charge of Rangers for seven months and 31 games – the shortest reign of a permanent manager in the club's history. How could it go so wrong?

His dealings in the transfer market that summer set alarm bells ringing. Signing three players from Austria Vienna was unusual, if not strange. The former Rennes coach recruited midfielder Libor Sionko and striker Filip Sebo from the Austrian club before returning for defender Sasa Papac. While Papac would have a good career at Rangers after a shaky start, Sionko was no more than average at best but impressive in comparison to £1.85 million Sebo, whose name would become a byword for incompetence in Scottish football. Sebo would be the lightning conductor for much of the criticism aimed at Le Guen in the initial few months and would be to the Frenchman what Konterman had been to Advocaat, although his robust style endeared him to the fans.

There was little inspiration to be found in Le Guen's other signings, try as the media might to talk them up. France under-21 international Jeremy Clement arrived at the cost of £1.1 million while Rangers took Manchester United defender Phil Bardsley on loan until the end of the year, to join fellow Old Trafford loanee Lee Martin. Lionel Letizi arrived on a free transfer from Paris St Germain while Sweden defender Karl Svensson cost a reported £600,000 from IFK Gothenburg. Less notable recruits included youngsters William Stanger and Antoine Ponroy, free from Rennes, and Dean Furman, a free from Chelsea. Le Guen's close-season work failed to impress either, and there were further indications that all was not going to run smoothly for him when Ricksen had to be sent home in disgrace from Rangers' pre-season tour of South Africa following an incident on a flight.

But there was still enough confidence in Le Guen for the Frenchman to be given the benefit of the doubt as season 2006–07 got underway. However, the former Paris St Germain player had the statisticians reaching for their record books to discover that after ten games it was the worst start to a season by an Old Firm debutant boss since John Greig's team won only two, drew six and lost two of their opening ten games in 1978–79. After a 2–1 win at Motherwell on the opening day, the first points were dropped in Le Guen's Ibrox debut as Rangers were held 2–2 by Dundee United. Further draws at Dunfermline and Kilmarnock led to early unrest among the Light Blues support, which increased with a defeat against Hibernian at Easter Road on 17 September, the week before the first Old Firm game of the season at Celtic Park. Former Rangers striker Kenny Miller – who would end up at Ibrox for the second time in the future – rubbed salt in the wounds of the travelling support when he ended his goal drought for the Parkhead club after Thomas Gravesen had opened the scoring for the home side.

Le Guen came under intense scrutiny. Against Inverness at Ibrox on 14 October his controversial decision to drop fans' favourite Allan McGregor for Letizi backfired when the French keeper gifted Graham Bayne the only goal of the game. More points were dropped. A 1–1 draw against Motherwell at home was followed by a 2–1 defeat at Dundee United in what was Craig Levein's first game in charge at Tannadice. However, it was the 2–0 CIS Insurance Cup defeat to First Division side St Johnstone at Ibrox which caused doubts to become fears. The shock defeat had Murray having to publicly back his manager after just five months in the job. Stevie Clark was one of many fans who believed Le Guen's credentials had been shot to pieces by the end of the St Johnstone game: 'It appeared he totally underestimated Scottish football and did little or no preparation before becoming manager,' he said. 'His signings were bizarre to say the least, it appeared the only club he had been watching prior to his appointment was Austria Vienna and he seemed hell bent on transplanting the starting 11 to Ibrox. He signed a Swedish centre half who could not defend cross balls and a striker, Sebo, who struggled to play, never mind score goals. The alarm bells should have been ringing in his first two games where we played some great football against Motherwell and Dundee United but lost very cheap goals in both games. But the St Johnstone game at Ibrox . . . was the turning point for me. Getting knocked out at Ibrox by a lower league opposition for the first time in our history was bad enough, but to be outplayed into the bargain was unacceptable.'

The defeat against Saints shook Rangers into action and, as their domestic form improved, a 2–2 draw at Auxerre secured their place in the knockout stages of the UEFA Cup. They had earlier beaten Livorno and Maccabi Haifa, and went on to defeat Partizan Belgrade in their final Group A game to finish top of the five-team section.

However, December was a domestic disaster for Le Guen. A 1–0 defeat at Falkirk came before the second Old Firm game of the season at Ibrox, which revealed signs of a rift between the Frenchman and Ferguson, who had expressed disappointment at comments from Le Guen playing down the importance of a skipper's duties. 'The role of the skipper isn't as important in France as it seems to be here,' the Rangers boss said. 'I don't believe captains are as important to the players as some people think. We had a chat about that and Barry knows my way of thinking.' Ferguson may have known Le Guen's views but he did not agree: 'I read what the boss said and wasn't happy with that comment,' he said ahead of the Old Firm game in which Rangers played well in a 1–1 draw. Speculation about a breakdown between the two men gathered pace and it was a far from fun festive season for the Ibrox men as they lost to a late goal at Inverness on 27 December before dropping two more points at home to St Mirren in a 1–1 draw three days later.

However, the gloom surrounding those results was nothing compared to the controversy on the first day of 2007 when the Le Guen versus Ferguson battle came to a head in spectacular fashion. Ibrox fans woke up on New Year's Day to discover that the Rangers captain had been dropped from the team for the SPL game against Motherwell at Fir Park the following day, with Gavin Rae, who had started only three matches that season, instated as skipper. The news led to a media frenzy and Le Guen, with great intrigue, said that he would reveal all after the Motherwell game which became something of a circus.

Television cameras outside Fir Park pre-match focused on Rangers fans who backed their No. 6 who had told the *Scottish Sun* the previous day: 'I will be cremated in the jersey I wore the night I was first made captain of Rangers. I have already decided that I will be clothed in that light blue shirt with my captain's armband on when they send me to that big dressing room in the sky. Morbid? Maybe, but the truth is that the arrangements for what I wear in my coffin are already made. That is the last will and testament of Barry Ferguson and it has been settled for a while now.'

Inside the ground, the travelling fans chanted Ferguson's name incessantly and when striker Kris Boyd scored the winning goal from the spot, he held up six fingers to the travelling support to show where his allegiance lay. The whole afternoon was a remarkable and unprecedented show of defiance against the manager of Rangers Football Club. 'It was an awful experience for anyone who cares about Rangers,' Stevie Clark recalled. 'We had players at war with the manager – Boyd made that clear with his goal celebration – and we had supporters at each other's throats.'

At the post-match press conference Le Guen calmly articulated his decision to drop Ferguson. 'He needs a new way of behaving,' Le Guen said of the Scotland midfielder. 'He has had too much [negative] influence in the dressing room. The fans might not understand, but I know this. When people undermine you, you have to act. I took a decision. After that decision, it is not up to me to say if I will be here during the following months. If I go, I go. But I want to do my job with respect.'

It was a classic manager versus player scenario; one which convention decrees is always won by the boss. Nick Harris wrote in the *Independent* of Ferguson: 'The reality is he's already toast, and looking for a club in England unless Le Guen's own number comes up first.' Which is exactly what happened. On 4 January, amid mounting speculation, Rangers announced that Le Guen had left the club by mutual consent with Murray quoted as saying, 'Having met with Paul it was clear that in the interests of the club we agreed jointly to him stepping down as manager.'

It appeared a meek surrender by Le Guen whose comments were rather anodyne in light of the furore around him. He said: 'I am disappointed to leave the club, but I think it is the best solution for all concerned. I would like to thank all the people who helped me and my team during my spell in Scotland. In particular I would like to thank the directors who at all times gave me their total support.'

David Edgar is one of many Rangers fans who was left with a sour taste in his mouth. 'No matter who won or who lost, it was always going to harm the club,' he said. 'Boyd publicly rebuked his manager's decision with that gesture after the goal at Motherwell. You don't do that sort of thing in public. It was the sign of players who thought they were untouchable. A poor attitude for a Ranger. I think he made fans aware of what the dressing room was like – I'm not sure that Ferguson ever regained the levels of popularity he'd had after that. If the players didn't like the manager, tough. We've all worked for a boss we didn't like.' However, Edgar believes Le Guen cut an unconvincing figure as Rangers' boss. 'He underestimated the game here,' he said. 'He thought it was worse than it actually is. He also couldn't relate to Scottish players – probably more their fault than his – and what little money he had, he spent badly. He never gave the impression of permanence. By the end, his leaving seemed like a mercy killing.'

Alex Anderson claims the club's reputation and image was

tarnished in the treatment of Le Guen, whom he believes would have got it right if given time. 'Key players rebelled against him and he was too mature to be dragged into a pouty, shouty reaction,' he said. 'Le Guen knew he was the outsider so he tried to bring round the likes of Boyd and Ferguson – players who both subsequently upset a bona fide Rangers legend in Walter Smith – but when he'd given Barry Ferguson enough time or enough rope to hang himself he struck like the classic Ibrox disciplinarian, like Bill Struth himself for God's sake. What happened thereafter is the most embarrassing and shameful moment in my 30-odd years as a Bluenose. The fans undermined Le Guen – with the help of the bloodthirsty tabloid media. Le Guen dealt with Ferguson expertly – his "this is not a whim" post-match speech at Fir Park on his last day displayed an intelligence, determination and degree of straightforward nous which we, as a support, demand of our managers – and he'd already been dropping Boyd, as Walter Smith would when he arrived back. But for the first time in Rangers' history the players and the knee-jerk element of our support were allowed to rule the day. Le Guen may never have been the manager we hoped for but when we got rid of him after six months something about the regal, establishment nature of our club was lost. What Le Guen represents for me is the day our more short-sighted fans became so powerful that they threatened the very nature and future existence of the club. No investor could ever appease such demands. His actual legacy, for me personally, is the night we played Partizan Belgrade in the UEFA Cup. For the only time in our history we were playing a dead rubber in a European group, not because we were already out but because we were already through. He was getting it right in Europe – Scottish domestic football follows all too easily after that.'

16
ALEX McLEISH — THE MANAGER OF TRANSITION

'I think it is strange that Alex McLeish is not held in as high esteem by Rangers fans as Martin O'Neill is at Celtic,' says former Light Blues striker Steven Thompson, brought to Ibrox by McLeish from Dundee United in January 2003. 'It is strange how some people get put up on a higher pedestal than others. Maybe Alex didn't get the accolades he deserved. But I think that deep down the Rangers fans will know that his achievements during his time at Ibrox were sensational. You look at the facts and they tell you all you need to know.'

After a glittering career as a centre half under Alex Ferguson at Aberdeen, McLeish became player-manager at Motherwell in 1994 for a year before retiring from defensive duties to focus solely on his managerial role. His first season at Fir Park saw the Steelmen finish second to Rangers. After struggling in the next two seasons he took over at Hibernian in 1998, but his new appointment came too late to prevent their relegation to the First Division. However, his entertaining Hibees team returned to the SPL at the first attempt and despite his record at Easter Road coming in for scrutiny latterly, he had impressed Advocaat enough for the Dutchman to recommend him as his successor.

McLeish arrived at Ibrox in December 2001, to allow the Dutchman to 'go upstairs' into the newly created and short-lived Director of Football role. 'It is stunning to be at this level and I suppose the pressure here will be quite enormous – I am relishing the challenge,' the new Rangers boss told the media at his unveiling.

McLeish's appointment was not greeted with any great enthusiasm by the Rangers support. The Barrhead-born man symbolised the post-Advocaat downsizing of the club, which now found itself in a perilous financial position. The lack of cash available, in relative terms, curtailed his own ambitions. Throughout his time in Govan the former Scotland defender had to work without the transfer funds available to his predecessors as he foraged in the Bosman market.

However, McLeish, who brought with him assistant Andy Watson, got off to an encouraging start in his new post. Rangers were too far behind O'Neill's Celtic side in the SPL when he arrived to be credible challengers but he captured both the Scottish Cup and the League Cup. McLeish's first full season in charge was even more successful when he became the sixth manager in the club's history to guide Rangers to the domestic Treble. The title was won in dramatic circumstances after both Old Firm sides went into the last day tied on points. At the end of a pulsating afternoon, a 6–1 win over Dunfermline at Ibrox saw Rangers pip Celtic, who won 4–0 at Kilmarnock, by one goal. The League Cup was retained with a 2–1 win in the final against Celtic and the Scottish Cup secured with a 1–0 victory over Dundee.

The following season, 2003–04, was surprisingly barren and McLeish blotted his copybook by losing five times to Celtic. However, there was a dramatic end to the 2004–05 season when another last-day championship battle between the Glasgow giants saw the title return to Ibrox. A 1–0 win for the

Light Blues at Hibernian, coupled with a shock 2–1 defeat for Celtic at Motherwell, gave the Gers a championship win which looked highly unlikely after they had fallen five points behind the Parkhead men with just four games remaining. Rangers also won the League Cup with a thumping 5–1 victory over Motherwell in the Hampden final.

Amid poor domestic form the following season, McLeish made history when he guided the Ibrox men to the last 16 of the Champions League, where they were defeated on the away goals rule by Spanish side Villarreal. Under McLeish's guidance Rangers had become the first Scottish team to progress through a European group stage but it was not enough to save the former Scotland defender's job.

Despite rallying towards the end of the year a Scottish Cup defeat by Hibernian at Ibrox in 4 February, and the subsequent 2–0 loss at Aberdeen, which left Celtic 18 points clear at the top of the SPL, accelerated McLeish's departure. After much speculation it was announced by chairman David Murray that the former Dons player would be standing down as manager at the end of that season, to be replaced by French coach Paul Le Guen.

In his last game in the Ibrox hot seat McLeish signed off with a 2–0 home win over Hearts, who had already clinched second place behind Celtic, and was given a decent send-off by the fans at the end of the game. He subsequently became Scotland boss for a short spell before moving to Birmingham in 2007, then Aston Villa in 2011. 'It's been a draining season, no doubt about that,' said McLeish after leaving. 'There has been a lot of pressure and it's never let up. I think it would have been interesting if there had been huge spending power. But at the time I came here, the chairman needed somebody who would relish the challenge, knowing there would not be much money to spend. I was the right man at the right time.'

Thompson revealed how McLeish kept calm under the normal stresses of being at Rangers while also finding himself the first Ibrox boss in decades to face budget cuts. 'There is huge pressure when you are a Rangers player,' he says. 'One of the things you learn very quickly is that you are expected to win every game. Other clubs don't have that expectation and you have to learn how to deal with that. There is even more pressure if you are the manager but Alex remained the same. He didn't seem to be riled or flustered when things weren't going so well and generally there was a calmness about him, which was good for the players. Alex had a good relationship with his players and that was one of his strengths.

'In the first year I was at Ibrox there were still a lot of big hitters in the changing room like Shota Arveladze, Ronald de Boer, Michael Mols and Michael Arteta,' continues Thompson as he explains the transition that was taking place at the club. 'One of the things I remember about those players is their professionalism; you could see why they were top players. Ronald de Boer had the most natural ability but Michael Mols could do special things and Barry Ferguson in the Treble season scored something like 17 or 18 goals. It annoys me when people have a go at him. Barry was one of the best players I ever played with and Birmingham fans would tell you how much he came to mean to them. The summer after we won the Treble a few players moved and perhaps the players who came, in like Nuno Capucho, Emerson and Paolo Vanoli, were not quite as good. But to win a Double in 2004–05 as Alex did with a pared-down squad was a magnificent achievement.'

However, there were undoubted lows as well as highs during McLeish's tenure. Inconsistency plagued Rangers during the trophyless season of 2003–04 and some things could not simply be put down to a lack of investment. After the CIS Cup win over Celtic in March 2003, Rangers fans endured an all-time record run of seven successive defeats in the Old Firm fixture. McLeish failed to build on the last-day title win in 2004–05 and in his last season Rangers chalked up a ten-match winless streak, the worst in the club's history, which might have seen him leave the club in December.

Stephen Smith, of the Rangers Supporters' Trust, recalls a

'very mixed bag indeed' under McLeish. 'You have the history made in Europe for being the first Scottish club to make the last 16 of the Champions League versus the worst ever run of results in the club's history,' he says. 'The Lovenkrands Cup final of 2002 and the 2002-03 Treble followed immediately by the sale of the Treble-winning squad. Lots of defeats against Celtic, a last-minute title thriller against the Pars in 2003 followed by a season when we won nothing and went backwards at an alarming rate and then Helicopter Sunday in 2005 – it was as if Rangers were bipolar. Occasional flashes of brilliance were probably overshadowed by too much mediocrity and tame surrenders to average but physical Celtic sides. He could pick a decent defender and was prepared to experiment with 4–3–3 and the occasional 4–2–4. Giving Ronald de Boer a free role in the last third, with Barry Ferguson encouraged to get forward, saw some of the best link-up play between midfield and front I've ever seen from a Rangers side. But signings like Jeffers, Nieto, Emerson, Capucho, Ostenstad and Bernard? Not up to scratch.'

Thompson remains eternally grateful to McLeish for giving him the opportunity to join Rangers and be part of the two last-day title wins in 2002–03 and 2004–05, which have gone down in Ibrox folklore. 'It was an amazing time in my career,' he says. 'I really enjoyed it. I was playing with some great players and I have treasured memories of Old Firm games and winning medals and you have to remember that it is only a small percentage of professionals who win anything during their careers. Both last-day title wins were incredible. After the game against Dunfermline in 2003 I said that level of drama would never be seen again but I was wrong, it happened again two years later. But the first one was special to me because I scored and it was the first trophy that I'd won. I remember the adrenalin that day, it was electrifying; I felt that I could have done anything. Then we won the Scottish Cup the following week so it was a surreal period for me and rather overwhelming.'

Thompson believes McLeish, by guiding Birmingham to their

League Cup final win over Arsenal at Wembley in February 2011, confirmed his status as a top-class manager. 'People might have expected Alex to win things with Rangers but he has to be given enormous credit for winning a domestic trophy in England with Birmingham against a team like Arsenal,' he says. That's another thing on his CV on top of a fantastic time with the Scotland national team. I won't have a bad word to say about him. But he won't be bothered by what people say about him anyway, he has proven himself and he has the CV to show it.'

Stephen Smith believes history should be kind to McLeish when assessing his time at Ibrox. 'I hope it recognises he was the first manager to be dealt a very poor hand by David Murray and unreasonably asked to work miracles,' he says. 'I hope it will also remember that he was a credit to the club in the dignified way he conducted himself with the media and he made a point of acknowledging the fans. The contrast between the highs and lows of Eck's tenure was enormous but he's a Rangers manager who won as many trophies as Martin O'Neill, including a Treble, and was the first manager to take a Scots side into the last 16 of Europe's premier competition.

'I think a Scot coming in, having managed Hibs and Motherwell, was a problem for some fans used to seeing figures like Souness, Smith and Advocaat in the dugout,' adds Smith. 'But most of our fans were patient, tolerant and ultimately benevolent to McLeish. If he were to return to Ibrox with his Villa side I don't think there's any doubt he'd be warmly welcomed.'

17
SMITH RETURNS

On 4 January 2007, Rangers announced the departure of Paul Le Guen after just seven turbulent months in charge. The Frenchman claimed his departure had been 'the best solution for all concerned' and there were few dissenters. David Murray admitted the Ibrox club had to stop a rot that had set in during Le Guen's brief tenure. 'You're driven by results,' he said. 'Rangers Football Club rises and falls on results. If you're in a hole, stop digging. And that's what we've done.' Murray turned immediately to former Ibrox boss, Walter Smith, by then Scotland manager.

Smith resigned from his post at Hampden, in some controversy, and on 10 January it was announced that he would be Rangers' new boss, almost nine years after he had left the club. 'I got a phone call out of the blue and I was genuinely surprised,' Smith said. 'People say you shouldn't go back and that I would damage my legacy but I don't have an ego that allows me to think I might damage whatever legacy I had left. Dick Advocaat, Alex McLeish and Paul Le Guen had all been the manager at

Rangers since I had left so the gap was big. But the main thing was whether or not I had the determination and drive I had the first time. I was getting day-to-day involvement again and the chance to replicate a successful period. I still felt I had it in me to meet that challenge. And the fact is Rangers is my team, they have always been my team.'

However, the SFA and a large section of the Tartan Army were unhappy about Smith's apparent desertion from his post and SFA chief executive David Taylor came out fighting. Smith had enhanced his reputation with Scotland who, at the time, were surprisingly top of their Euro 2008 qualifying group, ahead of Italy and France, the two 2006 World Cup finalists. The former Everton boss had visited the SFA offices at Hampden to deliver a resignation letter to Taylor – which was not accepted. Subsequently, the SFA confirmed its intention to take legal action against Smith for breach of contract and against Rangers for inducement to breach the contract.

Smith admits some misgivings but denied leaving his country in the lurch. He said: 'I was at the national team and we had come up the FIFA rankings. If it had been at the end of the qualification tournament it would have been easy but it was in the middle of that and I felt as though I was maybe walking out on something there. But if you're saying that there was only one person who can manage the team and that was me then you've got a problem. I think there are other people who can do the job, so I don't think you can say it was a bad day for the national team.'

Taylor knew he had lost his man but his attempt to maximise compensation did not go down well with Murray and an unseemly spat ensued. Murray was furious at the SFA's compensation demands. He said: 'They rejected our offer and we'll sort that out later. They came in with a figure which was totally unrealistic.' As is usual in these circumstances, an agreement was reached and the Ibrox club agreed to make a payment, reportedly around £400,000, to end the impasse.

What was much more worrying for many Rangers fans

was their team's performance on the park. In between Le Guen leaving and Smith returning, the Ibrox men, under the guidance of stand-in boss Ian Durrant, had been beaten 3–2 by Dunfermline at East End Park in the third round of the Scottish Cup. The Light Blues had been knocked out of the League Cup by St Johnstone earlier in the season, in what had been for many the low point of Le Guen's tenure, and were trailing Celtic by 17 points, which meant the SPL title race was effectively over.

On the plus side, Rangers were still in the UEFA Cup, facing Israeli side Hapoel Tel Aviv in what was a winnable tie, and there was time for Smith to strengthen the squad before the transfer window closed at the end of the month. Smith had announced that his assistant at Hampden, Rangers legend Ally McCoist, would be returning to Ibrox with him. More surprisingly, Kenny McDowall was recruited from Celtic as first-team coach as part of his plan to build afresh from the ruins of Le Guen. 'You normally don't get managerial jobs when there are no problems at a club,' Smith later explained. 'I don't know if Scottish football was a surprise to Paul, you would need to ask him, but it wasn't a nice environment. The foreign players and Scottish players weren't gelling as they should have done. So the first thing I did was ask Ally McCoist, Kenny McDowall, Ian Durrant – who was already here – and Jim Stewart to form my backroom team.'

Le Guen's departure had been swift, but a bitter aftertaste remained. Robert McElroy was one of many Rangers fans who felt the Le Guen experiment has been a missed opportunity. He said: 'Smith was welcomed back by the fans but I was very disappointed when Le Guen resigned. I thought he would come good. I thought he was different and could do well in Europe, which he did to an extent, but domestically it was a disaster. It comes back to the Scottish psyche. Le Guen obviously wanted his players to be professional sportsmen. The Boozegate incident [when Rangers duo Barry Ferguson and Allan McGregor were banned by the SFA for a drinking episode while on international duty with Scotland] exonerated Le Guen, although not everyone agrees. But I would sum it up as an opportunity lost.'

In contrast Jim Templeton, president of the Rangers Supporters' Assembly, was among many who were delighted by the news that Smith had been reappointed and said at the time: 'I think he'll be welcomed back with open arms. Obviously you'll never please all of them but the vast majority of supporters will be delighted to have Walter back at the club. The first thing he will bring is stability and organisation, both of which appear to have been non-existent at times this season, and he also brings his knowledge of Rangers Football Club. Walter is a man who is steeped in the club's traditions. He obviously has lots of rebuilding to do,' continued Templeton. 'Anyone who has been present at the majority of Rangers' games this season will realise that. But I think he'll make an immediate impression.'

Ibrox legend Richard Gough, Smith's captain during his first spell at Rangers in the 1990s and later at Everton, also made public his belief that his former gaffer was the right man for the job. 'The main attribute of Walter Smith is his management of the players,' Gough said. 'I can only talk from my own experience with Walter and he handled a lot of different characters very well back then. I don't think he has as mad a bunch as we had when I was playing but he will handle them well. He's good that way with players and players respect him. They will want to play for him and, judging from reports, that's what Mr Le Guen was lacking. It seems like half the dressing room didn't want to play for him, which is unusual in football.'

Smith was soon to show the strength of character that would become a feature of his second spell at the club, firstly by reappointing Ferguson as captain. 'Before recent weeks, Barry was captain of Rangers and captain of Scotland and there was not a question mark against him,' Smith told BBC Radio Scotland. 'A few aspects cropped up between then and now and I just think he's the best captain at the club and that's why he's back in the job again. He's captain now and I would certainly hope there would be no problems between himself and I in the future.'

Ferguson's spat with Le Guen had split the Rangers support to an extent and not all fans were pleased with Smith's decision. McElroy said: 'I wanted Ferguson out the door. I thought he was a troublemaker. You can't be certain what went on but you heard of him not adhering to Le Guen's tactics.'

But, as always in football, positive results act as a balm to any perceived irritant. Smith's first match in his second spell at Ibrox saw a 5–0 home win against Dundee United, with two goals from Kris Boyd and one each from Ferguson, Chris Burke and Charlie Adam. It was certainly an encouraging start but it was clear the squad needed to be refurbished. However, it was a vastly different financial landscape from the one Smith had helped paint in his first spell at the club. No longer would world-class players such as Brian Laudrup or Paul Gascoigne be enticed to Ibrox with wages equal to that of any club in Europe. However, some decent money was made available. Scotland defender Andy Webster was cleared by the SFA to join the Ibrox club on loan from Wigan after being at the centre of a lengthy registration dispute with former club Hearts. (His time at Rangers would prove to be a costly disaster and after a loan spell at Dundee United and numerous injuries, he returned to Tynecastle in January 2011.) David Weir joined from Everton, having signed a contract until the end of the season, and he was soon joined by former England defender Ugo Ehiogu from Middlesbrough.

Weir's arrival at the age of 36 inspired mixed feelings among the Rangers supporters, many of whom believed the player to be well past his best. John MacMillan, secretary of the Rangers Supporters' Association, summed up the views of many of his members at the time. He said: 'Under the circumstances, it's understandable that Walter has gone for Weir. We need someone with experience in the middle of the defence and we need some substance, which has been lacking all season. Hopefully he can stabilise things and maybe he can bring on

Karl Svensson at the same time. But I'm glad he is only signed until the end of the season. I was worried he would sign for 18 months or longer. It cannot be a long-term solution. We have to go for younger players in the future.' On reflection, Smith admits pragmatism lay behind the recruitment of Weir: 'The job hadn't changed that much when I returned,' Smith said. 'There are basic principles that you have to adhere to and we had to get in as many good players as we could. In my first time at Rangers, up until around 1995 when the television monies started to kick in to English football, we could compete with English teams for players but it was no longer possible so we had to look in different markets. We brought in Kevin Thomson, Davie Weir and Ugo Ehiogu to toughen the team up a bit and we got a good reaction right away. No disrespect to Davie Weir, because I couldn't hold any player in any higher esteem than I hold him, but if there was money available I would not have made that decision. But it wasn't perfect circumstances. We had a wee bit of money to get Kevin Thomson and we got experience with Davie and Ehiogu, they were good professionals. I had no fears with Davie – but I didn't think he would end up staying the same length of time as me!'

Thomson had completed his move from Hibernian at the end of January then admitted his ideal scenario would see teammate and flatmate Scott Brown following him to Ibrox. Thomson said: 'I would love to see Scott come here. It's looking like he will be staying at Hibs this time but I would be over the moon if he were to join me at Rangers.' Ironically, Brown would sign for Celtic the following summer and in time become the captain at Parkhead.

Meanwhile, midfielder Jeremy Clement signed for Paris St Germain and goalkeeper Lionel Letizi, who made eight appearances under Le Guen, was released from his contract. The day after the transfer window closed Motherwell striker Scott McDonald admitted he was 'completely and utterly devastated' following the Fir Park club's decision to block a move to Rangers. Motherwell boss Maurice Malpas refused to sanction the striker's £400,000 transfer to Ibrox, after allowing top goalscorer Richie Foran to move to Southend. McDonald told the *Daily Record*: 'To say I'm completely devastated is probably an understatement. It's so hard for me to take. At half past four, when my agent called to tell me what was happening, I was on top of the world. Six hours later and I'm on the floor. But it's up to Motherwell to call the shots. I'm under contract as a Motherwell player and there's nothing I can do about that.'

McDonald revealed a hope that Smith would renew his interest in the summer, adding: 'Hopefully I can get over this, keep playing well and then see where it takes me in the summer. My only hope is that Walter Smith will still want me then because it's not very often you get the chance to work for a man like that at a club like Rangers.' In the event, McDonald signed a pre-contract with Celtic in March for a reported fee of £700,000 and moved to Parkhead in the summer.

Rangers reached the last 16 of the UEFA Cup with a 5–2 aggregate defeat of Hapoel Tel Aviv but succumbed to Spanish side Osasuna over two legs at that next hurdle. However, it was indisputable that form had picked up and Smith's rejuvenated side ended the season in second place with a brace of wins over Celtic to offer encouragement for the following season.

Inevitably, there was more refurbishment in the summer. Smith's list of new recruits included: Roy Carroll (from West Ham on a free), Steven Whittaker (Hibernian, £2 million), Carlos Cuellar (Osasuna, £2.37 million, Amdy Faye (Charlton, on loan), Kirk Broadfoot (St Mirren, free), Alan Gow (Falkirk, free), Lee McCulloch (Wigan Athletic, £2.25 million), Steven Naismith (Kilmarnock, £1.9 million), DaMarcus Beasley (PSV, £700,000), Daniel Cousin (Lens, £750,000) and Jean-Claude Darcheville (Bordeaux, free).

Rangers, once again Walter Smith's team, began 2007–08, his first full season in charge since 1997–98, in fine form. They ended it after an exhausting schedule of 68 competitive matches, which included a memorable run all the way to the UEFA Cup final. On the way they scooped up both domestic cups and, after battling with the authorities over fixture congestion, were only pipped for the title by Old Firm rivals Celtic on the last day of the season. Amid a punishing European campaign Rangers battled on the domestic front, ultimately with mixed fortunes. On 16 March 2008, the Light Blues played in their first final since 2005 when they took on Dundee United in the CIS Cup final at Hampden. A thrilling encounter ended 2–2 after extra time, with both goals coming from substitute Kris Boyd who also scored the winning spot kick in a dramatic penalty shoot-out.

By the end of the month Smith's side had a ten-point lead over Celtic in the title race but the sheer number of games Rangers had to play before the end of the season made it a bridge too far for the Ibrox men. Gradually Celtic caught up and the two teams were tied on 86 points going into their final games on 22 May against Dundee United at Tannadice and Aberdeen at Pittodrie respectively. The Parkhead club were four goals better off which gave them a psychological advantage but goal difference was to play no part as Rangers lost 2–0 to the Dons while Celtic won on Tayside. There was something anti-climatic about Rangers' Scottish Cup final win over First Division side Queen of the South two days later at Hampden. Goals from DaMarcus Beasley and a double from Kris Boyd gave Rangers a 3–2 win and took the trophy back to Ibrox but the season was a case of what might have been.

The European run that season, however, will forever be etched into the minds of the Rangers fans and it began in the Champions League, where qualification was secured with victories over FK Zeta and Red Star Belgrade. In the group stage Rangers were drawn along with Barcelona, Lyon and Stuttgart and there were some encouraging results in the early stages with wins over Stuttgart and Lyon and a home draw with the superstars from the Nou Camp. However, a collapse in the second half of the campaign with three defeats meant Rangers finished third in the group and were left only with the consolation of a place in the UEFA Cup.

But Rangers gradually built up a head of steam in the competition by beating Panathinaikos, Werder Bremen and Sporting Lisbon before reaching the final thanks to a penalty shoot-out victory against Fiorentina in the semi-final second leg in Florence. However, there was to be no fairytale for Smith and the Rangers support who invaded Manchester on 14 May for the final against Zenit St Petersburg. The Russian side, managed by former Gers boss Dick Advocaat, were comfortable 2–0 winners.

'There are mixed emotions,' Smith admitted at the end of an exhausting season. 'You are delighted that you have taken a team to a UEFA Cup final and disappointed that you didn't win it. I remember it now more fondly than I did at the time and there is the frustration of not winning. But it was fantastic to be involved in. We had to play Saturday, Tuesday, Thursday then the Scottish Cup final. I don't think anyone has ever had to do that, so winning the league and UEFA Cup under those circumstances would have capped everything I have done. I wouldn't have given that season up for anything; the boys were fantastic. I still think it goes down as one of the best seasons in the club's history.'

While it is not unusual for English teams to prioritise competitions – which many pundits and punters implored Smith to do – he insists he was duty-bound to win every tournament entered. 'We ended up in a hell of a situation that year but how do you pick and choose?' said Smith looking back some years later. 'You don't and you can't pick and choose when you are trying to create a winning environment within your club. If you are creating a winning environment that means you have to win every game you play whether it's the first round of the Scottish Cup or the final of the League Cup. If you pick a team full of reserve team players for the League Cup or Scottish Cup then you are saying I am not bothered about that tournament. We were in Athens against Panathinaikos, 1–0 down with 20 minutes to go and Coisty said to me: "What are we going to do?" I said: "Well if we want to win domestically, we need to get beat," but you can't. So we make substitutions and we score and get through on away goals and it sets us up for a run that we wouldn't have given up for anything anyway. It obviously inhibited our opportunities for league success but I wouldn't have given it up or had it any other way.'

The following season, 2008–09, was almost the polar opposite with early European disappointment followed by title success. Scotland's continually plummeting European coefficient meant Rangers had to qualify for the Champions League, and in the second qualifier a 0–0 draw with Lithuanian minnows FBK Kaunas at Ibrox was followed by an embarrassing 2–1 defeat in the return leg. There would be no safety net of the Europa League (which had superseded the UEFA Cup that season) and thus Rangers' European campaign was over before the league season began.

There were more comings and goings at the club during that summer. Algerian defender Madjid Bougherra arrived from Charlton for £2.5 million before popular Spanish defender Carlos Cuellar was sold to Aston Villa. Pedro Mendes cost £3 million from Portsmouth and Steven Davis, having enjoyed a six-month loan spell at Ibrox the previous season, was also signed for £3 million from Fulham. Eyebrows were raised when young Irish striker Kyle Lafferty was bought from Burnley for £3.5 million while another relatively unknown player, midfielder Maurice Edu, cost £2.5 million from FC Toronto. Former Hearts striker Andrius Velicka arrived at a cost of £1 million from Viking, Aaron Niguez was brought in on loan from Valencia while Andy Webster completed his permanent move to Rangers from Wigan.

Smith again had to swim against the popularity tide when he signed Kenny Miller from Derby County for £1.9 million. The Scotland striker returned to Ibrox for the second time, having had a brief spell under Dick Advocaat. However, in the intervening period he had played for Celtic and scored against Rangers. Most managers would not have put themselves into that situation but Smith would not be swayed by the hysteria whipped up after stories of his imminent arrival had surfaced in the months before his move.

In February 2008, one fan was quoted as saying: 'I think it would go down like a lead balloon. You only have to look at the striking talent Rangers have at the moment. Daniel Cousin is still here for now, Jean-Claude Darcheville and Kris Boyd are doing a job and Lee McCulloch can also play up front. And I don't think you will find a Rangers fan who will say Miller is a better player than Nacho Novo – Miller would probably be seventh-choice striker if he came back. Anyone who has been at games knows the Rangers fans have made it clear he would not be welcomed back. We are looking to move on, not to take a step backwards.' Phone-ins, websites and message boards were kept busy with Rangers fans condemning the proposed signing and, during the Scottish Cup final win over Queen of the South, a large section of the Rangers support had chanted vociferously against Miller. The feelings of the fans could not have been made any clearer but the player duly signed, saying on his arrival to the club's official website: 'I'm over the moon. It's taken longer than I expected but I'm delighted. When a club like Rangers comes calling, it's always going to be hard to knock that back anyway. I worked with the manager Walter Smith and his assistant with Scotland. I get on really well with Walter and Ally both on and off the field and I felt they got the best out of me for the national team. I definitely feel I'm coming here a far better player than when I left first time around.' Miller had to put up with boos and jeers in the early months of his career but he proved every bit as strong-willed as Smith and two goals at Parkhead in the first Old Firm game of the season helped him assuage the Ibrox support. Mendes also scored his first goal for the club in a convincing 4–2 victory.

By the time he was sold to Turkish side Bursaspor in January 2011, the former Hoops striker had won over the Rangers fans. Smith though, who faced up to critics once again when he brought in controversial Senegalese international El-Hadji Diouf from Blackburn on loan as his replacement, took no extra pleasure from proving the doubters wrong. In explaining these unpopular decisions, Smith reveals something of his management style: 'Part of management is having the strength of character to say "I think this is the best thing at the present moment, I don't think we can get better." If you think it is for the benefit of the team you have to make those decisions. I never had any doubts that Kenny would come and do a good job for us. No one can say that he was anything other than excellent for us in his second time here.

'Satisfaction comes from winning. I don't get extra satisfaction in saying people didn't want me to sign this player but I have and it has worked out, because you make a lot of signings and it doesn't work out. There is always a balance there, you win some and lose some. No manager can look back and says that he hasn't made errors, but you do have to make decisions.'

Smith's decisions that season were proved right. Rangers won the title with a 3–0 win over Dundee United at Tannadice on the last day of the campaign. In one of the best performances of the season goals from Kyle Lafferty, Pedro Mendes and Kris Boyd brought the 52nd championship in the club's history back to Ibrox, the first title in four seasons. Having lost in the Co-operative Insurance Cup final against Celtic at Hampden in March, Rangers got the chance to make amends in the Scottish Cup final against Falkirk at the national stadium on 30 May. The Bairns had avoided relegation in the last day of the season with a win at Inverness but their luck had run out. A Nacho Novo strike in the first minute of the second half, just after the Spaniard had come on as a substitute, gave the Light Blues a 1–0 win to complete the domestic Double.

In contrast Rangers continued to struggle in Europe, despite being seeded in pot two of the UEFA Champions League group stage for the first time. The group, which included Sevilla, Stuttgart and Romanian champions Unirea Urziceni, was thought to represent a more than decent chance of making the knockout stages. Instead, there was more embarrassment, although the campaign began positively with a 1–1 draw against

Stuttgart in Germany. Thereafter, however, followed two consecutive 4–1 defeats at home to Sevilla and Unirea, the latter being one of the worst European results in the club's history. Rangers finished with a record low tally of two points.

More misery was to follow in the summer of 2009 when the full extent of the club's financial predicament became clear to the club and its supporters. In terms of transfers, it was a case of players moving out rather than bringing them in. Around a dozen players who had appeared for the first team including Barry Ferguson, Charlie Adam, Pedro Mendes, Brahim Hemdani, Christian Dailly and Alan Gow left the club while Jerome Rothen arrived on a season-long loan from Paris St Germain, the first signing in over a year. More significantly, David Murray stepped down as chairman and was replaced by non-executive director Alastair Johnston, who admitted his main priority was to find a buyer for the club.

Smith became involved in the internal politics, revealing to the consternation of the supporters that Lloyds Banking Group, to whom Rangers was in debt, was 'effectively running the club'. On 12 November, it was announced that the debt had risen to £31 million, an increase of £10 million from the previous year. The club was in some turmoil but at its AGM held at Ibrox the following month came some good news when it was revealed that Smith and his assistants McCoist and McDowall would continue to work without contracts when they expired in the New Year.

On the field, Smith was keeping Rangers ahead of the rest. In March, the spirit that he had fostered at the club came to the fore in the Co-operative Insurance Cup final against St Mirren at Hampden. The Light Blues were reduced to nine men when Danny Wilson and Kevin Thomson were sent off, but a Kenny Miller goal brought the trophy to Ibrox. Chances of a domestic Treble ended when Rangers lost 1–0 in the quarter-final of the Scottish Cup to eventual winners Dundee United in a replay. However, despite the turbulence of the season, the 53rd championship was captured on 25 April with a

1–0 win over Hibernian at Easter Road with Kyle Lafferty scoring the winner.

A month later, Smith ended speculation about his future when he signed a new one-year deal. However, he stated that he would be leaving at the end of the following season. Rangers would have a new man at the helm and that man would be Ally McCoist, who was confirmed as the next manager on 22 February 2011.

Many believe Smith's final year at the club was his best.

In the summer of 2010, despite having secured two consecutive titles, the Light Blues were far from favourites to make it three.

Celtic had finished the season strongly under Neil Lennon whose role as manager was made permanent following a spell as interim boss and the Irishman had money to spend.

There was on-going speculation about Rangers' financial problems and the club's search for a new owner.

The Govan club lost its top scorer, Kris Boyd, during the transfer window while the departure of Nacho Novo, Kevin Thomson and teenage defender Danny Wilson left the Light Blues squad somewhat depleted.

To that end, Smith signed striker Nikica Jelavic from Rapid Vienna for £4 million and James Beattie was signed from Stoke for a reported fee of £1.5 million. Manchester City winger Vladimir Weiss and Aberdeen defender Richard Foster arrived on loan. The squad was to be bolstered further in January by more loan signings in the shape of young Arsenal defender Kyle Bartley and Blackburn forward El-Hadji Diouf while veteran Northern Ireland international David Healy was signed until the end of the season from Sunderland.

However, as season 2010–11 got under way it was clear that Smith would rely on tried and trusted players such as goalkeeper Allan McGregor, defenders Madjid Bougherra, Sasa Papac and Steven Whittaker, and midfielders Lee McCulloch (whose season would be wrecked by injury) and Steven Davis. Veteran defender David Weir, who had turned 40 at the end of the season, was persuaded to skipper the side for another year.

There were to be seven Old Firm games in what was a controversial and at times acrimonious season. Rangers and Celtic both started the league campaign with eight straight wins before the first Old Firm derby in September at Parkhead which the visitors won 3–1 with a double from on-form striker Kenny Miller.

The Champions League was always going to prove difficult but in a group which included English champions Manchester United – who would reach the final – Spanish giants Valencia and Turkish side Bursaspor, Rangers finished third following a respectable campaign which saw them hold the Red Devils to a goalless draw at Old Trafford and only lose at home to Sir Alex Ferguson's side through a late penalty.

The Ibrox club parachuted into the Europa League which secured European football after Christmas. However, there was little festive cheer on the domestic front for the Light Blues fans as Rangers lost 2–0 at home to Celtic on 2 January, in what was the 40th anniversary of the Ibrox Disaster.

Adverse winter weather conditions had played havoc with the fixtures and Celtic headed into the New Year showdown with a one point lead over their city rivals at the top of the SPL which they stretched to four, although Rangers had two games in hand.

Moreover, the financial problems at Ibrox saw top-scorer Miller sold to Bursaspor for £400,000, a paltry sum for a player who had scored 22 goals for the club in six months.

The Gers support had been given a boost in January with the return of Jelavic from injury but when Scotland international Kris Commons opted to join Celtic rather than Rangers from Derby County, it appeared to many that the advantage in the title race was swinging towards Parkhead.

In between securing their passage in to the last 16 of the Europa League in February with an away goals win over Sporting Lisbon – a 2–2 draw in Portugal coming after a 1–1 draw at Ibrox – Rangers lost 3–0 at Parkhead in the SPL to leave them trailing by eight points. The Ibrox side still had two games in hand but Smith admitted improvement was needed if they were to retain the title.

He said: 'I don't think we have been playing that well since the turn of the year. We've been patchy with our form although we have managed to win some of the games so we will have to look at getting a better level of consistency about us. If we can gain that consistency, we always have the final Old Firm game of the season at Ibrox, which will take on importance if we can take on a level of consistency. We are going to have to search for something that will give us a lift in the remaining part of the season.'

It took all of Smith's experience to keep the ship steady as the season slipped in to March and especially after Rangers lost 1–0 to Celtic in their highly charged Scottish Cup fifth-round replay at Parkhead, the first game at Ibrox the previous month having ended 2–2.

Four days before the Co-operative Insurance Cup final against Celtic at Hampden, Rangers exited Europe with a 1–0 defeat against Dutch side PSV Eindhoven at Ibrox, following a goalless draw in the first leg in Holland.

Celtic were overwhelming favourites to pick up the first piece of silverware of the season but once again Smith proved he was the man for the big occasion. A Steven Davis drive and a fine extra-time strike from the impressive Jelavic gave the Light Blues a well-deserved 2–1 win.

After collecting his 20th trophy of his two stints at Ibrox, Smith said: 'They showed they have the desire to win. It won't do us any harm psychologically in the final stages of the season.'

However, Rangers then contrived to lose 3–2 in their next game at home to Dundee United, thus blowing their chance to go top of the table for the first time since Boxing Day.

Smith's men responded with five straight wins but the ascendancy was handed back to Celtic on 24 April at Ibrox. The seventh and final Old Firm game of the season ended in a goalless draw keeping the home side just one point clear but having played a game more than Celtic and with the Parkhead side six goals better off.

Georgios Samaras had his late spot-kick brilliantly saved by McGregor but the visiting fans cheered the final whistle in a manner which suggested that they believed the Gers' keeper's save had been irrelevant and that the title had been secured.

But there was another twist to come and it was the most significant of the SPL season. On the evening of 4 May, in what was their game in hand over Rangers, Celtic suffered a shock 3-2 defeat at Inverness to keep them one point behind the champions with both Old Firm sides having just three games to play.

It was the break Smith and Rangers needed and they took full advantage. Having beat Motherwell 5-0 at Fir Park in the wake of the goalless draw against Celtic at Ibrox, Rangers followed it up with a 4-0 home win over Hearts, watched by new owner Craig Whyte, whose takeover had been completed the previous day.

Title tensions were increasing by the game but Celtic responded the next day with a 2-0 win at Kilmarnock to close the gap to one point again.

On Tuesday 10 May, a nervy Rangers beat Dundee United 2-0 at Ibrox in what was to be Smith's last home game as manager. He was given a thunderous send-off by the Gers fans as he walked around the pitch in the pouring rain after the game but there was still work to be done as Celtic overcame Hearts 3-0 at Tynecastle the following night to ensure the title race would go to the last day of the season.

Rangers were to visit Rugby Park while Celtic were to host Motherwell. Before the Killie game Smith paid tribute to his squad, saying: 'We have been short of iconic figures that Rangers teams have had down through history. Over the past few years we have had former players saying we were a poor Rangers team so I don't think they have received the credit for their abilities. If they do win on Sunday then three league championships in a row would be an achievement that not a lot of players who have starred for Rangers have managed to achieve. They have worked really hard and put up with things other players would not have tolerated.'

His players responded magnificently as they wrapped up the club's 54th title in style.

The kick-off at Parkhead had been delayed by moments which meant Celtic's game against the Steelmen had just started when news filtered through that Rangers had taken the lead.

The rampant Ibrox men, in fact, were three up in seven minutes and ended up 5–1 winners. Striker Kyle Lafferty scored twice, either side of a Steven Naismith strike to ease any nerves among the massive Gers travelling support.

As Celtic cruised to a meaningless 4–0 win over Motherwell, the second half at Rugby Park saw Jelavic drive in a wonderful free-kick and Lafferty complete his hat-trick.

Rangers retained the title by one point which meant Smith signed off with 10 championships, and a total of 21 trophies, over his two spells at the Ibrox helm.

During the post-match celebrations at Rugby Park, Papac said: 'It's the best feeling of my life. It's a present for Walter. He is a great man. I would like to say thank you to him.'

In typically modest style, Smith deflected any praise that was coming his way. 'It's for the club, it's not for me,' he said. 'Everything you do is for the club. We've got a great bunch of lads who have worked extremely hard for us. They've been brilliant. I'm just delighted the team has managed to win – that's the main thing. It's always the main thing. I just feel it's the right time for me to leave and it's the right thing for Rangers.'

Reflecting on the troubled times he endured during his second spell as Rangers boss, Smith claimed that his spell in charge at Goodison Park helped him cope: 'Everton gave me that experience, twice in a three-and-a-half-year period,' he said. 'I was having to sell players months after buying them then bring older players back. It wasn't the environment in which I wanted to work but it taught me a lot as a manager. It was a lesson in crisis management in many ways and in how to handle it. I had a good idea what it was like to work within tighter confines.

'The credit for handling the situation doesn't go to the manager it goes to the group of players who have had to go out and win. The boys we had here were all really receptive and they deserved enormous credit for keeping the club successful during this period. I didn't get burdened with the intricacies; I was concerned with the team. I was concerned with how it would all affect the team – whether we had to sell players or could we bring any in – that was the only thing that affected me. Martin Bain [former chief executive] did a fantastic job keeping things at a decent level. We tried to keep together as good a group of players as we could and he deserves enormous credit for the way he has worked to keep the club going.'

Smith is assured of his legendary status. His advice to his successors is simple. He said: 'All Rangers managers face the same challenge – to win. It's that simple. You are surrounded by success, the history and tradition of the place is success and if you are taking over as manager that is exactly what you have to try to copy. It is as simple and as difficult as that. Just win. I would have that saying put up on every wall inside Murray Park.'

18
EUROPEAN NIGHTS

Rangers' reputation has been built on the club's record-breaking domestic success, but there has always been a desire for more glamour with European football providing it over the past 50 years or so. Title and trophy wins are celebrated and enjoyed but big European nights at Ibrox – under the floodlights and in front of capacity crowds – also remain long in the memories of supporters, players, coaches and commentators alike.

In his book *Rangers: The New Era* William Allison highlighted the club's first European tie against Nice in 1956, which ended in a first round exit following a play-off defeat in Paris. Allison noted that the innovative idea of European football had opened up 'new and inviting avenues that were to lead to some of the most glamorous adventures in the club's history, bringing new ideals, new ambitions, new commitments and more important, new standards – gold standards too.'

The Ibrox club had always welcomed the challenge of matches against foreign opposition. In November 1945, Russian side

Moscow Dynamo visited Ibrox as part of their tour of Britain. Despite the match being played in the afternoon, an incredible crowd of 90,000 turned up to see Rangers – wearing hoops – claw back a two-goal deficit to draw 2–2. It is a game that has gone down in Ibrox folklore (see chapter 8).

Of course, this tradition goes back even further. From the 1930s Rangers played friendly matches home and away against foreign opposition such as Sparta Prague, Benfica, Rapid Vienna, Barcelona and Valencia; games against English aristocrats Arsenal were also common, all of which whetted an existing appetite which the European tournaments would in time satisfy.

In the summer of 1962, a year after Rangers had reached their first European final, the Ibrox club flew to the Soviet Union for a three-match tour. The Light Blues returned unbeaten after a 3–1 victory over Lokomotiv Moscow, a 1–0 triumph over Dynamo Tbilisi of Georgia and a 1–1 draw with Dynamo Kiev (see chapter 10). During this Cold War period, when the Soviet Union was still shrouded in mystery, the tour caught the imagination of the Scottish public. Thousands of Rangers fans turned up at Renfrew (now Glasgow) airport to welcome the team back and caused some chaos when they streamed on to the runway after the plane had landed.

'There was always an excitement about European games,' said Robert McElroy, in the *Rangers Historian*. 'They were huge games. There was little or no television coverage of football and you knew little about these teams. Now you know everything about European opposition. The attitude then was if they had a foreign name then they must be good! European football coincided with regular floodlight matches and that was attractive in its own way. In the early European ties Rangers wore these unusual satin shorts, which looked great under the lights. However, in those early days there was always a lot of trouble on the park. The traditional British style of football with its hard tackling did not go down well with the Italians, Spanish and French. They were more accustomed to body checking which, in turn, did not go down well with the British. When Rangers played Fiorentina in the first leg of the Cup-Winners' Cup final at Ibrox in 1961, the Italian flag was burned and against Red Star Belgrade a few years later, there were incredible scenes on the pitch.'

The late Ken Gallacher, writing in *The Scottish Book of Football* in 1970, described European football as 'The Magic Challenge' and noted that by entering the newly formed European Cup in 1955 Hibs had been the first Scottish club to 'pioneer the glamorous road to the continental clashes that we know today'. Gallacher spoke of a 'brave new world that had been opened up' to Scottish clubs, though even by then the Old Firm were at the forefront of Scotland's challenge in Europe.

Rangers reached a European Cup semi-final and Cup-Winners' Cup final in the first five years of European competition with another two Cup-Winners' Cup final appearances in 1966–67 and 1971–72. As the rest of Europe caught up and overtook Scottish clubs, it would be a 36-year wait until the UEFA Cup final in Manchester in 2008. But during that time the greatest names in world football including Real Madrid, Inter Milan, Manchester United and Barcelona have been the visitors to Govan while 'Battle of Britain' matches against Tottenham, Wolves, Leeds and Newcastle United have had Ibrox packed to the rafters.

While Rangers have normally taken huge travelling support on their continental jaunts, the games at Ibrox have allowed more fans to enjoy memorable nights of excitement and high drama, including the European Cup-Winners' Cup semi-final against Bayern Munich at Ibrox on 19 April 1972.

The German club were one of the finest sides in Europe at the time, a team on the cusp of greatness. They boasted players such as Sepp Maier, Paul Breitner, Hans-Georg Schwarzenbeck, Franz Beckenbauer, Gerd Müller and Uli Hoeness, all of whom would help West Germany beat England 3–1 in a European Championship qualifier at Wembley in the same month before going on to win the 1972 European Championship and the 1974

World Cup. Willie Waddell's side survived a battering in Munich to hang on for a 1–1 draw which set up a potential glory night for the second leg.

Some of the 80,000 Gers fans who would pack Ibrox were still making their way into the stadium when Sandy Jardine cut in from the right before sending a left-footed shot past the bemused Maier to gave Rangers the lead with only a minute on the clock. Youngster Derek Parlane, deputising for injured skipper John Greig, scored the second before the break with a shot that crashed in off the underside of the bar. There was no way back for the rattled visitors who unravelled further as Ibrox rocked to the sound of 'Barcelona Here We Come', a reference to the Nou Camp final the following month.

Iain McColl, one of the founder members of the Founders Trail, watched the game through a child's eyes. 'I had only just turned seven but that night is as fresh in my mind as if it had happened last week,' he said. 'The excitement had been building for a number of days, I had never seen my dad so edgy as the day of the match approached. Celtic were also playing that evening against Milan at Celtic Park in the semi-final of the European Cup. What an honour it was for the city of Glasgow, which saw 150,000 football supporters converge on the two stadiums that day. I recall being stood on the vast open terrace at the Celtic End of Ibrox down at the boundary wall. Because I was so small, Ibrox rose above me like the Coliseum, the noise of the 80,000 crowd literally rattled inside your stomach as the teams emerged from the tunnel. I had been to a few games at Ibrox before but this was different, very different. The tension and excitement was etched on the faces of many around me. I was aware that for us to reach the final in Barcelona it would take an incredible effort against what was an impressive group of players that Bayern Munich had in their side.

'I need not have worried, the Rangers played like men possessed that evening and I can still see Sandy Jardine and Derek Parlane's magnificent efforts fly into the net at my end of the ground. The final whistle came in a match that seemed to fly past. I vividly remember being hugged by elderly men, complete strangers, some in tears, and one said to me: "I've waited all of my life for this, son." Myself and Dad made our way home riding on a tidal wave of joy. Later that evening the news came through that Celtic had failed to make their final on penalties. A perfect day. It was never going to be viable financially for myself and Dad to travel to Barcelona for the final, so that night at Ibrox was my own personal European Cup-Winners' Cup final. Looking back, just to be part of something so special and unique in the club's history fills me with an incredible amount of pride – a real "I was there" moment and never to be forgotten.'

Robert McElroy has witnessed most of the European nights at Ibrox but admits the game against Bayern was special. 'My first European game was against Eintracht Frankfurt in 1960, the semi-final of the European Cup,' he said. 'There have been some great nights, Bayern Munich in 1972, Juventus in 1978, Dynamo Kiev in the 1980s, it's very difficult to choose one. But maybe I would pick the Bayern Munich game because that was a great result. It was amazing, given the quality of the players Bayern had in their team.'

The Cup-Winners' Cup victory of 1972 remains the pinnacle of Rangers' European achievements. Continental clubs with superior technique allied to pace and power caught up and overtook the Ibrox club and although Aberdeen and Dundee United flew the flag for Scottish football in the 1980s, it became the case that no Scottish teams could be confident of a run in any of the European competitions. However, occasional nights of magic lit up the gloom.

Six years after the Bayern match, in an amazing European Cup first round tie against star-studded Juventus at Ibrox, Rangers overcame a one-goal deficit for the first time in Europe to have the ground shaking to its foundations. A 2–0 win, thanks to goals by Alex MacDonald and Gordon Smith, took the Gers through to the next round where, in equally dramatic circum- stances, they disposed of PSV Eindhoven only to be halted at the quarter-final stage by German side Cologne.

As Rangers' domestic form stuttered in the early 1980s, the club's European ambitions were held in abeyance. In 1984, a 3–1 win over Inter Milan in the second leg of the second round UEFA Cup tie at Ibrox was stirring but futile as the Italians, with future Celtic manager Liam Brady pulling the strings in midfield, always looked in control and ran out 4–3 winners on aggregate.

When Graeme Souness arrived as player-manager in 1986, Rangers' European ambitions were quickly reassessed and raised. A year later, after the SPL title had returned to Govan for the first time in nine years, there was a never-to-be-forgotten European Cup first round tie against Dynamo Kiev. With the Ibrox pitch controversially narrowed by Souness to negate the dangerous wing play of the highly talented and highly rated Ukraine giants, Rangers overcame a 1–0 first-leg defeat to win 2–0 on the night.

Some say it was the best atmosphere ever experienced at Ibrox, including president of the Rangers Supporters' Assembly, Andy Kerr: 'It was the second season of the Souness era and we had won the league in his first campaign. We had many new high-profile players and here we were setting off in the European Cup with great optimism,' he recalls. 'The draw pitched us against a very strong Kiev side and we did well to hold them to a 1–0 defeat in the first leg. The build-up to the second leg was manic and the match was a complete sell-out. On the night the stadium was bouncing. Mark Falco scored early on to level the tie and the roof nearly came off. We then went ahead early in the second half with an Ally McCoist goal and the reaction was as if we had won the cup. Thereafter, we tried to stifle the game with our experienced players – no doubt based on Souness's experience of similar situations with Liverpool – but it only served to heighten the tension. We allowed them more possession and defended deep and that last 20 minutes seemed like a lifetime. I can well remember the release of tension when the final whistle eventually blew.

It's hard to believe but we actually thought that beating such a good team meant we could win it – such was the enthusiasm generated by the Souness revolution! Overall, the emotions of that evening, the high expectation, the atmosphere, the victory and the promise of what was to come was a heady mix and makes it stand out so much for me.'

Steve Clark recalls that night with ease – and the fraught ending with unease. 'The ultimate night for me was the Dynamo Kiev game where for 90 minutes Ibrox was a wall of noise,' he said. 'That Kiev team was packed with Russia internationals. I was in the West Enclosure that night and the last ten minutes seemed to last forever, you could have cut the tension with a knife. But just to be part of that crowd that night was something special.' However, despite getting past Gornik Zabrze with rather more ease in the second round, Rangers were beaten by a tough Steaua Bucharest in the quarter-finals.

Kiev proved to be the European highlight of Souness's time at Ibrox. By the time he had left to be replaced by his assistant Walter Smith in 1991, Rangers' rejuvenation had been mostly confined to the domestic scene. However, the fans were to enjoy several pulsating European nights in season 1992–93. The newly revamped European Cup provided a classic Battle of Britain tie when Rangers were paired with English champions Leeds United in the second round.

Leeds had in their side future Celtic boss Gordon Strachan, Gary McAllister and Eric Cantona and such was the fear of crowd trouble it was decided that travelling fans would be banned from both games. However, that did little to flatten the atmosphere in the first leg at Ibrox – although McAllister's wonderfully executed first-minute volley initially did: 'There was a distinct eerie silence when I scored after just a minute with a full volley from just outside the box,' former Scotland skipper McAllister said. 'But then we lost two bad goals from set pieces. Both of them came from corners and our goalkeeper John Lukic was complaining about the low lights on the main stand. The noise was deafening but what I remember was not the noise when we walked out but just before the referee blew to signal the start of the game, the build-up, the crescendo of noise was amazing. I remember that myself, Gordon Strachan and Gary Speed, my two midfielder partners, looked across at each other and thought "Hello, what is going on here" and we knew then just how important this game was to Rangers. It is the loudest I have ever heard at a game, it made the hairs on the back of my neck stand up. It was certainly a very memorable game, there is not too often in your career you are involved in games like that when there is so much at stake.'

Peter Drury, whose commentary provided the soundtrack to the television coverage of Rangers' journey to the UEFA Cup final in 2008, was working for BBC Radio Leeds that night – and the memory has stayed with him. He said: 'It was my favourite Ibrox European night partly because it was my first and I was exposed to that raw noise that I'd never experienced before but also because I was one of very few Englishmen in the ground! At the time, I was a young reporter/commentator and I will never forget the moment when Gary McAllister thundered a wonder-goal past Andy Goram very early in the game. Although a few "under the radar" Leeds fans did give themselves away with their instinctive celebrations, there was, otherwise, the most silent silence I have ever witnessed during a football match. It lasted about three seconds and then a deep growl started emanating from all four sides of the ground, which developed into a roar and then into the most extraordinary tidal wave of retaliatory noise! After that, I recall John Lukic losing the ball in the floodlights for the equaliser and Coisty, of course, snatching the winner. Rangers won at Elland Road, too . . . needless to say, more Rangers fans managed to get in that night.'

When Rangers fan Elaine Sommerville takes a trip down memory lane, she invariably ends up at Ibrox on the night the English champions from Yorkshire came to town. 'When I think of my favourite European nights I change my mind,' she says. 'There is the 2–0 win over Juventus in 1978, the 2–0 win over

Dynamo Kiev, the 2–2 draw with Marseille in 1992 and the 1–1 draw with Inter Milan in 2005. But I think I'll go for the game against Leeds. Obviously the chance to get into the first Champions League group stage made it a special prize and Scotland v England added to the pre-match hype. I can still remember the atmosphere at the game, which was electric, even with no away fans. The silence after Leeds scored in the first minute was so strange. Then after the shock the noise returned and the atmosphere was fantastic. The two goals before half-time meant the noise level was high through to the end. Of course, that was only the first leg but qualifying after another win at Elland Road was really special. It gave a much better picture of Scottish football as most of the English press had assumed Leeds would win through easily. But I could have made a case for all the games I picked.'

Alex Anderson, co-author of *Barcelona Here We Come* and *The Advocaat Years*, is in no doubt the visit of Leeds United will forever remain one of the great European nights in Govan. 'When we became the first British team ever to play in the Champions League proper – something even Man United can't take off us! – will always stay with me because of the atmosphere,' he said. 'Okay, it was quickly killed by Gary McAllister and I left Ibrox that night with a sense of foreboding because Leeds, of course, had the away goal. However, I've never experienced noise like it before or since – and I've been to a Milan derby! I was down the very front of the Govan and I always remember being unable to comprehend how Leeds full back Tony Dorigo could jump up and down on the spot so calmly because, as he was waiting for the ref to start the game, the noise was beyond loud. It was white noise. It was a physical force of noise. It was "Hullo, Hullo!" – a song which may have had to go but when it did the atmosphere before European games in Govan was never quite as loud – and you felt it almost knock you over. The East and West Enclosures seemed full of 10,000 crazed trampolinists. Ibrox had a smaller capacity then than now and the open corners of the Govan meant the acoustics weren't as great as at present but, by God, I've never experienced football passion like it. That was a crowd who knew Britain was watching and who wanted Europe to see we were the best in Britain.'

Expectations grew quickly following the dismissal of the English champions. The eight second-round winners were split into two groups with the winners meeting in the final. Rangers were drawn with Marseille, CSKA Moscow and Club Brugge and there was no shortage of confidence around when the French side travelled to Glasgow on match day one. The visitors were packed with stars including Fabien Barthez, Basile Boli (who would later move to Ibrox), Marcel Desailly, Didier Deschamps, Alen Boksic and Rudi Völler and indeed it looked like a mismatch as the Ligue 1 side raced to a two-goal lead through Boksic and Völler. The Light Blues were being outclassed but in a remarkable turnaround two goals in two minutes by substitute Gary McSwegan and Mark Hateley had the rain-soaked stadium in raptures.

Anderson jokes that the excitement generated by the fight-back provided a potential health hazard. 'Aleksei Mikhailichenko did a step-over at 2–2 which, had it led to a goal, would have killed me,' he said. 'I was only 23 years old at the time and pretty healthy but coming back from 2–0 down to 2–2 in the space of two minutes had my heart pounding at an unnatural rate. It was a night of hugging strangers when Hateley made it all-square. I was again down the front of the Govan and it was directly in front of me – just yards away, with Marseille's great team rocking, that Aleksei left his marker for dead and piled towards the box. Nothing came of it but I knew if we'd scored a third my head would explode. I still wish it had. What a way to go.'

The result imbued Smith's side with confidence and, en route to a domestic Treble that season, they remained unbeaten in Group A and went within a goal of making it to the Champions League final. A victory in the return game in Marseille would have ensured a final appearance against AC Milan but they could only forge a 1–1 draw. Ultimately, Marseille topped the group and beat the Italians 1–0 in the final with a Boli goal, although the French club's achievement was later tarnished with allegations of match fixing.

After the exhilarating European campaign of 1992–93 came some fallow and frustrating times for Rangers when Ibrox was often a graveyard against the elite and not so elite of Europe. When former Holland manager Dick Advocaat took over from Smith in 1998 it was hoped that the good times in Europe would return to complement the regular domestic success.

Indeed, the Dutchman helped restore the club's continental credibility. Rangers lost to Parma in the third round of the UEFA Cup in 1998–99 and watched the big-spending Italian outfit go all the way to win the competition. However, the Light Blues would get their revenge the following year when they met in the third qualifying round of the Champions League. Parma are not by tradition one of the big clubs in Italy but during that period they were one of the most cash-rich clubs in Europe and boasted Gianluigi Buffon, generally recognised as one of the finest goalkeepers in the world, Italian international Fabio Cannavaro and his French defensive partner Lilian Thuram. However, Advocaat had returned a confidence to the Ibrox club, which manifested itself in a pulsating first-leg at Ibrox where goals from Tony Vidmar and Claudio Reyna stunned the visitors, who could only claw one goal back in the return game.

Iain Duff, author of several books on Rangers, recalled the night when the Little General perhaps won his famous battle in light blue: 'In 30 years of attending European games at Ibrox, I have never known such a tremendous atmosphere,' insisted Duff. 'Before the game, Advocaat had urged the fans to act as a 12th man and they responded in style, generating so much noise the players could barely hear each other speak as they took to the pitch. From the moment the players walked out to the strains of Tina Turner's "Simply the Best" the supporters lived every minute of the action. The atmosphere inside Ibrox was matched by the players' performance – probably the best I have ever seen from a Rangers team in Europe. Advocaat's team were at the peak of their powers and that night they destroyed the best Italy had to offer.'

Parma were unable to cope with the high-tempo, skilful football that Rangers produced that night and in the end were lucky to escape Ibrox with just a 2–0 defeat. The first goal came from the most unlikely of sources but when Australian left back Tony Vidmar's deflected shot hit the back of the net, the roar shook Ibrox to its foundations. There was a similar reaction in the second half when Claudio Reyna added a second goal. It says much for the performance that night that there was some disappointment that Rangers hadn't won even more convincingly. After a 1–0 defeat in Italy, Rangers progressed to the Champions League proper and performed well against Bayern Munich, Valencia and PSV Eindhoven. They didn't quite manage to reach the heights of the Parma game, although the 4–1 demolition of PSV at Ibrox on another fervent and memorable night came close, and narrowly failed to go through to the next round. However, after countless disappointments in Europe, that victory over the Italians was one that would live long in the memory.

Rangers failed to build on the early European optimism generated by Advocaat and in the intervening years the European landscape has changed dramatically with competitions expanded in order to generate even more money, which has become even more disproportionately distributed. Only a few superpowers can win the Champions League and the European future for the Old Firm looks to be in the second tier of European competition, whatever it may be called. For the rest of Scottish football, Europe now looks to be an irrelevance.

Indeed, McElroy, a veteran of the European scene at Ibrox, detects a growing apathy. 'I think we are getting blasé about European football,' he said. 'There are too many European games these days – it takes 19 games or so to get to a Europa League final. That's too much. When Rangers and Celtic were winning European trophies they played a maximum of nine games. You can play more than that before Christmas these days. One season Motherwell played six games and they still couldn't get out of the Europa League qualifiers.'

However, now and again, a moment or a match at Ibrox can recapture the magic and not only for the home support. When Manchester United were the visitors in the Champions League in 2003, a rare Phil Neville goal after five minutes was enough to give the Red Devils victory. However, the former England defender remembers the occasion for more than his goal. He said in an interview with the *Glasgow Herald* in September 2010: 'I must confess that despite my career having taken me to some unbelievable sporting arenas around the world and having savoured remarkable atmospheres, playing at Ibrox was one of the best experiences of my life. When the Champions League anthem played the hairs on the back of my neck literally stood straight up and I have never, ever heard noise like that crowd made that night.'

19
EUROPEAN FINALS

'I have a collection of medals at Ibrox from the four European finals Rangers have appeared in,' says former Gers defender Sandy Jardine, who now works in the commercial department at the club and whose search for historical artefacts and club memorabilia is on-going. 'Alex Scott's medal from the 1961 European Cup-Winners' Cup final came up for auction and I went along and bought that. I donated my medals from the 1967 and 1972 Cup-Winners' Cup finals and Walter Smith donated his medal from the UEFA Cup final in 2008. I had them framed and put in the Blue Room along with an accompanying story.'

Hibs had been Scotland's first representatives in Europe when they entered the inaugural European Cup in 1955–56. The reached the semi-final where they were beaten by Stade de Reims. Of course, the tournament was won by Real Madrid who dominated its early years. However, for the next three seasons it was Rangers who flew the Lion Rampant in the tournament. In 1959–60 they reached the semi-final where they were beaten 12–4 on aggregate by a good Eintracht Frankfurt side, who themselves lost 7–3 to Real Madrid in the famous Hampden final, the Spanish club picking up the trophy for the fifth successive time.

Initially, the European Cup was contested only by the champions of the respective countries and the first attempt by UEFA to expand its portfolio brought about the Cup-Winners' Cup tournament which was put in place for the start of the 1960–61 season. This tournament was for the winners of domestic cup competitions. Rangers finished third to Hearts and Kilmarnock in the Scottish First Division in 1960 but beat Killie in the Scottish Cup final to qualify for the inaugural competition, which had a difficult birth.

Many countries did not have domestic cup competitions and then, just as now, among those that did it was often not taken too seriously by the bigger clubs. Consequently, only ten teams took part in the first competition with the Spanish and French Cup winners as notable absentees. But Rangers was a club keen to expand its horizons and was delighted to get a place in the inaugural tournament. Scot Symon's side defeated Ferencvaros of Hungary 5–4 on aggregate in the preliminary round to reach the last eight, where they thrashed German side Borussia Mönchengladbach 11–0 over two legs. In the semi-final Rangers were paired against then English giants Wolves in an encounter that would be written into Ibrox folklore. Goals by Alex Scott and Ralph Brand in the first leg in Govan gave the Scots a cushion for the return game at Molineux where the fighting spirit of the visitors, backed by a huge travelling support, ensured a 1–1 draw and spawned the terracing song, 'When the Rangers Came to Wolverhampton Town'.

The two-legged final was against Italian side Fiorentina who had beaten Dinamo Zagreb in their semi-final. The first leg was at Ibrox on 17 May 1961. The Rangers team had been strengthened during the season with the addition of a young Jim Baxter, but top scorer Jimmy Millar was out with a back injury and Robert Hume took his place. Rangers lined up as follows: Billy Ritchie, Bobby Shearer, Bill Paterson, Harold Davis, Eric

Caldow, Jim Baxter, Davie Wilson, Ian McMillan, Robert Hume, Ralph Brand, Alex Scott.

Coppa Italia winners Fiorentina, managed by Hungarian Nandor Hidegkuti, travelled to Glasgow in confident mood. The visitors had several Italian internationals in their side, including goalkeeper Enrico Albertosi, who went on to play in the 1966 World Cup in England and the 1970 World Cup final against Brazil in Mexico, and Swedish winger Kurt Hamrin who had played for his country in the 1958 World Cup finals.

The Rangers support had quickly taken to European football and 80,000 fans squeezed into Ibrox to witness an ill-tempered game in which Luigi Milan scored twice for the visitors, the first after only 12 minutes, to make the second leg a formality.

The home side had the chance to equalise six minutes after the opener when Austrian referee Erich Steiner awarded McMillan a dubious penalty but Caldow put the spot-kick wide. 'In those days the keeper was not allowed to move, but he was practically out on the penalty spot by the time Eric hit the ball,' McMillan told the *Scotsman* years later. 'We felt a wee bit aggrieved. And as we pushed forward we were obviously leaving some space at the back, and they took advantage. I think we were a bit unlucky in that we dominated the play for most of the first game and they relied on breakaways.'

In the return leg ten days later at the Stadio Comunale, Milan scored again after 12 minutes to effectively finish the contest. Scott levelled on the night on the hour mark but Hamrin added a second to make the score 4–1 on aggregate.

Edinburgh-born Jardine had joined Rangers as a 15-year-old straight from school when the club was enjoying the novelty of those early European experiences. 'Players like Ritchie, Shearer, Caldow, Baxter and Brand were all still at the club when I arrived,' he said. 'They had done really well to get to the final that season and had been involved in the first Battle of Britain against a very good Wolves side and beating them was a great result. To be honest Fiorentina were the better team in the final and the Swedish player, Hamrin, was excellent. But you have to remember that European football was a trip into the unknown in those early days. There was a novelty about the games.'

First-team football was still a novelty for Jardine when the Light Blues reached the Cup-Winners' Cup final again six years later. As it turned out 1966–67 was not a great year for the Ibrox club, beginning with the infamous shock 1–0 Scottish Cup defeat to lowly Berwick at Shielfield, which led to Jardine getting his chance. 'I came into the team after Berwick Rangers and my first European game was against Real Zaragoza when we won the tie on a toss of the coin, after drawing 2–2 on aggregate,' he said. 'In the previous round Rangers had beaten Borussia Dortmund who had beaten Liverpool in the final of the Cup-Winners' Cup the previous season. In the semi-final we had good 1–0 wins against Slavia Sofia home and away.'

The shockwaves from Berwick, though, were still reverberating by the time Rangers travelled to Nuremberg to play Bayern Munich. Strikers Jim Forrest and George McLean had been blamed for the Scottish Cup defeat and didn't play for the club again. On-form striker Alec Willoughby was overlooked by manager Symon for the final and centre half Roger Hynd was selected as centre forward despite having played less than a handful of games all season. It remains one of the most puzzling decisions in the club's history. In addition, the day before the final, Rangers chairman John Lawrence criticised the Ibrox team, and to add to the pressure on the players, Old Firm rivals Celtic had won the European Cup the previous week, capping the domestic Treble they had already secured.

Rangers faced a Bayern side that included Franz Beckenbauer, Sepp Maier and Gerd Müller, players who would help the German side win the European Cup three times in the following decade while helping West Germany win the European Championships in 1972 and the World Cup in 1974. On top of that, Bayern were effectively playing in their own back yard. 'Nuremberg, where the game was to be played, was just 50 miles up the road from Munich so it was like a home game for them,' said Jardine. 'I remember coming out for the warm-up before the game and there was about 8,000 Rangers fans already inside making a terrific noise and I was thinking, "We are going to have a good support here tonight." By the time we came out for the kick-off there were 70,000 inside and we couldn't hear our supporters because of the noise the Bayern fans were making with their horns.'

Symon's side that night lined up as follows: Norrie Martin, Kai Johansen, David Provan, Sandy Jardine, Ronnie McKinnon, John Greig, Willie Henderson, Dave Smith, Roger Hynd, Alex Smith, Willie Johnston.

Despite being outnumbered on the terraces Rangers were far from intimidated on the park and they were more than a match for Bayern. However, Symon's bizarre decision to play Hynd came back to haunt the Ibrox club. He was a willing workhorse but he missed a sitter from close range when the game was goalless although he did have a 'goal' controversially ruled off for a challenge on Sepp Maier. Hynd was forever to be blamed, unfairly given that he made no claim to be a striker, for Rangers' eventual defeat.

Franz Roth scored the crucial goal in extra time to take the cup the short distance back to Munich. It was Bayern's first European trophy but would not be their last and Roth himself would score again in the 1975 final against Leeds United in Paris and in the 1976 final against St Etienne at Hampden.

Having just broken into the team months earlier, Jardine had a different perspective on the defeat than some of his more experienced teammates. 'Players like John Greig and Willie Johnston were so disappointed,' he recalls. 'I was just happy to be in the final. I was naive, thinking there would be plenty more. I had just turned 18 and I think I was the youngest player to have played in a European final at the time. After the game I wanted to swap shirts with Franz Beckenbauer. At that time Bayern did not have the pedigree that they do now, they were just taking off as a European force. But Beckenbauer was the big name because he had played against England in the 1966 World Cup final at

Wembley. Our dressing room was full of disappointment. I left it and walked into the Bayern dressing room, which was celebrating their first European trophy in what was their first final, and walked over to Beckenbauer and asked to swap shirts and he said yes. I got it framed and it must be worth a few bob these days although there were no distinctive or commemorative badges on the strip. He was complimentary about my performance afterwards, which was encouraging. I watched a DVD of the game recently and we murdered them. We were far the better team but couldn't score and of course Roth got their goal.'

By the time Rangers reached their next European final – again it was in the Cup-Winners' Cup – five years later, Jardine had been changed from an inside forward to a right back by Willie Waddell, who had taken over from David White in 1969. Under Waddell and assistant manager Jock Wallace, a poor domestic season in which Rangers finished trophyless ran in tandem with a successful European campaign in which Rennes, Sporting Lisbon and Torino were overcome before a reunion with old foes Bayern in the semi-final.

Jardine remembers that Rangers survived a battering in the first leg in Munich. He said: 'We got the biggest tanking of our life in the first game in Munich: not only did we not get out of our own half, we didn't get out of our own box. Bayern were a great team by then. But by the second half on their own ground against us, they had shot their bolt. Jock Wallace had us very fit and in the last 20 minutes it was us who were on top and we came away with a 1–1 draw.'

The second leg was played on a unique night for Glasgow and for Scottish football as Rangers fans headed for Ibrox at the same time as Celtic fans made their way to Parkhead for the European Cup semi-final, second leg against Inter Milan. Many Rangers supporters lucky enough to have been at Ibrox that night to witness one of the club's truly great victories (see chapter 18) also made it home to see Celtic lose to the Italian champions on penalties as the Hoops' match had kicked off half an hour later.

The famous Ibrox Trophy Room

Ibrox *c.*1960

Ibrox in the early 1970s

Ibrox *c.*1930s

Seats going into the enclosure, 199.

The new stadium complete

Aerial view of Ibrox stadium

The Marble Hall

Below: The statue to the victims of the three disasters at the stadium

Left: The Club Deck under construction, 1991

THE MANAGERS

Bill Struth in his office at Ibrox

Scott Symon

Graeme Souness

David White

Jock Wallace

Willie Waddell

William Wilton

Dick Advocaat

Alex McLeish

Walter Smith

Paul Le Guen

The City of Manchester Stadium packed with Rangers fans before the 2008 UEFA Cup final between Rangers and Zenit St Petersburg

Left: Rangers fans in full voice in Manchester

The Rangers side that played in the club's fourth European final

Premier League champions 2010–11

Craig Whyte

Nikica Jelavic is grabbed by
Steven Naismith after scoring
the winner against Celtic in the
2011 Co-operative Insurance
Cup final at Hampden

Steven Naismith leads training followed by
Steven Whittaker, Steven Davis, Kyle Lafferty,
Andrew Shinnie and Thomas Kind Bendiksen

Ally McCoist begins life as the Rangers manager. A living legend as a Light Blues striker, he is captured after scoring against Celtic and Hibernian and (middle) he celebrates a Rangers goal in his former role as assistant manager

Memories of that night are clear in Jardine's mind: 'It was a great achievement to beat Bayern 2–0 at Ibrox,' he said. 'I scored in the first minute with a shot that deceived Maier and then a young Derek Parlane got the second.' The German side did not take defeat well. In the second half, with the tie slipping away, and the stadium rocking to 'Barcelona Here We Come', the Germans lost their composure. Colin Jackson recalled a spat between Maier and Beckenbauer at a Rangers corner ending with the latter walking out of the penalty box 'like a big kid in a huff – he didn't want to know'. Colin Stein was also aware of dissent in the Bayern ranks. 'Beckenbauer swore at me in English when I kicked him on the ankle,' he said. 'He was so frustrated. I knew then that we had them.'

Another set of old adversaries, Moscow Dynamo, stood between Rangers and a much-coveted first European trophy. However, there was as little information available about the Russians in 1972 as there had been for the famous match 27 years earlier. 'It was the time of the Cold War and it was difficult to find out anything about Russian football,' said Jardine. 'So Jock Wallace went over there to see them play and came back with pictures of all their players. Before the game he handed them out so we would know who were playing against and he told us how they would play. So we were as prepared as we could be.'

Around 25,000 Rangers fans travelled to Barcelona, many leaving Scotland for the first time. Jim Shirkie remembers: 'I had never been abroad – we used to go to Blackpool for our holidays – and I had never been on an aeroplane before either so there was a mixture of nerves and excitement.'

Greig passed a late fitness test and Jackson failed one so Waddell's side lined up: Peter McCloy, Sandy Jardine, Willie Mathieson, John Greig, Derek Johnstone, David Smith, Tommy McLean, Alfie Conn, Colin Stein, Alex MacDonald, Willie Johnston. Despite the win over Bayern in the semi-final Jardine recalled only a quiet optimism in the Rangers dressing room before the game: 'Even after beating the favourites we didn't think the final was a formality,' he said. However, a formality is exactly what it looked like before the hour mark. The Rangers fans could barely contain themselves – and many didn't – as they watched their heroes race into a two-goal half-time lead with strikes from Stein and Johnston, who looked to have wrapped it up minutes into the second half when he made it 3–0.

Stein recalls the celebrations following his opening goal in the 24th minute. 'I started running and Dave Smith picked me out,' he said. 'I ran through with the centre half close to me and whacked it into the top corner. I turned away to celebrate and there was nothing but Rangers fans on the park.' The classy Smith also set up Johnston for his first goal five minutes before the break with a cross that 'Bud' turned in with his head. 'I came in from the wing and when Dave pulled it on to his left foot I knew where the ball was going,' Johnston said. 'And I knew where I was putting it, just a glance to put it into the corner.' The third goal was a simple punt down the park by McCloy which caught the Russians out, leaving Johnston to run through and score. Johnston said: 'I definitely wasn't offside; I was giving them five yards of a start. I could have taken it in further but decided to hit it early because the keeper wasn't ready.'

It seemed to be all over, but Rangers' season had ended weeks earlier, their fitness had deteriorated and they ran out of steam. The Russians, who had only a handful of fans cheering them on, came back with two goals and Waddell's side were hanging on for the final whistle. Jardine is one of the few players who insist the result was never really in doubt. 'We played really well in that game and even though they came back strongly, I didn't think we were ever going to get beat,' he said. 'It was a fantastic feeling to win it, especially for me, John Greig, Willie Johnston and Dave Smith who had played in 1967.'

Rangers fans were equally euphoric and invaded the park, not for the first time that night, on the final whistle. Instead of clearing the pitch to allow the presentation, the Spanish militia began striking out at anyone in blue and white and a battle ensued. Consequently, Ibrox skipper Greig was presented with the trophy deep in the bowels of the Nou Camp, which left a bitter taste. 'One of the officials handed the trophy to me with hardly a word and then we were back on our way to the dressing room,' he said. 'It was one of the greatest nights of my career but in the end it was a real slap in the face for Rangers.'

The next day over 20,000 fans turned up in the rain at Ibrox to see Rangers return with the trophy which, due to the crowd trouble, they were not allowed to defend the following season. The Ibrox club were banned from Europe for two years, later reduced to one on appeal.

Jardine would continue his career at Ibrox, winning more honours and international caps, before moving to Hearts in 1982 where he eventually co-managed the club along with former Rangers teammate Alex MacDonald. But by the time Rangers reached their first European final 36 years after Barcelona, Jardine was back working behind the scenes at Ibrox, safe in the knowledge that he had played during the halcyon years of Scottish football. 'The 1960s and early 1970s were the golden age of Scottish football,' he said. 'Not only did Rangers and Celtic get to finals but you had Dundee, Kilmarnock getting to semi-finals and Dunfermline getting to quarter-finals. From 1967 until 1972 I got to two finals, one Fairs Cup semi-final and two quarter-finals. For a small country we were punching well above our weight. Only later do you look back and think it's not as easy as all that.'

It certainly wasn't easy for Rangers in Europe after 1972 and there were many disappointments before the UEFA Cup final appearance in 2008. Jardine was involved in the build-up to the showpiece occasion against Russian side Zenit St Petersburg, which was to be played at the City of Manchester Stadium, home of Manchester City.

European football had expanded over the years and while only ten teams had entered the 1960–61 Cup-Winners' Cup tournament, 88 teams were involved in the 2008 UEFA Cup competition. The Champions League, the successor to the European Cup, had become mostly the preserve of the European powerhouses and the final was taking place between Chelsea and Manchester United in Moscow a week later.

Walter Smith, in his second spell as Rangers manager, was to come up against the man who had succeeded him at Ibrox in 1998, Dick Advocaat. The Dutchman had failed to turn Rangers into European heavyweights during his three-and-a-half years in charge, despite spending big, but he was enjoying the same largesse at the nouveau riche Russian club, and had taken them to their first ever European final.

Over the years the appetite of Rangers fans for European fare has increased. There had perhaps been several hundred fans in Florence, around 8,000 in Nuremberg, and approximately 25,000 in Barcelona. All of which were dwarfed by the 200,000 who mobilised for Manchester. In the eyes of Rangers' supporters, wherever they were in the world, the biggest event in the club's recent history was taking place in the City of Manchester Stadium and many were determined to get as close as possible to the event.

'There was a huge contrast between 1967, 1972 and 2008,' said Jardine. 'I was the players' liaison manager at the time of Manchester. I had to help look after them. Commercialism had grown and there were also a huge amount of corporate guests to look after and everyone at the club had to make sure it went successfully.' Jardine was one of several former Rangers players who swelled the capacity crowd of 44,000, of which four-fifths were Bluenoses.

Another major difference in the 2007–08 European campaign was the convoluted nature of the route to the final. It began in August 2007 with victory over Zeta Golubovci from Montenegro in the second qualifying phase of the Champions League. Once qualification was achieved, Rangers were drawn in a group alongside Barcelona, Lyon and Stuttgart. Ibrox fans harboured no great hopes but wins over Stuttgart and Lyon were encouraging as was the home draw with Barcelona. However, Rangers lost their last three matches, which left them third in the group and the consolation of a place in the UEFA Cup.

The lingering disappointment of another Champions League failure took some time to disappear and consequently the initial knockout rounds of Europe's second-ranked competition were low-key. It wasn't pretty to watch for the most part but Rangers forced their way past Greek side Panathinaikos and Werder Bremen of Germany before meeting Sporting Lisbon in the quarter-finals. After a goalless draw at Ibrox, classic breakaway goals from Jean-Claude Darcheville and Steven Whittaker in the second leg had the Govan men facing the hitherto unlikely prospect of a European semi-final against Fiorentina.

The first leg was at Ibrox and in keeping with the cautious approach of previous games, there was an expectation that Rangers would concentrate on keeping a clean sheet and it proved to be the case as a goalless draw was played out. Commentator Peter Drury, like most neutrals, was not enthralled by what he was seeing. 'The football was not sparkling, it was functional,' he said. 'Walter Smith had a game plan with the lone striker and he made it work. The first game against Sporting Lisbon was a classic example of the style of football Rangers were playing. It ended up 0–0 but it was almost minus goals. I thought then that it was over but then you had Whittaker going through like Lionel Messi to score the second goal in Lisbon. It made no sense.

'The semi-final first leg against Fiorentina at Ibrox was almost a carbon copy of the game against Sporting. But from my notes, I see that Barry Ferguson and Kevin Thomson were suspended, and Burke, McCulloch, McGregor, Beasley, Adam and Naismith were injured. You had names like Jordan MacMillan in the squad, names that, with due respect, should not have been near a European semi-final. I also noted that Rangers had a game against Celtic in between the two legs. So you have to put it all into context. In Florence, although Rangers were battered for most of the game, I remember thinking, "this is going to happen". There was a sense of destiny about it. When Cousin was sent off, after picking up his second booking of the night for clashing with Liverani in injury time, I was almost angry. I remember feeling he had been inexplicably stupid and that he had blown it for Rangers, a feeling that stayed with me when Ferguson missed the first penalty in the shoot-out. But Alexander then saved from Liverani and when Christian Vieira missed his penalty, I thought it was back on and then, of course, Novo scored the winner.'

The little Spaniard's winning penalty sparked an immediate stampede for tickets for the final as Rangers fans realised Manchester was probably going to be a once-in-a-lifetime occasion. Andy Kerr, president of the Rangers Supporters' Assembly, said: 'I knew there would be people looking for tickets but the demand surprised me. I came under siege; dozens of people I knew – or barely knew – were on the phone to me. Again and again I heard the words, "I know it's unlikely but . . ."'

While fans made arrangements for the trip to Manchester the players remained embroiled in a fixture backlog. On the night before the final Rangers had already played 63 games, 18 of them in Europe, and there had been a battle with the authorities who had refused to extend the season sufficiently to help the Ibrox club.

Smith admitted that a European final appearance had not been under consideration for long. 'The European competition isn't one that we thought we would get this far in so it's a nice surprise for us and hopefully we will do well,' he said. 'You start to think about the final and realise just how much it means to everyone. It starts to take over everything else and it has done for the last few days. We had a difficult weekend [winning in an SPL game against Dundee United that the SPL would not postpone, despite requests] and had to concentrate on that match but now that we are here we will try to win this trophy.'

Advocaat's achievement in guiding cash-rich Zenit to a European final against Rangers was laden with inescapable irony and he admitted that the game would be a special one because of his Ibrox connections. 'I've said from the beginning that I would love to play Rangers in the final and it's great that it will happen,' he said. 'It is a major achievement for Rangers and for us, and I look forward to seeing David [Murray] and Walter in Manchester. My wife and I had a wonderful time in Scotland. I enjoyed my time working with David and I'm very happy for Walter that he managed to get through to the final.'

Advocaat knew what he was up against. Smith had played with a lone striker throughout the European run and with Cousin suspended it was Darcheville who got the nod, as expected, ahead of top scorer Kris Boyd, who had to settle for a place on the bench alongside semi-final hero Novo. Smith's side lined up as follows: Neil Alexander, Kirk Broadfoot, David Weir, Carlos Cuellar, Sasa Papac, Brahim Hemdani, Steven Whittaker, Barry Ferguson, Kevin Thomson, Steve Davis, Jean-Claude Darcheville.

Aside from the loss of suspended striker Pavel Pogrebnyak, Advocaat's side were at full strength and Malafeev, Aniukov, Krizanac, Shirokov, Sirl, Tymoschuk, Zyryanov, Denisov, Faitzulin, Fatih and Arshavin were given a cheer by the 9,000 or so Zenit fans, most of whom had flown over directly from St Petersburg.

Alexey Morozov was one of the few Russian supporters who flew to London before getting a train north and, although he had anticipated that Zenit fans would be outnumbered, the extent of the disparity surprised him. Rangers fans had invaded Manchester and the surrounding areas and broke all records for the number of people travelling to a sporting event. 'Scotland is much closer to England than Russia and Rangers fans did not need to take a plane to get to Manchester, so I expected to see crowds. However, I was stunned to see the sheer number of Rangers fans in the city centre. Most of them were peaceful and I was even offered a Rangers scarf – however, I politely refused to accept.'

Drury took his place in the commentary gantry alongside regular co-commentator Jim Beglin and relished the occasion: 'I knew how desperate Rangers fans were to get tickets and I was neither a Rangers fan nor a Scotsman. If there was an Olympics for getting tickets then Scottish football fans would win the gold medal. There will be thousands of individual stories about how fans got their tickets and we knew there would be more than the official allocation inside the stadium, some of whom would have got there by hook or by crook. If the final had been in the Maracana stadium, the Rangers fans would have sold it out.'

The noisy and colourful Light Blues fans who, judging by the evidence of the banners on display, had come from all over the world, were not expecting their side to roar into a three-goal lead as they had done in Barcelona. If victory were to come it would come via a sound defensive display which had characterised the run to the final. Consequently, there was little panic as Zenit controlled possession and looked more purposeful and no surprise when the first-half ended goalless, although the Russian side might have had a penalty for a handball by Broadfoot just before half-time.

The second half unfolded along similar lines with Rangers taking no chances, but Zenit midfielder Igor Denisov eventually got the breakthrough in the 72nd minute following a one-two with the wonderfully talented Andrei Arshavin, the highest paid player in Russian football who would eventually move to Arsenal. The Rangers support looked for their side to throw off the shackles in search of an equaliser but it was not in the team's European DNA. Novo, on for Sasa Papac after the loss of the first goal, had a real chance to level near the end but he blazed over the bar. Lee McCulloch replaced Hemdani, and Boyd, who would finish the season with 27 goals, came on for Whittaker with four minutes remaining but it was too little too late. In stoppage time Konstatin Zyryanov sealed the Zenit victory with a close-range tap-in after being teed-up by Fatih Tekke.

The Ibrox club's disappointment was compounded when it emerged that some Rangers supporters had fought running battles with police in the city centre during and after the game. But the Light Blues fans inside the stadium applauded both teams before leaving the Russian supporters to celebrate becoming only the second Russian side to win the competition, after CSKA Moscow in 2004–05.

Like most of the Rangers fans, Walter Smith had no complaints about the result. 'Over the tournament we've worked very hard to get to the final – there was not that much in it overall and we had a few chances ourselves,' he said. 'Zenit looked the more offensive team but obviously I'm disappointed to have lost. We've had a terrific tournament – it doesn't take away the disappointment but in the end I can have no complaints.'

Jardine still believes Rangers should have had more help with their preparations for the final. 'The players played a record amount of games that season, 68, and 19 games in the European run was also a record,' he said. 'I think we had to play nine games in three weeks. Scottish football, be it the SFA or the SPL, did not do the club any favours. Zenit had been given three weeks off by the Russian FA. We were left to get on with it and the final was a game too far for the players. They were an exceptionally good side but we didn't do ourselves justice.'

In the midst of Scotland's seemingly inexorable slide down the European rankings at club level it was an unlikely European final appearance. As the battle to improve the UEFA coefficient becomes harder many believe it could be quite some time – if ever again – that a Scottish side reaches a European final, including Jardine. 'That night in Manchester I looked back to the previous finals Rangers had been in,' he said. 'It highlights your achievements because Rangers get to plenty of finals in Scotland but it is totally different in Europe. You never say never . . . but it's getting harder. The coefficient in Scotland is dropping and money is dictating everything. The clubs with the biggest turnover get to the European finals. It could be very difficult for Rangers and other Scottish clubs in the future.'

20
IBROX

'You can feel the history as you walk around here,' says Mary 'Tiny' Gallacher as brilliant June sunshine streams through the window of the manager's room at Ibrox and spreads itself across the desk which once belonged to the legendary Bill Struth.

Tiny is an intrinsic part of that history.

Nowadays a tour guide at the stadium, her family's involvement with the Govan club and Ibrox dates back to 1929, the same year that Glasgow-born architect and engineer Archibald Leitch's new main stand was opened. The red-bricked building remains the grand centrepiece of a stadium that has been almost totally revamped in the intervening years.

Tiny knows every nook and cranny of the main stand, now named the Bill Struth Main Stand, and she recalls stories told to her by her gran who, among myriad duties at Ibrox, washed and darned the strips as well as weeding the pitch. 'My grand-mother lived just across the road at that time,' Tiny recalls. 'She told me that Rangers used to send the strips out to be washed but had decided to do it at the stadium so she and another lady were asked to do it. They had a kind of small steamie downstairs with tubs, washboards and a mangle. She also did the darning and sewing of the strips, which at that time had to last the whole season. My mother, Lizzie Love, then started working at the club and for 50 years Rangers Football Club was her life. My sister, Irene Love, and I came in after her and we are still here.'

While Tiny's family can lay claim to around 80 years of service at Ibrox, the club, of course, dates back another half century or so and the Light Blues played at several other locations (see chapter 2) before moving to the first Ibrox. The new ground was officially opened on 20 August 1887, with Preston North End invited up from England to take part in a challenge match that attracted a healthy crowd of 18,000. The Light Blues lost 8–1 and the game ended prematurely following a pitch invasion.

But things were moving fast for the Glasgow club on and off the pitch, and during the 1898–99 season Rangers became a limited company, the newly appointed board immediately agreeing that the first Ibrox was too small for the increasing support and the club's ambitions so the decision was taken to move a few yards to a new Ibrox. Britain's foremost football stadium architect Leitch was invited to create a bigger and bolder stadium and his idea was certainly big and bold as he proposed an 80,000-capacity stadium at the cost of £12,000.

The new ground, with its 1,700-capacity pavilion and wooden-built terraces, opened on 30 December 1899 with a 3–1 win over Hearts. It appeared Rangers had found a home fit for purpose, fit for a club looking to become the biggest and best in Scotland. However, just three years later a tragedy occurred during an international match between Scotland and England. When part of the wooden west terracing collapsed under the strain of too many fans, 25 people were killed and over 500 injured. It was football's worst disaster at that time and brought about a criminal investigation, in which Leitch's reputation did not escape unscathed.

Perhaps curiously given the situation, Leitch was tasked with undertaking the considerable and costly work needed to improve safety at the stadium, with the main refurbishment being the replacement of the wood and steel terraces at each end by solid earth embankments. The capacity was set at 25,000 and then in 1910 extended to accommodate over 60,000, a figure that would increase even further over time. Leitch was responsible for designing stands at many other grounds, including Arsenal, Celtic, Manchester United, Everton, Tottenham Hotspur, Chelsea and Aston Villa, but arguably the pinnacle of his career was the 10,500-seater stand at Ibrox, which included a standing enclosure capable of holding more than 15,000 fans. It was officially opened on 1 January 1929 with a 3–0 win over Celtic.

Journalist Iain Duff was moved to write *Temple of Dreams: The Changing Face of Ibrox*, a well-researched book about the stadium published in 2008 to critical acclaim. 'The idea for the book first came to me when Arsenal moved from Highbury to the shiny new Emirates stadium in 2006,' he said. 'Like Rangers, the Gunners are a club with a long and rich history and their old ground reflected this. In an era of dreary and characterless new stadiums, Highbury's closure left Ibrox – and in particular its magnificent main stand – as the last remaining example of a bygone age. Arguably, no other football stadium in Europe, possibly the world, has such a rich history of triumph and tragedy. These days it boasts state-of-the-art modern facilities that rank alongside the best in the world but its wood panelled entrance lobby, famous marble staircase and glittering trophy room evoke memories of a distant era.'

Duff's book charted the history of Ibrox, from the early days, through the creation of Leitch's stunning main stand in 1929 to the present day five-star facilities. 'The statistics relating to the construction of the stand were impressive. Contractors used more than one million red bricks, 536 tonnes of cement, one thousand tonnes of steel, nine-and-a-half miles of timber battens and two acres of flooring and linings. The wooden boards used would have stretched almost 38 miles if laid end-to-end.' Former diplomat Archie McKenzie brought up yards from Ibrox in the 1920s, remembers when the stand was built and recalled in his book *It's Rangers For Me?* how Old Firm tribalisms were being shaped even then. He said: 'We had a family friend who sometimes took me to the new stand which was always a great pleasure. Old Firm games were always special occasions in the 1920s and 1930s but I don't think segregation was enforced. At Ibrox, the Rangers fans concentrated in the Copland Road end and while the Celtic fans tended to drift towards the other end.' Certainly, by the time the new main stand was open, the Old Firm derby was on its way to becoming one of the most passionate rivalries in world football.

There were 118,730 packed in to the stadium on 2 January 1939 to see Bill Struth's side beat champions Celtic 2–1 on their way to wresting the title back from Parkhead. This remains the record attendance for a league match in Britain and Tiny's granny would have made sure that Struth and his players looked their best for that game. 'My gran was always talking about Bill Struth,' said Tiny. 'He stayed over in Copland Road but partly lived in the manager's office. My gran used to wash and iron all of his shirts. She did Jim Baxter's as well, but that was under different circumstances, namely lipstick. She told me that after Mr Struth's wife passed away, he stayed more often in the office. He used to take tea without milk, which allowed him to get a wee half of whisky with it.

'My mother was also here when Mr Struth was here but Scot Symon was her favourite and she loved Jimmy Millar. Also working at Ibrox with my gran and mother was my uncle, who was head groundsman. During the summer people would come in and wash the place from top to bottom to get it ready for the new season. My mother told me that they would also have to weed the pitch. Everyone would get down on their knees in a line and go along picking out any weeds that were sticking up through the grass. Imagine that happening now? There certainly weren't many staff as such. My mother had keys to Ibrox but there was a man called Bobby Moffat who would open the stadium up. He was a chauffeur at the club. I first came to work here in 1967 as a part-time cleaner. I was about 18 or 19 and already married. There were seven or eight women who cleaned the stand. I only went full time when Mr Waddell became the manager two years later. He was my favourite. He was very straight. He never held a grudge and if you worked a bit harder he would slip you a few pounds extra. I was really upset when he passed away. His wife still comes to the stadium and talks about "my Willie".

'Jock Wallace was a bear of a man and it was he who asked my mother to make the players something light to eat after training and that's how the catering side of things began. The directors used to eat here before games and everything had to be pristine and polished. My mother used to make soup and a roast for about eight or nine of them. But we only had a small kitchen from where we had to provide hospitality for around 400 people, split between the directors' box and members' club. The catering facilities have expanded the length of the stand and that is just one of the many changes that have happened over the years. There used to be a big communal bath in the dressing room but that got removed after Graeme Souness came in. However, even then there weren't that many people working here and the strips didn't get washed every day. Some players would tell you they had to put on dirty tops to go training over at the Albion.' When Souness arrived at Ibrox as player-manager in 1986 the ground had undergone a part-refurbishment but for a long time after the main stand was erected Ibrox had changed little. It had remained a huge bowl-shaped stadium with sweeping terraces, populated by steel crush barriers. Floodlights had been installed in the early 1950s and the roof was extended above the terracing opposite the main stand.

It was in 1959 that then manager Scot Symon had the idea of building the Trophy Room. Pictures from that era show that it was positively sparse in comparison to now but it has always been a source of pride. In his foreword to Rangers – The New

Era by William Allison, published in the 1960s, former chairman John Lawrence praises Symon's initiative in gathering together 'many trophies and gifts collected over the years in this country as well as Germany, France, Italy, Spain, Portugal, Denmark, and elsewhere'. Lawrence, who makes several references to the birth of the club as being in 1873, talks about how 'the glittering silver and crystal of our cups and vases, the glow from the golden football on the silver base, gifted by Real Madrid, to the sheen of the intricately carved caravels presented to us by Portugal's pride, Benfica, can have a magnetic appeal.' He continues to wax lyrical about what would become the jewel in the Ibrox crown, saying: 'None can pass through this room without, if he be a true Ranger, being swept away by a wave of intense pride in the feats of the club.'

Another prized exhibit housed in the Trophy Room is the Loving Cup. The cup was one of 30 made at a pottery in Stoke-on-Trent and was presented to Rangers by the president of the Stoke City club following a match between the teams for the benefit of the widows and orphans of the Brymbo Colliery Disaster Fund. The match took place in October 1937, three months after a fire and associated explosions had killed 31 miners and injured many others in the Staffordshire coalmine.

The cups were originally produced to commemorate the coronation of their Majesties King George VI and Queen Elizabeth in May that year. They were given to all of the then 22 English First Division clubs on the understanding that they would use them every New Year's Day for drinking the king's health. Another was presented to the king himself. The cups have three handles each in the form of a heavily gilded Staffordshire knot. One panel is the Royal Arms. Round the rim and base is an inscription indicating its purpose. Rangers' Loving Cup is almost certainly one of the few remaining, and probably the only one still used in the New Year tradition for which it was intended.

In the 1960s when he was assistant manager, Ibrox legend Willie Thornton tended to the Trophy Room and oversaw its development into a stunning visitors' attraction. Today, Rangers great Sandy Jardine performs this role and ensures that it has pride of place in the stadium tours.

In the days of the vast terracings the supporters were not well served by facilities. A roof was put over part of the Copland Road terrace in 1966 but was woefully inadequate, while the quirky, castellated press box that was perched on top of the main stand, disappeared. Robert McElroy claimed lack of cover was at the forefront of fans' minds in the 1960s and 1970s. 'I started going to see Rangers in the late 1950s, early 1960s when Ibrox was an austere place. I remember my father being upset when they got rid of the press box and replaced it with a steel structure. It was a unique feature of the stadium and he was furious that they had got rid of it without even announcing their intentions. I went to the main stand occasionally but it was almost as if that was a place for a better class of supporter. I do recall there was a lot of debate over the lack of cover in the ground. There was a limited cover put on the Copland Road end, and that was almost an afterthought. Celtic Park had more cover and the whole of the "Rangers end" there was covered. The Centenary Stand was built on the cheap in 1973 and didn't go down well. It was just benches and it helped kill the atmosphere. People wanted to go back to the terracing but within five years the development of the stadium had begun. After it was complete, segregation at the stadium was easier to organise. Before that, especially in the 1960s, there was segregation at Old Firm games but it was voluntary segregation. Games would not be all-ticket, apart from the main stand. In the late 1960s, the enclosure and stand would have mixed company at Old Firm games.'

It would have been a relief to the staff at Ibrox that more games were not made all-ticket. Campbell Ogilvie was general secretary at Rangers when Ibrox was far from the busy place it became. He said: 'There weren't many backroom staff at the club in the 1970s. There was Frank King, myself, Laura the secretary, one telephonist, two ticket staff and the Love family.'

Reverend Stuart McQuarrie, unofficial chaplain to Rangers, recalls a time when Old Firm fans could mix together at Ibrox when Celtic were the visitors. He said: 'In the early 1970s I would go to the game with my Celtic supporting pal Liam. It is incredible to think that if in those days you had a ticket for the Rangers end you could still get into Ibrox – and Celtic Park – at the opposite end. Liam and I would go in and stand around the halfway line talking to each other. There was no physical demarcation but at quarter to three we would go to opposite ends of the ground and meet up later in the city centre.'

Traditionally there had been less of a mix in terms of gender. Football stadiums were traditionally male domains but Elaine Sommerville was one of only a few thousand Rangers fans who had a season ticket in the early 1970s. She remembers her first trip to Ibrox as youngster. She said: 'My dad took my sister Christine and I to the main stand and I couldn't believe the size of the stadium. But I never stood on the terracing. I was only allowed to go to the enclosure because my mum thought it was less rough there. I got my season ticket in 1974, in section M in the main stand, nearer the Celtic end. There was no specific seats in those days, it was first come, first served.'

Sommerville's reference to a less constrained system of crowd control is confirmed by lifelong Rangers fan George Wells who remembers Ibrox in the 1960s. He said: 'My earliest memory was a pre-season friendly defeat against Arsenal in 1967–68, sitting on the wall in the "Derry" [the popular enclosure across from the main stand] and ending up on the pitch when bottles were thrown. I would get lifted over the turnstiles by my father. If I was with my pals we would be outside asking random adults to do the honours. It cost two shillings to transfer from the terracing to the enclosure in front of the stand. On the track in front of the Derry and behind both goals would be little blue invalid cars. The half-time scores would go up on wee boards on the walls behind the goals but you would need to buy a programme to see which letter corresponded to which particular game. Lots of alcohol was being consumed but we would be more concerned with collecting "ginger" bottles at the end of the game to take back to newsagents to get money back on them. I recall great walls of noise and almost continual singing from the Derry, even if it was only a couple of hundred singing, there always seemed to be a song being sung.'

If young fans could not get a lift over then other methods of entry had to be employed. 'You could get a lift over the turnstiles when I first went to see Rangers,' Drew Fails recalled in *Down the Copland Road*. 'When we got too big, me and my mate Saucy Ross would go along the disused railway lines, put up the old sleepers and climb over the wall where the old smelly toilets used to be.'

Iain Duff discovered during his extensive research on Ibrox that the stadium was used for more than just football. 'I was surprised at the number of non-football events to have taken place at Ibrox over the years,' he said. 'In 1917 George V visited Glasgow to honour heroes of the war and Ibrox was chosen as the venue. Shortly before the start of the Second World War there was another royal visit when George VI and Queen Elizabeth performed the opening ceremony of the 1938 Empire Exhibition in front of a crowd of 100,000. Eleven years later, Winston Churchill chose Ibrox for a gathering of Scottish Tories while US evangelist Billy Graham held a rally at the stadium in 1955 attended by 60,000 followers. In more recent times the Boys' Brigade held their centenary celebrations on the Ibrox pitch while countless stars have held concerts at the ground – most notably Frank Sinatra, Elton John and Rod Stewart.'

There was a tragedy in 1961 when two fans lost their lives in a stairway crush following a drawn Old Firm game but lessons had not been learned. On 2 January 1971, 66 fans were killed in a stairway crush after another Old Firm game had ended in a 1–1 draw (see chapter 21). The club was in shock and after Willie Waddell stepped down in 1972 as manager to take an executive role at the club, he set about the task of transforming the stadium completely with safety paramount, although it was a slow process.

In 1973 the Derry was filled with benches and renamed the Centenary Stand (note that the club were still going with the formation date of 1873 at that time) but it was no more than a temporary measure. It was clear that rebuilding rather than refurbishment was required. Waddell took most of his inspiration from the box-shaped Westfalenstadion, home of Borussia Dortmund, which had been opened in 1974 for the World Cup in what was then West Germany.

Planning permission was granted in 1977 and Rangers were ready to start a radical rebuilding programme, which would eventually see three sides of the famous old stadium demolished and three new state-of-the-art stands erected. The Copland Road Stand, (the 'Rangers end') was completed in 1979 and originally accommodated 7,500 spectators (later increased to around 8,000). An identical stand at the opposite end (the Broomloan Road Stand) was completed in 1980. The following year, a bigger stand, where the Derry once stood, and accommodating around 10,500 spectators, was completed and unimaginatively named the Govan Stand.

Campbell Ogilvie remembers that the costly transformation of the stadium did not automatically guarantee big gates. 'We had this new 44,000 capacity stadium but we weren't doing particularly well on the pitch at that time,' he said. 'Our average attendance was around 19,000 and, of course, we were listening to the joke about us building the stands the wrong way round – facing the pitch!'

The arrival of Graeme Souness as player-manager in 1986 rejuvenated the club (see chapter 13). New owner David Murray, who came two years later, facilitated the spending of big money on the team and also expanded the stadium, which was proving to be too small for the crowds which were flocking back. The main stand, awarded a Category-B listed status in 1987, was untouchable but in 1991 another tier (the Club Deck) was added and the last standing areas of the stadium, the East and West Enclosures at the front of stands, where the hardcore, vociferous Rangers fans had made their home, were seated to take the capacity to just under 47,000. The corners between the Copland Road Stand and the Govan Stand and Broomloan Road Stand and Govan Stand, were filled with seats with screens situated above and the capacity nudged up again to just over 51,000.

The stadium is now a hybrid of history and modernity, the ageless manager's office and famous Trophy Room sitting alongside the Waddell, Thornton and McPhail suites in the main stand. The Meiklejohn, Morton, Symon and Woodburn suites are situated in the Govan Stand. The main stand was renamed the Bill Struth Main Stand in September 2006 to commemorate the 50th anniversary of the death of the club's most celebrated manager.

As the stadium evolved over the years, so did Tiny's role and when the club's Murray Park training ground at Auchenhowie was opened in 2001 she stayed behind at Ibrox to act as a tour guide. 'We have tours on Fridays, Saturdays and Sundays during the close season,' she said. 'We have people from Canada, USA, Australia – every corner of the world. All kinds of people come, soldiers, exchange students, groups from Romania, all sorts. We have people who are dying and it is their last wish to see around the stadium and when you look at their faces and they are so happy it makes you cry. The tour takes about an hour and a half. We start in the Media Room, go out and up the stairs past the bust of Mr Struth, into the Blue Room – which has paintings of the former chairmen, captains and managers – then along to the manager's office, directors' box, members' club, Trophy Room and then down the stairs to the first team dressing room before going down the tunnel. Everyone wants to run on to the park at that point but they can't, they aren't allowed.

'There are so many stories to be told,' adds Tiny. 'The manager's room still has a bowler hat on the hat stand. Mr Struth used to have a canary in a cage and you can see the hook from which it hung. But the Trophy Room and the tunnel seem to be the bits of the tour that people like best. I don't have a favourite myself but I think the Trophy Room is gorgeous.

Everything about it says "wow" and that's what you hear from kids when they go in. I got an award from UEFA in 2001 for working behind the scenes. I think it must have been the club who nominated me. The award is in the Trophy Room and I'm very proud of it.' As we make our way down the marble staircase, Tiny reveals a rather startling statistic: 'I've been here 43 years and I've never watched a full game. I've seen the kick-offs but I haven't seen a full game because we are always working.'

21
DAYS OF TRAGEDY

The cover of the official match day programme for the Old Firm fixture of 2 January 2011 carries the image of a crumpled Rangers rosette attached to a traditional club scarf which is tied to a terracing handrail. Below are the words '2 January 1971 – Always Remembered'. The 40th anniversary of the Ibrox Disaster was observed both before the match and the following day at a memorial service held at the stadium and attended by family and friends of many of the victims. Ten years before, a statue was unveiled of club captain on the day John Greig along with plaques bearing the names of the 66 supporters who perished in the 1971 disaster and also those who died in tragedies in 1902 and 1961. The victims in 1971 were crushed to death on the stairway 13 exit at the north-east corner of the stadium following a Rangers–Celtic match which had ended in a 1–1 draw with both goals being scored in the dying moments. Then Chairman Alastair Johnston remarked in the match programme: 'The Ibrox Disaster is something that will never go away and neither should it. We know every one of these people who passed away or were injured were Rangers fans. They were all part of the family if you like and their loss was felt by and affected an awful lot of people'.

The 1971 disaster was the worst involving sports spectators that the British Isles had known until then. In terms of the death toll it surpassed the previous major football match tragedies of Bolton in 1946, and the one at Ibrox back in 1902. The latter case, which occurred during a Scotland–England international, was the result of the collapse of a section of the west terracing. It resembled the 1971 case in respect of the crucial factor of crowd pressure. The experience of spectators at large football matches in Britain changed very little from the beginning of the 20th century to the years nearing its close. Crushing was common and fans often lost control of their movements while watching the game and leaving the ground afterwards.

Following Ibrox in 1971 crowd safety issues began to be addressed more purposefully and new legislation was introduced. Rangers set about the radical reconstruction of Ibrox into a predominantly seated stadium by 1981, and an all-seater by the mid-1990s. However, it was only after the Hillsborough disaster of 1989, which eclipsed 1971 in terms of loss of life, that the character of crowd culture in British football changed in general.

The 1902 disaster claimed the lives of 25 people while the number of injuries was over 500. It came only two years after the new Ibrox stadium had been opened, and as the *Rangers Historian* makes clear, the staging of the international match was viewed as official recognition of the ground as a 'Coliseum of Football'. Although built close to the previous Ibrox ground, the new stadium bore little resemblance to its predecessor in terms of scale and design. It was a symbol of Rangers' growth and of the club's success in putting behind it the struggles of its early decades. The attendance on the day of the match was over 68,000; a huge turnout in the context of the time yet not by any means the estimated capacity of the ground. It appears, however, that many tried to gain access to the high vantage point afforded by the west terracing and overcrowding ensued. The pressure on the wooden construction proved too much and gave way to send hundreds hurtling some 40 feet to the ground below. One witness said that the terracing had collapsed 'like a trap-door'. Following an 18-minute delay the game, astonishingly, was permitted to resume. Parallels may be drawn in this respect with the Heysel tragedy of 1985.

The occupational profile of the dead and the injured reflected the game's popularity among the manual working class and the particular presence of the local shipbuilding and engineering industries. This was to be a constant feature of Ibrox crowds throughout the century. All the dead were male and the great majority under the age of 40. A criminal trial brought against the contractor in effect served as a fatal accident inquiry. The contractor was acquitted and the architect, Archibald Leitch, managed to restore his damaged reputation in the years ahead, most notably, of course, through the construction of Rangers' famous red-brick grandstand in 1928. Wooden terracing constructions were henceforth scrapped, and terraces at football grounds built on solid earth foundations. The capacity of Ibrox was reduced to 25,000 while rebuilding took place and by 1910 the ground was once again holding crowds of 60,000 plus. However, a shadow was cast over the club for at least a decade and playing concerns were sacrificed to dealing with the consequences of the disaster for the victims' dependants, and for the club in general. To help raise the money necessary for the rebuilding work, Rangers made 22 players available for transfer at the end of the season.

The capacity of Ibrox gradually increased during the post First World War era and on 2 January 1939 a club record crowd of 118,730 saw Rangers beat Celtic 2–1. The official figure is probably an underestimate, and over 30,000 were reported to have been locked out. The *Glasgow Herald* describes hundreds of fans sitting 'disconsolately on the reverse slopes of the terracing unable to penetrate within watching distance of the game and unable to leave the park'. This indeed was the scene at the east terracing, 'the home of Rangers' partisans, their blue favours reflecting the strong winter sunlight with good effect'. The paper also commented that the charity collection at half-time was out of proportion to the crowd on account of tightly packed thousands being unable to find 'sufficient room to extract money from their pockets'. Despite the discomfort the crowd was reported to be in good humour and sang 'A Guid New Year' with gusto.

It was indeed remarkable that only cases of fainting were reported in addition to the tragic case of one fan, Joseph Somerville, who had fallen trying to jump a crash barrier amidst crushing. This fan was later to die of his injuries in hospital, and his fate has generally not received the same attention as the victims of the other accidents. In fact, the massive attendance was if anything looked upon with pride by the authorities at the time and even greater attendances were predicted. Rangers manager Bill Struth stated afterwards that Ibrox actually had space for 20,000 more and that it was simply a case of packing the people in the right way. He suggested, to this end, that big matches should be all-ticket.

Ibrox attendances never again topped the 'Ne'erday' fixture of 1939, although there were instances of crowds in excess of 100,000 in the immediate post Second World War years. The famous encounter with Moscow Dynamo in 1945, which captured the imagination of the whole country, attracted at least 90,000, while certain matches against Celtic and Hibernian resulted in lock-outs after the six-figure crowd mark was passed. Even in the 1960s Ibrox boasted crowds of over 90,000, and the norm for Old Firm games at the stadium was 80,000. The official attendance on 2 January 1971 was in fact 80,057. Spectator safety was simply not given the consideration it should have been by the football authorities in general or any of the clubs. Moreover, historians have shown that at government level, the Scottish Office lacked knowledge of football, and held preconceived notions about football fans. Civil servants were in general much more concerned about issues around crowd behaviour than safety. This got in the way of a proper assessment of the risks that were being run and of due consideration of the question of whether football grounds should be licensed.

In 1961 it should not have been such a surprise that there was crushing on the exit stairway at the north-east corner of Ibrox following an Old Firm clash which led to the death of two fans. In March of that year a higher than anticipated crowd showed up for a midweek cup tie against Motherwell. Over-crowding and crushing at the top of the east terracing led to scenes of panic: as the *Evening Times* report described it: 'the top rim of the terracing was a seething, pushing battleground. Women and boys were shouting hysterically for breathing space.' A police report on the scenes later advocated that fixtures likely to prove a big draw should be limited to 80,000, and this indeed was done for the Rangers v Wolves European Cup-Winners' Cup tie which followed shortly afterwards.

For a long time clubs, fans and police had been aware of the amount of crowd pressure which could build up at the back of the terracing and on a steep stairway such as the one which was later to become known as 'Stairway 13' after the passageway number that it backed on to. Moreover, all those familiar with Ibrox knew that this exit was the most popular given its proximity to the Copland Road underground station and the area where most supporters' coaches were parked.

In 1961 only a wooden handrail down the middle divided the stairway. The brother of one of the two victims, George Nelson, testified to the Fatal Accident Inquiry that he had been coming down the packed staircase two or three minutes following the final whistle when his brother 'stumbled' and people began falling in front of him. The brother of the other victim, Thomas Thomson, referred to 'a bit of a bottleneck' at the top of the stairway, which led to them being separated. When he was halfway down he heard people shouting to fans to turn back. A friend of Thomson told the inquiry that he had fallen but had managed to get up again but that he had 'absolutely no control' going down the stairs. An ambulanceman remembered calling for help some ten minutes after the end of the match by which time the police were holding the crowd back at the top of the stairs. There were some 70 people injured, and this witness was of the view that there would have been more had it not been for the police keeping control. An engineer who inspected the stairway an hour after the accident noted that part of the wooden handrail had been knocked down, and the fencing on the south side of the stairway, which gave out to the grass verge, had been partly knocked down. The engineer ventured the opinion that the stair, although in 'reasonably good state of repair', should be 'a different construction entirely'. A police inspector testified that it was 'not normally' part of their duty to control the manner of exit of the crowds, and that the breaking of the fences eased the pressure. Finally, and perhaps most significantly, a police sergeant agreed in his evidence that 'a possible change in the future would be to have police stationed at the top of the terracing to control the exit of people.' The two victims, like those of the 1971 disaster, died of traumatic asphyxiation.

There are indeed many points in common between 1961 and 1971. Both matches featured late equalising goals for Rangers against their oldest rivals, and fans on both occasions exited the ground in a state of delirium. On both occasions the accident happened some minutes after the game had ended. On both occasions it was the crush on the stairway that resulted in people stumbling and falling and causing a forward surge of bodies. And at both inquests the pressure of the crowd at the top of the stairs was identified as a crucial factor with the pleas and shouts of fans on the stairs to those above to turn back falling on deaf ears.

However, in 1961 many fans had been able to escape the crush by scrambling through the breaks in the side fence to the safety of the grass verge. This fence was put back in place and, in all likelihood, was strengthened after another accident, in which around 30 people were injured, after the Old Firm fixture of 2 January 1969. Again, it appears on this occasion that fans were able to escape crushing by breaking through to the grass verge. In September 1967 there was yet another incident after another Old Firm encounter, which resulted in some minor injuries and a twisting of the steel handrails installed by Rangers as part of their scheme of improvements following the 1961 tragedy. The club had concreted the stairs as well as dividing the exit into seven passageways by means of the rails, and Rangers were indeed praised for undertaking such a programme of action.

At the 1971 inquiry former team manager Scot Symon recalled the perception on the part of all interested parties that the improvements had served the purpose of making the stair safe. It is indeed interesting to note that Symon was responsible at the time for the maintenance of the stadium as well as team matters. As for the reputation of Ibrox, it is worth quoting the words at the 1971 inquiry of the then Secretary of the Scottish FA, Willie Allan: 'In my opinion Ibrox Stadium is one of the best-maintained football grounds in Scotland and the last place I would have thought an incident such as happened on 2 January 1971, would have occurred.'

With hindsight, however, it can be concluded that it was the design of the stairway rather than its condition that should have received most attention. This applies too for the 1969 incident after which there were meetings between Rangers officials, the police and the Glasgow City Council engineers, which failed to produce any consensus of opinion or clear recommendations. The design was that of a 'waterfall staircase' with landings between flights of steps. At the 1971 inquiry several witnesses testified to the dangers of fans increasing their speed when on the landings and in losing their footing. In addition, after the disaster experts agreed that it would probably have helped if the stairs had fanned out from the first landing from the top, or had been reconstructed into a 'zigzag' style with regular turning points.

The other issue, probably the most crucial one, which might have been addressed years earlier, was that of overcrowding at the top of the stairway at the end of the match. This had been identified as the cause of the 1961 accident. The pressure from the top was so intense that it led to crushing on the stairs. This was again what happened in 1971. Witnesses recalled frantic shouts to fans at the top to hold back but that it was futile. Fans were simply swept forward and had no way of checking their forward surge. The problem was that there was no means by which the flow of fans towards the exit could be regulated or broken up.

The inquiry into the 1961 tragedy spotlighted the need for police and stewards to direct fans at the top of the terracing but this never seems to have been properly addressed. It was only after the 1971 disaster that the club engaged an engineering firm, who suggested the building of a wall at the top of the terracing to prevent the convergence of so many fans at the one time on the stairway. This simple expedient was put in place and proved effective during the seasons that remained before the demolition of the terracing and the construction of the new all-seated Ibrox.

During the inquiry in 1971, senior police officers stressed that their interpretation of their role on match days was to curb disorder, and that no effective control could be exercised over departing crowds at exits. The Chief Superintendent of the Govan division of the Glasgow police stated: 'There is always crushing leaving football matches, normal rushing, they seem to enjoy it and can take it. If we see any person in danger or anyone liable to fall, or anyone being injured through this crushing we would have a duty to act. Until we see this danger we don't act.' If this evidence in retrospect seems somewhat cavalier, it needs to be remembered that the fans did expect a 'rough and ready' spectating experience, and in many cases derived great thrills from the big occasions when the huge crowd would create an electric atmosphere. They were prepared to put up with the discomforts, the restricted views, the flying missiles, and the safety risks because of the sheer exhilaration of attending such a match. Even smaller clubs like Motherwell and St Mirren possessed grounds that could hold big crowds in this era.

Another police witness, Superintendent Angus MacDonald, acknowledged that the police had a responsibility to prevent dangerous crowd pressure developing and to try to arrange for the crowd to be spread as evenly as possible. It was, however, admitted by his superior that there were no policemen detailed to go to the exit stairways at the end of the game. The police's priority, as is clear from the inquiry evidence, was the prevention of hooligan behaviour, and many officers were instead instructed after the match to take up positions outside the stadium in case of fighting between rival sets of fans. When it became clear that an accident had occurred on the stairway some officers who remained inside the ground were directed to the top of the terracing to prevent overcrowding at the head of the stairs. By this time, however, it was too late. As was pointed out by the advocate for the relatives of the deceased at the Fatal Accident Inquiry, the police were admitting responsibility where there was danger to life on the one hand, and on the other saying that they were powerless to control departing crowds. Some have suggested that police could at least have been positioned at the top of the terracing to attempt to spread the departing spectators as evenly as they could down the different lanes of the stairway. The inquiry found that the crowd pressure was far greater in the first three lanes of the stairway looking up, while the ones furthest away from this point were relatively free of crowd pressure.

What became apparent at the inquiry was the profound lack of clarity pertaining to the responsibilities held by the police and the club regarding safety, and the ambiguities surrounding the issue of crowd disorder and where it could be said to have overlapped with that of crowd safety. As with the later Hillsborough disaster, there was much confusion of the issues of crowd behaviour and safety. The inquiry into the tragedy in 1961, moreover, had concluded that crowd pressure at the top of the stairs had been the crucial factor in the accident, and a police sergeant who gave evidence then agreed that police in future should be stationed at the top of the terracing to control the exit of people. The events of 1971 demonstrated that the lessons of the 1961 tragedy had not been absorbed, even after the further warnings of 1967 and 1969.

It should be observed that the police did call a meeting after the 1969 accident when concerns over safety were raised. Indeed this meeting was the focus of much attention at the inquiry in 1971 and at a subsequent court case taken against Rangers by the family of one of the victims. While the police evidence concerning the meeting was presented in a clear and informative fashion, the Rangers officials who were questioned about it were vague in their recollections, and failed to demonstrate that the club took the safety issue seriously enough in the aftermath of the third serious incident on the same stairway. It was this failure, combined with the evidence of the board minutes, which led the Sheriff presiding over the later court case to lambast the club for the manner in which it conducted its business and kept records. The club's dignity and good name was only salvaged by the organising ability and strength of character shown by the team manager of the time, the legendary Willie Waddell. Moreover, it would be Waddell's vision of a new Ibrox that would be pursued and eventually realised.

The 1969 meting about the staircase involved the police, a Rangers director (probably David Hope), and the Glasgow Corporation Master of Works and his deputy. Ideas were floated about the redesign of the stairway, the replacement of the side fence with handrails was discussed, and the vital issue of crowd pressure at the top of the terracing was addressed in relation to schemes for a tunnel to provide an alternative exit, and the division of the terracing to enforce a more even use of all exits. However, the impression that emerges out of the inquiry is of insufficient agreement being reached as to any one idea, sharp discrepancies between testimonies as to what was suggested, and no significant pressure being exerted on Rangers by the police or the Master of Works to adopt a specific scheme to improve safety. There was no follow-up meeting after the 1969 accident before the disaster two years later.

Both the police and the club, as expressed by respective representatives at the inquiry and the court case, were keen to describe the factor of crowd behaviour as something which could not always be predicted. It was said that any measures taken in relation to it could not be assured of success. The consumption of copious amounts of alcohol at the 2 January 1971 match was reflected in the profusion of cans and bottles on the terracing afterwards, yet this was not in itself unusual, and certainly not if the factor of a Scottish New Year was borne in mind. Moreover, the relative absence of alcohol among the victims was clearly recorded at the inquest. Some fans may well have been drunk and this may have influenced their behaviour when departing, but it is doubtful that it was more than a peripheral cause.

Perhaps more pertinent was the intoxicating drama of the closing moments of the match and the mood of jubilation it produced among the Rangers fans. It might also be recalled that news of Aberdeen's late winner in their match that day (scored by former Ranger Jim Forrest) provided further cause for celebration. At the time the Dons were Celtic's closest challengers for the league title. The Rangers chairman, John Lawrence, was convinced that the fans' euphoric state had much to do with what happened. A police superintendent described the scenes on the terracing as follows: 'The excitement was tremendous, jubilation, they were singing, shouting, they were jumping up and down, waving their arms, hugging their friends, the terracing was in an uproar. I would say it was football mania at its highest.' Certainly it is important to be aware of the feverish emotions generated by an Old Firm match with all its traditional overtones of tribalism and religiosity. The scale of the police operation on 2 January 1971 was well in excess of the suggested measures for the management of such a crowd contained in the report of the Lang Inquiry into football crowd behaviour published in 1969. Ironically, the crowd on the day was exceptionally well behaved with police making only three arrests for drunken conduct. Before the incident-packed climax to the match it was being considered as one of the quietest Old Firm contests in the history of the fixture. Such, though, was the ecstatic mood of the fans exiting 'the Rangers End' in the wake of Colin Stein's dramatic equalising goal that the testimonies of eyewitnesses concerning the significance of this factor in the disaster's occurrence have to be given weight. Exiting the stadium was a hazardous business even if the mood of the crowd was sober.

Yet it must be reiterated that there had been precedents. The circumstances of the 1961 fatal accident bore an uncanny resemblance to that of 1971. On the former occasion the departing Rangers fans were in a similarly rapturous mood after a late goal. In 1967 and 1969 the fans were in celebratory spirits following victory over their greatest rivals. Once more it is difficult not to draw the conclusion that the potential problems posed by a large exiting crowd should have been addressed more seriously, especially if happenings on the field had created a mood conducive to recklessness. Again it is pertinent to ask why the problem of crowd pressure at the top of the stairway, identified in the inquiry of 1961, was not thoroughly investigated.

If complacency was evident, it was symptomatic of a wider culture of neglect, and of a tendency on the part of the civil authorities to pass the buck, in effect, to the Scottish FA and then to the clubs themselves. No legislation was passed to enforce clubs to take safety measures, and this in turn reflected the absence of a consensus of opinion in Britain generally regarding standards of ground safety.

The findings of the Fatal Accident Inquiry into the Ibrox Disaster of 1971 spared Rangers, and other parties, from blame. However, in 1974 the club was condemned as negligent by the Sheriff presiding over the test case brought by the wife of a victim of the 1971 tragedy, and she was awarded over £26,000 in damages. By this time it was crucial for the salvaging of the club's reputation and public image that the plans to modernise Ibrox be carried through to completion.

The Disaster Inquiry should have laid to rest the theory which took root following the tragedy that fans rushing back when they heard the roar for Stein's last gasp equalising goal collided with other fans leaving after the final whistle. No evidence to support this emerged at the inquiry; indeed, there was the contrary testimony of many witnesses that the events occurred some five minutes or more after the end of the match. Witnesses testified to seeing fans falling forward: 'it was as if a hole had appeared in the ground' said one; there was no question of waves of fans making their way back up the stairs. Nevertheless, the theory tended to be recycled in accounts of the day for years afterwards much to the annoyance of those who had been there and knew it to be a complete fabrication. It is only as a product of recent campaigns on the part of the fans to have the causes of the disaster properly understood and its victims properly remembered that this 'explanation' of the tragedy has lost its credence.

The victims of the disaster were overwhelmingly adult male manual workers. Their occupations reflected Glasgow and west-central Scotland's heavy industrial character, and indicated the extent to which football remained the workingman's pastime in the 1970s. There were welders, platers, panel-beaters, machine operators, sheet metal workers, plumbers, electricians, boilermakers, fitters and steelworkers; in addition there were several young apprentices of various trades. Of the many witnesses who gave evidence at the Fatal Accident Inquiry, most of whom attended the match and were close to the tragic events, the social profile was identical: overwhelmingly male manual workers, predominantly skilled or semi-skilled. This indeed was the occupational profile associated with Rangers' bedrock support since its emergence as a major force in Scottish football in the late 19th century. Moreover, 1971 may well have been the peak of this social group's concentration among the Rangers support. Research into the club's base of support in the 1980s showed that the predominance of the manual class in general, and the skilled section of it in particular, had shrunk significantly. This research also found that as the club modernized and improved its facilities, and society was reshaped around new technology and the service industry, Rangers drew fans from a wider geographical radius, attracted substantially more white-collar workers and probably more females.

There was one female victim of the 1971 disaster: Margaret Ferguson from Stirlingshire, an 18-year-old machinist. Just weeks before, Margaret had actually visited Rangers centre forward Colin Stein's home bearing a gift for the striker's newborn daughter. Her passion for Rangers was simply all consuming. The youngest victim, nine-year-old Nigel Pickup, had travelled up to the game – his first – from Liverpool after having journeyed from Canada where his parents had taken up residence. Recently Rangers fans have raised funds to place a black granite stone of remembrance at Nigel's grave in Liverpool.

Perhaps the most heart-rending aspect of the tragedy, to those uninvolved, was the deaths of five teenage schoolfriends from the village of Markinch in Fife: Peter Easton aged 13, Ronald Paton, Mason Philip and Bryan Todd, all 14, and Douglas Morrison aged 15. The mother of one of the boys, Peter Easton, contributed movingly to a BBC programme to commemorate the 30th anniversary of the disaster. More recently, fans have contributed to the restoration of a memorial stone for the boys. Jim Archer, who stays in Fife and made the original plea for funds, says that the response from fans worldwide raised the remarkable sum of over £5,000. 'Everything was done with the blessing of the boys' families, that was important, and we kept them informed of our progress. We bought a new stone to put alongside the original one, and also donated shields and trophies to be used as prizes at Auchmuty High School, which the boys had attended.' A memorial bench was also purchased for the churchyard at Markinch Parish Church.

The Ibrox Disaster's impact was felt globally, a point made by the Rangers physiotherapist of the time, Tom Craig, in the television documentary. It reverberated throughout the Scottish diaspora, perhaps especially in Canada and Australia where Rangers and Celtic supporters' clubs formed a link with home. The Scottish actor John Cairney, a Celtic supporter, has provided a moving recollection in his autobiography of the profound impact of the disaster on exiled Scots and on his fellow Scottish entertainers who were touring Canada at the time, including the legendary singer and avid Rangers fan Andy Stewart. In addition, the tragedy profoundly affected the thousands of Rangers supporters in nearby Northern Ireland, the province at this juncture in the midst of its own agonies of political violence and sectarian strife.

A song in honour of the victims was penned shortly after the disaster by the Scottish folk-singer Matt McGinn who was from an Irish Catholic background. It proclaimed 'the Old Firm united' and 'no Billy, no Dan' and its first verse ran as follows: 'New Year bells had been ringing/All Scotland was singing/The old year had died and the new had been born/As the news of disaster from Ibrox came spreading/The news that would cause a whole nation to mourn.'

In the immediate aftermath of the tragedy there were indeed signs of a softening of the Old Firm rivalry. The joint efforts of the two clubs encouraged supporters to make conciliatory gestures. Players and officials of both clubs attended memorial church services for the victims at St Andrew's Roman Catholic Cathedral and at Glasgow Cathedral. Both clubs gave generously to the Lord Provost of Glasgow's Disaster Fund, and later in January took part as a Rangers and Celtic 'select' team (which also included George Best and Bobby Charlton as guests) against a Scottish international XI in a special match in aid of the fund held at Hampden Park. Willie Waddell's swift organisational response ensured that Rangers were represented at every funeral where their presence was welcomed. Celtic officials and former players were also present at the memorial service marking the 40th anniversary.

The next Rangers home game following the disaster in 1971 took place as scheduled two weeks later. Stairway 13 was closed and the atmosphere among the smaller than usual crowd of 26,000 was sombre. It would be some weeks before the traditional vibrancy of the terracing returned and for some people things would simply never be the same again. There are many testimonies of fans who decided to give up attending matches. It was as if such fans took the view that they had literally been flirting with death on a weekly basis and that the time had come to take no more such risks.

As the years passed it seemed that the Ibrox Disaster was destined to be quietly forgotten, at least in terms of public recognition and visible reminders. At the time of the tragedy, as a Rangers fan later observed, 'the public reaction was of quiet shock, nothing like the more recent disasters at Bradford, Heysel and Hillsborough.' The coming together of both Old Firm clubs in mourning gave way before long to old antagonisms, evident for instance at the Scottish Cup final between the clubs in May 1971. Indeed, the disaster came to be invoked more often in an offensive fashion by some who were antagonistic to Rangers, including some Celtic fans but particularly, from the 1980s, by followers of Aberdeen. The latter twist was ironic in the light of the Rangers fans' lusty choruses on the day of 'The Northern Lights of Old Aberdeen' in reference to the tussle between Aberdeen and Celtic at the top of the league table. The disaster, like that of the Manchester United Munich air crash of 1958 and other tragedies, itself fell victim to squalid supporters' rivalries.

However, commemoration of a well-meaning and respectful kind came to the fore as the culture of mourning underwent radical change in Britain in the 1980s and 1990s. Pivotal here was the reaction to the Hillsborough disaster of 1989 and the visual demonstration of tokens and symbols of supporters' grief. One commentator on the Hillsborough phenomenon observed that the overnight decoration of the Leppings Lane entrance at Hillsborough with football memorabilia was 'a popular rite largely without parallel' in 20th century Britain. This new attitude to public mourning was to reach its apogee in 1997 with the tragic death of Princess Diana. For football fans, Hillsborough seemed to provide the example to follow in mourning the subsequent deaths of victims of other tragic occurrences or of players and managers who had attracted adulation at specific clubs. Thus, in the case of Rangers, there were huge displays of supporters' tokens of respect and affection following the deaths of former winger Davie Cooper and former manager Jock Wallace in the 1990s. This kind of ritual had never before been observed following the deaths of ex-players and managers who had attained similar legendary status.

This changing pattern of behaviour came to focus on the Ibrox Disaster. By the time of the 20th anniversary many Rangers supporters were beginning to put pressure on the club to honour the memory of the victims. The line taken by the club for many years – that the new Ibrox stadium was in itself a memorial to those who lost their lives – was regarded increasingly by fans as inadequate. On 2 January 1991, when Rangers again faced Celtic at Ibrox, the fans paid their own tributes by laying scarves and other mementoes at the disaster site. A commemorative plaque, organised by the management of the club in response to popular demand, was also unveiled in the fateful corner of the stadium.

The continuing pressure exerted by supporters for a more prominent and visible memorial finally resulted in the com- mission of a statue that was unveiled at a special commemorative service at Ibrox to mark the 30th anniversary in 2001. The statue was of the club captain of the period, John Greig who still recalls 2 January 1971 as the worst day of his life. Opinions differ as to whether a statue of a player, however much of a club legend, was the most appropriate tribute. However, there was consensus around the decision to make the memorial in honour not only of the victims of the 1971 disaster, but also of those of 1902 and 1961. 'The players, managers and directors come and go,' wrote the editor of the Rangers supporters' fanzine *Follow Follow* at the time of the statue's unveiling, 'but the faceless and nameless crowd is the raw material out of which the club is made. Sadly those who died in the disasters did not remain faceless and nameless. Remember them all and the reasons why they died.'

Such sentiments also informed the events marking the 40th anniversary. At the memorial service Rangers Chief Executive Martin Bain said in his address: 'It is a matter of eternal sorrow that lives have been lost at Ibrox on more than one occasion. Forty years on, the Ibrox disaster remains a tragedy beyond belief. It is unthinkable anyone should set off for a football match and not return. That 66 were not to return was and still is an unimaginable horror. Our thoughts and hearts are with those who lost their lives that day and our message to them is a simple one: we will always remember.'

22
THE FANS

Rangers are by far the best-supported club in the history of Scottish football. The club appears to have attracted a sizeable following from its very earliest days. Even through the trying times of the first two decades, with only a shared league title to boast of, crowds continued to come whether to Glasgow Green, Burnbank, Kinning Park or the first Ibrox Park. Indeed, the construction of the present Ibrox was largely due to the need to accommodate the growing legions of fans.

From the beginning of the 20th century when attendance records became more formalised, Rangers' average crowd has been at the top in all but a small minority of seasons, as David Ross's book *The Roar of the Crowd* documents. Moreover, most other clubs' attendance records have been set when Rangers have been the visitors. Even when the team was suffering lean times on the pitch the attendance figures, more often than not, were the highest in the land. Thus the term 'loyal' is not one without meaning.

A famous Rangers song, recorded in the 1960s by the

comedian and fervent Bluenose Lex McLean, begins with the line, 'Every other Saturday's my half day off, and it's off to the match I go.' It could be said with some certainty that the advent of an institutionalised leisure time – Saturday afternoon – at the height of the industrial age in late 19th-century Britain was the key factor in the rise of football as a spectator attraction. Rising incomes also played a part, but the sense of liberation felt by the average factory worker at the Saturday lunchtime siren was the oxygen of the game's popularity. Workers got into the habit of spending Saturday afternoons at the match, and employers and clergymen and others more privileged began to appreciate the value of football, and organised sport in general, to a more contented workforce and healthier society. The growth of the game was notable for such attempts at 'social control', yet it was also powered very much by the working class itself. Football became an economic success story but it was no ordinary business. Very quickly it came to be about sentiment, local allegiances, community spirit and tribal honour.

In 1899 when Rangers became a limited company, membership and shareholding records indicate that the strongest support for the club came from the skilled manual occupational group. Tellingly, in a landmark book which took the pulse of the city at this time, *Glasgow in 1901*, the typical skilled craftsman is portrayed as a member of a Rangers supporters' brake club (named after the horse-drawn brakes, or buses, that carried them to the matches) who discharges all the pent-up frustrations of the working week at the match on Saturday. In this respect it is important to note that Rangers' location in the Govan district, close to the shipyards and heavy engineering factories of the River Clyde, was an integral part of the club's identity. It was natural that Rangers should draw a lot of their support from the working class of the area and, indeed, from other such districts across the river like Partick. In the *Supporters' Association Annual* for 1954 there is a magnificent photograph of the Ibrox pitch taken from the main stand with a forest of shipyard cranes in the background. The accompanying commentary noted these cranes, the shipyards, 'the dear Clyde', and 'the works of all descriptions'. It remarked that 'the majority of players and supporters are men of industry'; 'we are reminded here that without industry all would fade, spires and stadium, all would become as a dream.'

Rangers and their supporters, therefore, are intimately linked to the industrial growth and might of Glasgow as a city – the second city of Empire in the late 19th and early 20th century era. Even by the 1970s, long after the city's industrial zenith, the profile of the Rangers support was heavily skewed towards the skilled manual worker sector. Scrutiny of the occupations of those killed or injured in the Ibrox Disaster in 1971 (see chapter 21) reveals welders, platers, panel-beaters, engineers, boilermakers and so on. This demonstrates that the core support base of the club, in socio-economic terms, remained remarkably constant during the first century of its existence. It was only in the 1980s, reflecting the broader societal trend in the shrinkage of the skilled working class and the expansion of the white-collar sector, that the supporter profile changed. By the 1990s the modernisation and commercialisation of the club, the improvement in facilities and the alteration in society's work and leisure patterns resulted in a fan base that extended over a wider geographical radius and included more white-collar workers. It was also by now a more female-friendly environment, although there had always been significant numbers of female fans and the increase, if such it was, was not all that marked.

In qualification of this it should be said that Rangers' appeal went well beyond Glasgow from at least the turn of the 20th century, and that the club's support has also included many from the poorer semi- and unskilled working class as well as some well-heeled business figures. Membership and shareholder records offer an insight into the nature of the typical fan who wished to demonstrate his or her allegiance or had the means to do so. However, they do not account for the many who simply turned up to watch on a Saturday and had nothing to do with the club's affairs otherwise. A survey of Rangers fans conducted in 1983 revealed significant levels of unemployed, probably reflecting the closure at the time of many industrial concerns. Even by 1990, when the survey was repeated and wider economic conditions had somewhat improved, there were many unemployed fans, particularly among those who habitually stood in the remaining terraced part of the ground, 'the enclosure'.

Early observers noted the passion of the Rangers supporters. In March 1897 the journal *Scottish Sport* commented: 'The Rangers following is now the largest, and perhaps the most enthusiastic, in Scotland. On Saturday they had several thousand with them at Greenock.' The article went on to note: 'The Rangers "special" for Greenock beat all previous records. Never before in the history of football did such a crowd journey from St Mungo.'

This illustrates that the railways were playing an important part in the development of football as a lucrative business with knock-on effects for other industries too. However, it was another method of transport – that of the horse-drawn brakes (or charabancs) – which caught the attention of observers and seemed to symbolise even more colourfully the appeal of the game. While most football clubs had supporters organised into brake clubs, it was Rangers and Celtic (in existence from 1888) supporters who turned them into veritable travelling circuses, complete with banners, flags, bugles, horns, ricketies (rattles) and other paraphernalia. By the 1920s such was the level of disorder associated with the brake clubs that there were police clampdowns and numerous court cases.

This, it might be said, was an early manifestation of what would become known as football hooliganism. In reality, the growth of popular enthusiasm for the sport, combined with the development of club allegiances in a competitive context, always carried with it the potential for trouble, or 'rowdyism' as it was labelled in the early years of the game. Attempts at social control came up against the tendency on the part of fans to get carried away, often on account of being drunk. The problems, of course, recurred in every decade of the 20th century, and continue today. The more popular the club the greater the likelihood of its fans getting into bother. In Scotland, the Old Firm of Rangers and Celtic dominated on the playing pitch in terms of honours, and off the pitch the behaviour of their followers likewise posed the biggest problem for the authorities. Indeed, in 1909 after a Scottish Cup final replay at Hampden had ended in a draw, Rangers and Celtic fans rioted together in the apparent belief that they were being conned into returning for a third game. The fans fought a two-hour battle with the police and set fire to turnstiles. In the 1920s, through his written address to the fans in the club's annual handbook, manager Bill Struth made regular pleas for better behaviour.

With the Old Firm, however, there was the added layer of religious and in some ways political rivalries. In his book *The Roar of the Crowd* David Ross speculates that a developing Protestant identity around Rangers in the early part of the 20th century helped to sustain the high level of the club's support during fallow years on the pitch. It is indeed widely agreed by historians and commentators that Rangers had also come to assume the role for many people as Scotland's Protestant response to Celtic's Irish Catholic challenge. As historian Bill Murray has made clear in his groundbreaking book *The Old Firm*, Celtic were formed by and for the Catholic community of Glasgow which closely identified with its Irish immigrant history and with the Irish Nationalist politics of the period.

Neither club – Rangers or Celtic – had at this time practised religious exclusivism in the matter of players (although Celtic's policy was initially and briefly an all-Catholic one), but there is little doubt that the respective managements and supporters were willing to allow different identities and causes of a religious and political nature to take root and grow alongside the struggle for playing supremacy. Some more cynical commentators have suggested that both clubs recognised that an 'Orange versus Green' rivalry was good 'box office'.

Certainly, the Irish influences in Glasgow and the west of Scotland were reflected in this football rivalry. Celtic set out expressly to mobilise support from the Irish Catholic community and in this they were almost instantly successful, soon eclipsing the other 'Irish' team to the east, Hibernian. Rangers, it seems, began to draw upon the support of Ulster Protestant immigrants: in the 1870s and 1880s much Irish immigration to Scotland was of this kind, attracted by the possibilities of work in the shipyards on the Clyde. Rangers' association with local industry could only have made such developments more likely. Certainly, by 1912 when the controversy over the issue of Irish Home Rule was threatening civil war in Ireland, Rangers were linked to the Unionist anti-Home Rule cause just as Celtic were identified with the Irish Nationalist position.

The Irish troubles were also a key factor in the deepening antipathy between the fans of the two clubs after the First World War. There were several serious incidents involving the Irish Republican Army (IRA) in the west of Scotland, and a policeman lost his life after a shoot-out in Glasgow in 1922. Religious tensions in Scottish society in general increased in the inter-war period with notable controversies over issues like education and mixed marriages. The social historian Andrew Davies has investigated the Old Firm supporters' rivalry in this era and has found substantial evidence of social disorder around the brake clubs (largely motorised by the 1920s) and the railways with rival mobs carrying out ambushes and attacks. The Orange Order – originally a Protestant secret society in Ulster – had been established in Scotland from around 1830, but it was in the post First World War years that it grew most substantially, and became much more than an organisation for Irish Protestants in Scotland. In the inter-war period Rangers players and officials occasionally attended Orange functions, and there seems little doubt that many supporters became members of the institution. Old Firm matches carried a clearer Irish political significance after the First World War, and came to emblemise the 'Billy or a Dan?' street culture of a religiously divided city.

It needs to be added that for many fans of both Rangers and Celtic the fusion of football with religion and politics was – and is – a matter of profound regret. It may have made the rivalry unique, certainly in Britain, and supplied much of the intensity of the fixture; nevertheless, the social costs were high and as time went on Rangers' reputation suffered on account of the club's de facto adoption of a 'Protestants only' signing policy of players. As society's values changed and Rangers came to be linked to something increasingly viewed as unjustifiable, the club tended to adopt either a stonewalling or a defiant stance. This bolstered the views of those fans for whom Rangers were considered to be champions of a Protestant 'cause' or way of life. As the situation evolved, it became the stock in trade of the club's directors to say that the supporters would not accept a change to the practice while simultaneously encouraging, by lack of action, those fans to be fundamentalist in their attitudes. Eventually it required the intervention of the intrepid figure of Graeme Souness (see chapter 13) to sort the matter out.

The religious question and the Irish political overtones were a constant backdrop to the Old Firm, and to the behaviour of supporters. After the Second World War there were numerous disturbances at matches with bottle-throwing a particular problem. The authorities attempted, usually unsuccessfully, to prevent the flaunting of flags and emblems, and in the Old Firm context even the national Union flag was regarded as provocative. Celtic clashed with the Scottish FA in 1952 about the flying of the flag of the Irish Republic at Parkhead, an affair in which Rangers actually lent support to their rivals. Attendances at Rangers v Celtic games in the 1950s and 1960s were often limited to minimise trouble.

However, it was at matches in England and abroad in the late 1960s and early 1970s that Rangers supporters' behaviour captured adverse British and international media attention. Hooliganism at Newcastle in 1969, Manchester in 1974 and

Birmingham in 1976 tarnished the club's name, while the scenes at Barcelona following the triumph in the European Cup-Winners' Cup final in 1972 were also used, if unfairly in this case, to condemn Rangers. The media condemnation, moreover, was invariably accompanied by criticism of the club's apparent practice of signing only Protestant players. In the wake of the fans' excesses at Villa Park in 1976, general manager Willie Waddell publicly dissociated the club from such a policy. In retrospect, this appears to have been a stalling tactic to alleviate the intense pressure the club was then under.

Waddell, in fact, spent much energy both as manager and then general manager in addressing the hooligan problem. He was a member of the McElhone Working Group on the issue in 1976–77, which laid much stress in its report on the role played by alcohol and on the need for better education and improved facilities at grounds. In the latter respect at least Rangers were taking important steps to raise standards for the fans with the gradual reconstruction of Ibrox. The McElhone report also revealed that although this was generally considered to be a particularly bad period of misbehaviour on the part of Rangers fans, Celtic's support had a worse overall record in terms of offences and arrests. The fans of both clubs were also to blame for the riot at Hampden after the 1980 Scottish Cup final, yet the criticism fell more heavily on Rangers – once more largely because of the player policy.

It was also the case that the Troubles in Northern Ireland from the late 1960s entrenched some fans' prejudices more deeply. Certainly, songs, chants and flags and emblems seen at the stadium came to reflect the Ulster situation. Orange songs had long been sung by many Rangers fans but in the 1960s, and especially after the eruption of political violence in Northern Ireland, the repertoire became cruder. From this point on the club has endured many difficulties – culminating in a UEFA case in 2007–08 (at which Rangers were fined just over £13,000 by UEFA for discriminatory chanting by fans in both legs of a Champions League tie against Villarreal) – on account of fans choosing to sing such songs, often at the expense of club songs. Most pertinent in this regard has been the singing of 'The Billy Boys', a song about a Protestant street gang from inter-war Glasgow. Many outside observers have arguably read far too much into the singing of such songs; yet the fans have often not helped themselves or the club they love by insisting that certain blatantly sectarian songs are essential to their 'tradition'.

As Rangers and their support grew into a famous Scottish institution many good club songs emerged. 'Follow Follow' is the best known and dates at least to the 1920s, but there are many others such as 'There's Not a Team Like the Glasgow Rangers', 'Who's That Team They Call the Rangers', 'As I Was Walking Down the Copland Road', 'Every Other Saturday' and 'The Rangers Over Here'. Some draw on popular hymns, others on Scotland's rich folk and music hall traditions. Perhaps no other club has inspired such a profusion of praise in song. This is to say nothing of songs about legendary heroes such as Alan Morton: 'Oh Charlie Shaw [Celtic goalkeeper] he never saw where Alan Morton pit the ba'; Willie Waddell: 'Nature bestowed all her gifts with a smile, the right foot, the left foot, the "noddle", when you can buy all these wonderful things, then you can buy Willie Waddell'; and Woodburn: 'But they'll never stop us singing, Follow Follow is our cry, and the name of Willie Woodburn in our hearts will never die.'

Many, many more purely Rangers songs are staples of supporters' bus journeys, albeit they are never heard reverberating around the stadium. And it is to this remarkable heritage of song and folklore that groups of fans turned to encourage the singing of club anthems and to redress the balance in the fans' repertoire that had led to so much criticism. The fans' group 'The Blue Order' conducted a highly effective campaign, which saw such songs as 'Wolverhampton Town' (celebrating the great victory of 1961) and 'The Blue Sea of Ibrox' become better known and more frequently sung in recent years.

Such developments have revealed a more complex picture than many Rangers critics tend to suggest. Rangers fans have found themselves regularly pilloried in the media as bigots. Yet when there are attempts to survey the opinions of fans on matters such as religion and politics, the results – as evidenced in Ronnie Esplin's book *Down the Copland Road* – are highly diverse and often confound the stereotypes. Indeed, the caricature bigot is hardly visible in such evidence. Many critics appear to pursue an agenda against Rangers fans that makes no allowances for the tribalistic 'wind-up', motivations which would be routinely used to excuse the behaviour of the fans of other clubs. In much of the contemporary reporting of football fans' behaviour in Scotland, it appears that the singing of certain songs is considered of far greater significance than actual thuggery.

Serious 'state of the nation' inquiries into the Old Firm phenomenon or more specifically what Rangers are said to represent, can also overlook the rich vein of humour which goes with this particular territory. The anecdotes of the fans in Stephen Walsh's *Voices of the Old Firm* are salutary reminders that sectarian divisions in Scotland are not on the same scale as those in Northern Ireland. Indeed, Walsh's collection should be required reading for anyone about to pronounce on the supposed political or social significance of football in Scotland.

Rangers fans were no slouches in the developing terracing fan culture of the 1960s onwards when pop songs would be humorously adapted, and irreverent chants popularised. If the Kop at Liverpool displayed superb wit in serenading an opposition goalkeeper who had blundered with the song 'Careless Hands', then the Rangers fans who sang 'Don't Walk Away Rene – we're going to stuff you on Wednesday' to Hearts striker Rene Moller after a drawn cup tie, were equally deserving of what would now be termed 'respect'. In the 1960s and 1970s the fans at Ibrox took the tune of a famous hymn and turned it into a football anthem the rest of Britain copied: 'We'll Support You Evermore'. They tweaked the New Seekers' 'I'd Like to Teach the World to Sing (The sash my father wore)' and riffed on Deep Purple's 'Black Night' with appropriate references to the team. The Derry choir possessed a repertoire more extensive and inventive than any other terrace including the fabled Kop. As the writer John Burrowes put it, the Rangers choir was 'unrivalled for the lustiness and originality of its songs'. 'Like a leaderless zigzag of starlings in high flight,' Burrowes wrote memorably, 'they could switch from song to song, chant to chant, insult to insult, in uncanny orchestrated unison at precise and appropriate moments during a game, as though some unseen conductor had unfolded a giant cue board before them.' It is no exaggeration to say that the fans deserved as much credit as the players for the salvaging of matches that were slipping away, or the snatching of often improbable victories. They specialised in the singing of battle hymns in adversity, and in morale-boosting defiance. For those who grew up following the Gers in the decades before the transformation of Ibrox into an all-seated arena, the memories of packed terracings, thunderous roars and stirring singing are indelible. The sea of blue that a packed Ibrox often presented in these years was simply awe-inspiring.

All-seated stadiums have struggled to match the terracing experience for atmosphere and sheer thrills, although Ibrox has still proved to be an intimidating venue on European nights as the testimonies of opponents from teams such as Marseille, Villarreal, Monaco, Parma, Leeds United and Manchester United all serve to show. It might be added that the Old Firm clashes too have lost little of their spice and clamour.

Initiatives on the part of supporters groups like the Rangers Assembly have done much in recent years to bring the ordinary fan closer to the club and to bring to light episodes in Rangers' history which have been neglected or under-appreciated. There has been vigorous debate about the club's identity, the way it is run and the way it should respond to criticism. In the age of the Internet fans have been encouraged to be more proactive in expressing opinions and challenging critical portrayals of the club. Since the 1980s fanzines, like *Follow Follow* (begun and still run by Mark Dingwall), and more recently websites have been forums for intense debate and discussion about Rangers on the pitch and off with a sometimes high level of informed comment on business and finance, politics and culture as well as team formations and performances. The *Follow Follow* fanzine also led a vigorous if unavailing campaign to prevent the standing enclosure at Ibrox being seated in the early 1990s.

In the pre-digital age and pre-season-ticket culture, it was the Rangers Supporters' Association that was responsible for expressing the fans' viewpoint. It is fair to say that for the most part the association did this in a low-key and uncombative manner, and there was nothing like the pressure which today can be exerted by the fans' lobby on the directors and management. The association, which was founded in 1946 and quickly became the largest federation of supporters' clubs in Britain, was nonetheless an important channel between club officials and players and the supporters. It received high praise in this connection from George Young, legendary team captain in the post-war era, in whose autobiography it was stated that the association had some 10,000 members by the end of the 1940s. The association also initiated annual supporters' rallies, which the players and management always attended. These were large and entertaining gatherings and were usually compered by Rangers fans in the world of showbiz such as Lex McLean and Ross Bowie. The association and its individual branches did much impressive charity work, a situation which, of course, continues today among supporters' clubs and groups. In the post-war years through to the 1970s, the association and its many branches organised travel to follow Rangers wherever the team ventured; moreover, there was the bi-annual Wembley trip for the Scotland–England international. For most supporters' clubs the Wembley outing was a major operation and this reflected the extent to which the Rangers fans formed the backbone of the support for the Scottish international team prior to the 1980s.

Supporters' bus trips to matches became a subculture in itself, and websites in recent years have featured regular items on famous and infamous excursions on the part of buses such as the Kinning Park Loyal, the Bridgeton Loyal, Newmacher Red White and Blue, Thornliebank True Blues, Girvan Valley RSC, Linwood No. 1 and Edinburgh Union Jack. Billy 'Monty' Montgomery of the Nithsdale Loyal has recently been to the fore in promoting a better appreciation of the club's history and image. Some supporters' buses are impeccably run and stand for no rowdy conduct; others, which can usually be heard before they are seen, have acquired a more raffish and dubious reputation. The terms 'bonkers' and 'mental' are routinely applied to these buses in fans' discussion boards. In all buses, however, there is a deep sense of camaraderie and fraternal bonding. Travelling with Rangers over the years has produced much comedy gold; the stories could fill another book. One might be told here to convey a flavour of these trips and the richness of the cultural exchange involved. When at a stopover in France en route to a match in Switzerland, a well-educated and hungry fan ducked into a cafe and ordered a ham sandwich. Some minutes later he was joined by some of his fellow supporters from the bus and asked how he managed to be served such a tasty treat. 'Just ask for Jambon', the fan replied to which one burly member of the gang shouted to the barmaid: 'Hey, hen, gie's wan o yer jumbos!'

The characters among the Rangers support past and present are legion. For many years Bob Moffat was 'Mr Rangers of Northern Ireland'; no one did more to stimulate the growth of the fan base in the Province in the 1950s and 1960s. Bob's pub, The Four Step Inn on Belfast's storied Shankill Road, was a shrine to Rangers before it was destroyed by a bomb in the early 1970s as the Troubles tore Ulster apart. Andy Bain, who lost a leg in the Second World War, still followed the team home and abroad; his remarkable loyalty has been highlighted by comedian Andy Cameron whose 'patter' over the years has probably owed much to his own immersion in the colourful world of the ordinary fan. *Rangers Historian* editor Robert McElroy went 18 years without missing a single match and has compiled a complete record of the team's matches for which every other fan owes him a debt of gratitude. The late Garry Lynch rivalléd McElroy in his dedication, clocking up in one season a total of 143 matches involving Rangers sides from the first team to the Youth XI. Stuart Daniels of the Kinning Park club probably holds the record for trips abroad: it stood at over 70 some ten years ago. Stuart was born, in his own words, 'within the sound of the Ibrox roar'.

Then there is Davie Edgar, whose book *21st Century Blue: Being a Bear in the Modern World* provides a hilarious, sane and proud sketch of his passion for the Rangers family. Davie closes his book by saying that Rangers should never settle for being just another club but always strive to do better: 'This is who we are. This is what we do. I was born a Ranger and I'll die one, and I couldn't be happier.'

That Rangers could never be regarded as just another club was dramatically illustrated in May 2008 when around 200,000 supporters converged on Manchester and surrounding areas for the UEFA Cup final. If ever a commentator spoke prophetically it was ITV's Peter Drury at the moment when Nacho Novo's penalty in Fiorentina sealed Rangers' passage to the final: 'Manchester brace yourself . . . Rangers are coming! The Scots are heading for Manchester and you know what? Manchester may not be big enough!' The Rangers fans simply swamped the city drawn by the burning desire, as UEFA President Michel Platini himself said, 'to be close to their club in one of the most crucial moments in its history'. They came from all over the world and by means of every kind of transport. The vast majority knew there was no chance of getting a ticket for the game at the 44,000 capacity City of Manchester stadium. They just wanted to be there.

The day was to end in disappointment, and in some shambolic scenes of crowd disorder that dredged up the familiar criticisms of the club, its support and its image. In their own country Rangers are not a fashionable institution among opinion-formers, notwithstanding the transformative recent history of the club and its enduring appeal to the mass of humanity who travelled from Scotland or who remained to cheer at home on this landmark occasion. In a crowd of such magnitude there were always likely to be bad elements, and the amount of alcohol consumed was genuinely mind-boggling. However, when the tumult had died down and the more balanced of observers started to put events in their appropriate context, it became possible to view the whole event primarily as the most remarkable display of support for a football team imaginable. It was testimony to something noted all those years ago by the *Scottish Sport*. From the 19th century to the 21st century Rangers and their fans were still setting records.

23
THE BOARDROOM

In 1899 Rangers became a limited company. Since then the club has been officially run by its various chairmen and directors. As in any large organisation there have been disagreements, factionalism and internal politics. However, few fans have grasped the detail of boardroom politics, and few indeed have seemed to want to know. It was observed, for example, that during the power struggle taking place inside Ibrox in 1947 no fans were on hand anxious to be informed of the outcome, whereas thousands would have been there if the team had been playing even in a practice match.

This sums up the perspective of the average fan, and it has changed only to a limited degree over the years. Only when the playing fortunes of the club are obviously linked to the boardroom, as in recent times, have more than a small minority taken more than a passing interest.

Yet a 'biography' of the club has to include some reflections on the men in dark suits as well as the players in the blue shirt. Several chairmen and directors have been engrossing characters in their own right, while decisions at boardroom level have inevitably had the broadest repercussions. Moreover, the history of Rangers Football Club has involved power struggles analogous in many ways with the dramas on the pitch.

In the first decades of the club's history, there were many comings and goings in the personnel who held office. The club's early struggles, particularly in relation to finance, were reflected for example in the censuring of the treasurer for the 'careless discharge of his duties' in 1882. The unfortunate man then did the decent thing and resigned. The club did not have its troubles to seek when its match secretary in the early 1880s, John Wallace MacKay, brought it into disrepute by association with his shady dealings. Sections of the press, particularly the *Athletic Journal*, hounded Rangers on account of MacKay's influence at the club.

Some stability was established by the 1890s, not least due to the masterly administrative skills of William Wilton, the match secretary at this time. Wilton, of course, would become the club's first manager after the transformation of 1899.

Rangers' first chairman of the board was James Henderson who had been president for the year 1898–99 under the old arrangements. There were eight directors. Henderson was also a member of Govan Parish Council and later Glasgow City Council, and he was renowned for his work among the poor children of Govan. Rangers indeed had by now a notable record of helping charitable causes, among them, incidentally, Catholic charities. The club's minute books show that matches were played for the benefit of the unemployed in 1886, and donations made to help the Unemployed Relief Fund for the Kinning Park area.

Henderson passed away in 1912 and was succeeded by Sir John Ure-Primrose. Ure-Primrose has become posthumously controversial, viewed by critics of Rangers' ethos as an intolerant and sectarian-minded figure. This school of thought bases its damning conclusions on Ure-Primrose's Freemasonry, his regard for empire, and his identification with the Unionist cause in the struggle over Irish Home Rule.

Ure-Primrose began his association with Rangers in 1887. He was exactly the kind of man the club – and other football clubs at the time – wished to attract. He was a prominent local councillor and magistrate, and a successful businessman and flour-mill owner. In 1902 he became Lord Provost of the City of Glasgow. He was also a member of the Ibrox United Free Church. Any football club would have seen the benefits of having such an influential man connected with it. Ure-Primrose was decidedly typical of the municipal ethos of the time: the stress on civic values and the improvement in facilities and services provided by local government. For Ure-Primrose it was not about Rangers winning or losing, as he put it at the club's 'Jubilee' event of 1923, '. . . all he was concerned about was the sport and its influence on the general welfare.'

This was also still a time when Glasgow's mighty export industries prospered through the imperial markets they reached, and a time when the idea that the connections of empire powered social progress at home were current. Ure-Primrose was representative of a business class strongest in the west of Scotland, which saw the United Kingdom's success as underpinned by Union and Empire.

The politics of this group were Liberal Unionist. Many like Ure-Primrose had been Liberal Party supporters, and had broken with the party over its decision to pursue Irish Home Rule. Such was the significance of the Irish issue in the late 19th and early 20th century that British politics underwent a process of realignment with Liberal Unionists, like Ure-Primrose, entering into an alliance with the Conservatives. This alliance, in Scotland, was formalised by the creation of the Unionist Party in 1912, the year Ure-Primrose became Rangers chairman. From this point till the mid-1960s the Unionists, although linked to the Conservatives in the rest of Britain, had a separate identity in Scotland. Increasingly in this period the main political battle in Scotland was between the Unionists and the Labour Party with the Liberals fading into the background.

The Scottish National Party, formed in 1934, did not really become a political force until the late 1960s. When the Unionist designation was consigned to history in Scotland in the mid-1960s and the name Conservative formally assumed, the party's fortunes began a long downward spiral. It is significant that Donald Findlay, when Rangers vice-chairman in 1997, suggested that the party revert to its old name and accentuate its separate Scottish identity.

Ure-Primrose, like other chairmen who came after him such as Bailie Duncan Graham and Councillor John F. Wilson, and the patrons of the club from the 1920s through to the 1950s, industry magnates Lord Weir and John Cargill, were essentially paternalist figures whose politics sought to defuse social class tensions and promote co-operation in industry. They undoubt-edly saw in sport and recreation ways of bridging class divides and providing entertainment and outlets for energy and passion at the end of the working week. It was probably no accident that the Independent Labour Party (ILP) newspaper, *The Forward*, published in Glasgow, should take a jaundiced view of the appeal to the working class of leisure pursuits such as football and horse racing.

The outlook of the Rangers chairmen and patrons was that of the chairmen of many other football clubs. These men – and it was always men – were a conservative breed. Their own economic interests were well served by football; not usually through massive sums of money being made, rather the part played by the sport in working-class culture that many on the left wished some radical political thinking would supplant.

In 1946 when the Rangers Supporters' Association emerged, the secretary of the Cathcart branch in Glasgow wrote to Lord Weir, still a club patron and still a major employer with the family pump manufacturing concern based in Cathcart. In his correspondence the branch secretary asked if Weir would become honorary president of the branch, pointing out that this would encourage the supporters' club to maintain high standards of behaviour and highlighting the fact that most of the branch members were in Weir's 'employ' at Cathcart. The request typified a certain 'respectable worker' perspective, and the Unionist party's success in Scotland – it won over half the popular vote in the 1955 election – was to a great extent reliant on its appeal to a significant section of the working class in those years. There is little doubt that many such workers would have been Rangers fans.

On the other hand, there were many Labour-voting Rangers fans for whom the patronage of a Lord Weir was a matter of indifference or even embarrassment. Supporters' records show that there were clubs and branches who were happy to meet in, and be associated with, Labour Rooms just as others met in Unionist Rooms or Orange Halls. Moreover, Rangers have had notable Labour politicians as supporters over the years such as two Labour Lord Provosts of Glasgow, Tom Kerr and Andrew Hood, and more recently ministers in the British and Scottish governments like Adam Ingram, Gus MacDonald and Andy Kerr.

It is relevant to mention the political outlook of those chairmen and directors who were involved in local and national politics; the club even had a Westminster MP among its directors between 1950 and 1955 when W. Gordon Bennett sat for the constituency of Glasgow Woodside. However, it is equally important to stress that there were chairmen and directors who attained their positions on account of their knowledge of the game and service to it and not for any influence they may have exerted beyond the sport. William Craig, a director of the club and briefly its chairman from its time as a limited company till his death in 1923, had also been a member of the general committee that oversaw the club's affairs before it was incorporated. He was also a vice-president of the Scottish FA, a body that many Rangers officials were to serve over the years. The *Rangers Club Handbook* of 1924–25 provided a description of Craig's style: 'In meeting situations of difficulty, he showed a comprehension of facts and a plain manner of dealing with them which allowed of no evasions by would-be fencers.' After they stopped playing both Alan Morton and later George Brown were to serve as Rangers directors for over 30 years.

One former Rangers player whose playing days encompassed the years 1910 to 1922, wing half James Bowie, went on to become first a director then club chairman upon the death of Duncan Graham in 1934. Bowie occupied the chair until 1947 when he was in effect deposed by a 'coup' engineered by manager Bill Struth. This was one of the most dramatic episodes in the club's history and it did not involve a ball being kicked.

What is known is that Bowie had proposed that Struth step down as manager at the end of the 1946–47 season, or at least appoint an assistant who would take over in due course. Bowie was fully respectful of Struth's immense contribution to the club's success but was concerned about the manager's declining health. He was prepared to offer Struth a seat on the board, or if he continued as boss with an assistant, to have the club's constitution altered to allow the manager to also serve as a director. However, Struth was not contemplating retirement yet and interpreted this as a threat to his position. In the light of the changes regarding the right of the manager to be on the board, and the coincidental enlargement of the board from three to five members, Struth set about exploiting the new situation. Working with the club secretary William Rogers Simpson and local Councillor John F. Wilson, Struth acquired the support of the most important shareholders and targeted Bowie. At an extraordinary general meeting on 12 June Bowie was ousted as chairman and Simpson, Struth's ally, installed in his place.

As Robert McElroy in his expert analysis of these events in the book *Ten Days That Shook Rangers* and in the pages of the *Rangers Historian* has argued, this bitter struggle marked a major turning point in the club's history. From then on control of Rangers Football Club would lie with those who owned large amounts of club shares, or were able to command the backing of big shareholders. The tradition of boardroom power being conferred as a reward for past loyalty and service, whether as administrators or players, was at an end. As McElroy has observed, the events of 1947 enabled the later takeover of the Lawrence Group and then the succession of David Murray. Bowie styled himself as the champion of the small shareholders, and claimed that the principles of loyalty to and love for the team and the sport were being sacrificed for financial interest.

This was unfair to Struth whose loyalty to Rangers was unquestionable. Nevertheless, Struth set in train events that would see financial clout at the club taking increasing precedence. As George Brown put it in his evidence to the Ibrox Disaster Inquiry: 'It was after that [1947] that the share issue was doubled and eventually redoubled so that in the end it was possible to obtain very substantial holdings in the company.' Brown added that he had only held on to his position as director – this was 1971 – by avoiding 'any form of intrigue'. When Struth eventually came under fire from supporters in 1953, it was suggested that the root of the problem was the 'business' attitude of the directors and management.

In truth, Rangers had long prized the prestige of being associated with successful businessmen like Ure-Primrose. However, there had been a balance between financial considerations and sporting idealism, which was allowed to tip up in 1947. In luring the wealthy house-builder John Lawrence on to the board in 1954, Rangers were further encouraging the percolation of business values and conduct into their affairs. Lawrence became chairman in 1963 but he was an unpopular figure. The changing times resulted in much less deference among ordinary fans being shown to the figures of authority at the club. Fans were decidedly unimpressed when they read at regular intervals of the chairman sealing business deals abroad while the team were playing crucial matches at home. When Scot Symon and then Davie White were sacked, Lawrence came in for some personal abuse from fans over the way the club's image had sunk.

It should be said in Lawrence's defence that he often made the correct public gesture on behalf of the club, however

274 THE OFFICIAL BIOGRAPHY OF RANGERS

unpopular it might have been among some fans. In 1967 he was present to welcome back the Celtic team who had won the European Cup, an act of courtesy not reciprocated when Rangers returned triumphant in 1972. Lawrence was also genuinely appalled at the machinations resorted to by those who wished to prevent David Hope succeeding him as chairman in 1973. The plotters got their wish by creating divisions over Hope's wife's religion and rumours about Hope himself, and Matt Taylor succeeded Lawrence instead. Rae Simpson, son of William Rogers Simpson, occupied the chair from 1975 through to 1983, but he was largely a figurehead. In 1975 Lawrence's grandson Lawrence Marlborough joined the board.

In the event it fell to Marlborough to stop the rot of the early 1980s when the club's playing fortunes were at an all-time low, crowds were dwindling to alarming levels, and the board appeared riven by factionalism. Although he had resigned from the board in 1983 he had retained his large shareholding and he reached agreement two years later with director Jack Gillespie to sell him his holding to enable him to gain effective control of the club. He installed David Holmes as his voice on the board with instructions to bring about radical change. The 'Souness Revolution' duly followed. Two years into the Souness era, steel magnate David Murray bought out the Lawrence Group and assumed control of Rangers. Murray was to oversee the most successful period in the club's history.

The club were now piloted into a completely different financial stratosphere, and few fans would deny that it was an exciting time. For a while nothing seemed too ambitious for the club, a state of affairs which was well in keeping with its history. It could be said that Murray simply tried to reconcile these traditions with the new highly commercialised world which sport was moving into. The chairman did not stint in making available money for transfers and for wages to lure players who would not otherwise have looked twice at the Scottish game. Rangers quite simply did not deliver at the highest level of the game during this period of largesse, and it was clear it could not go on indefinitely. Murray could not bring about the wider cultural change the club needed in order to take a step up. In the 1990s with every passing season the fans would hanker more and more after the goal of nine championships in a row to equal Celtic's feat in the 1960s and 1970s, and ten-in-a-row to finally beat it. It did not matter that the comparison was a false one: that five- or six-in-a-row under the arrangements of the Scottish Premier League in the 1980s and 1990s was at least the equivalent of nine under the old 34 games a season, 18-team league of the earlier period. The fans would not be satisfied till this old score was settled.

This was not the mentality for a serious performance on the European stage. Only once, in season 1992–93, did Rangers deliver that performance and even then it fell just short. The club needed to be backed to the hilt in its desire to conquer Europe as the overriding priority. In the event too many fans were parochial and even in a curious way uncomfortable about the benefits of success at the top level. As it turned out Rangers drained themselves physically and mentally achieving the nine consecutive titles while hardly registering in the Champions League. The same fans turned on Murray in the first decade of the 21st century as Rangers' debt spiralled to unsustainable levels.

Certainly there were pertinent questions to be asked of Murray's stewardship by this time although he did underwrite a £51 million share issue in a bid to get the club back on an even keel. Certainly the agenda of the fans' groups was constructive. Certainly the question of whether the model of ownership was best for the club needed to be discussed and debated openly. Certainly it was reasonable to ask the club to show that they did not just regard fans as customers, and that they were well aware that Rangers was a sacred institution and not just a business. However, many fans need to ask questions of their own outlook when the opportunities were knocking in more abundant times.

24
ALLY McCOIST

You have to take a deep breath before listing Ally McCoist's achievements as a Rangers and Scotland striker. He was signed by John Greig from Sunderland in June 1983 for £185,000 and in the following 15 seasons at the club 'Super Ally' broke record after record, including the Rangers record for league and European goals. The former St Johnstone player, who had signed for the Perth club straight from leaving school in his home town of East Kilbride, was the Light Blues' leading scorer nine times and was the first Scottish player to win the European Golden Boot – an award he retained the following season.

McCoist made his Rangers debut against St Mirren on 20 August 1983. He scored his first goal for the club in a 4–1 League Cup win over Queen of the South a week later and it took him just 27 seconds in his Old Firm debut at Parkhead the following week to find the net. But John Greig would not get the benefit of McCoist's goalscoring prowess. Poor results meant the former Rangers skipper made way in October that year for former Ibrox boss Jock Wallace who returned to the hot seat.

The following March, McCoist scored a hat-trick against Celtic in a 3–2 League Cup final win at Hampden and finished the season with 20 goals in 47 appearances. That hat-trick against the Parkhead club should have made him an instant hero. However, 11 months later, on 16 February 1985 during a 1–0 Scottish Cup defeat by Dundee at Ibrox, McCoist found himself on the receiving end of the supporters' wrath. He missed a series of chances and the frustration of the fans boiled over and the Copland Road stand reverberated to 'Ally, Ally get tae ****'. That game would have finished a lesser player. However, McCoist showed that he was a man of substance and bounced back almost immediately, scoring ten goals in nine games at the end of the season to become top scorer at the club for the second successive year.

McCoist initially flourished under Graeme Souness, who took over as player-manager from Wallace in 1986. However, there was a highly publicised personality clash between the two men and the Scotland striker found himself on the bench for much of the 1990–91 campaign, earning himself the nickname of 'The Judge'. This time, though, the fans were behind McCoist although it appeared for a time that the striker might leave the club. However, it was Souness who left Govan in controversial circumstances weeks before the end of season 1990–91 to return to Liverpool to become manager of the Anfield club.

By the time McCoist left Rangers at the end of season 1997–98 he had scored 355 competitive goals for the club in 581 appearances, winning ten league winners' medals, nine League Cup winners' medals, and one Scottish Cup medal. He was one of only three players to win all nine-in-a-row titles under Walter Smith – the others being Richard Gough and Ian Ferguson – and in the dark blue of Scotland McCoist scored 19 goals in 61 appearances.

The desire to keep playing led to a brief spell at Kilmarnock in the twilight of his career. When he eventually hung up his shooting boots he became a television personality before returning to the game as assistant manager to Smith with

Scotland. McCoist had no hesitation in accepting Smith's invitation to join him when he slipped into the Ibrox hot seat for the second time in 2007.

While much has been written about McCoist's upbeat personality, little heed has been paid to the incredible mental strength which saw him through some tough times, none more so than that infamous afternoon against Dundee. Sitting in the manager's chair at Murray Park before training, McCoist breaks out into uncontrollable laughter when the subject is brought up. And then laughs some more before reflecting on what he concedes to be a pivotal moment in his Ibrox career. 'I will never forget the Dundee game,' he said. 'In many ways I wouldn't swap it. It was a fantastic, hurtful experience. You have to laugh about it now but it was tough.' McCoist laughs some more. 'To be fair, I missed some chances that day. I am not saying what the fans did was justified but I did have a howler. I remember Bomber [John Brown] – who was playing for Dundee that day – coming up to me at the end of the game and growling, "keep your head up". I am still not sure if it was encouragement or a threat! But I did keep it up and kept plugging away.

'The football graveyard is littered with players who couldn't play with the Old Firm,' McCoist continues. 'It is not an easy place to play. It is a unique environment. Rangers and Celtic fans expect their team to win every game and I mean every game – with the exception of Barcelona. Our fans will settle for a draw – in the Nou Camp! That's just the way it is and if you can't handle that then it's obviously not going to happen for you.'

McCoist has lived with expectations all his football life and, like a lot of Old Firm players, admits that the fear of failure was much more powerful than the joy of winning. 'We won a lot of things, but for me it was more a fear of losing than the desire to win that kept me going,' he said. 'Very seldom did we win anything and I was absolutely euphoric and delighted rather than feeling relief. You would be thinking, "Imagine if we hadn't won that?" There can't be any other country in the world where when you win something you don't say, "On you go ya dancer" but "Thank God we won that."'

Had McCoist left Ibrox at the time of his spat with Souness then who knows how his career would have panned out. However, Rangers fans can be thankful that his determination to succeed came to the fore again. Ironically, he believes the backing of the Gers support during that period might have worked against him. 'I have spoken to Graeme about that a hundred times – and I still say to him that I should have been playing,' smiles McCoist. 'But although I didn't agree with it, I know he was doing it because he thought it was best for the club. He believed that was the way. Maybe he was trying to teach me a lesson but I guarantee it was for the best for the team and I can see it a lot clearer now from where I'm sitting than I could at the time. A lot was made of it but we got on fine and we talk away, no problem. Falling out with the manager happens all the time.' He continues: 'Perversely, I don't think it helped that the fans were behind me – I hope they take that the right way – because the only thing which would have affected his decision was me with performances. He wouldn't be influenced by anyone else and so in that respect, while the fans were fantastic to me, they wouldn't have affected Graeme's decision. He is strong-willed and he didn't think I should be playing and was sticking to his guns. I don't think he was being stubborn. If you are stubborn it can affect your decisions and that can't be a good thing. I think he was just strong-willed.'

While the insatiable demand for constant domestic success sucked much of the joy from title and trophy wins, the European arena, where Rangers were more often than not the underdogs, brought a greater sense of excitement and achievement. McCoist was involved in many big European nights for Rangers and like many Light Blues supporters, he recalls the two games against Leeds United in 1992–93, when Rangers won 2–1 home and away against the English champions to qualify for the newly formatted Champions League, as a highlight. 'I will never forget the atmosphere in the game against Leeds United at Ibrox if I live to be a hundred,' he says. 'It was unbelievable. I remember looking across to Gary McAllister, David Batty, Gary Speed walking out the tunnel and they were just looking at each other. There was no way we were going to sit back and defend. You were not allowed to defend at Ibrox then. The fans wouldn't allow it. That has changed. In the UEFA Cup run in 2007–08, the fans were brilliant, they came to Ibrox knowing we had to keep it tight at the back. But that was unheard of years ago. When the first whistle sounded it was the charge of the Light Brigade.'

Both clubs agreed that no away fans would be at either game but McCoist laughs at the memory of the Light Blue interloper he spotted outside Elland Road. 'The away game was also fantastic,' he said. 'We weren't supposed to have any fans at the game. We drove up to Elland Road and the place was swarming with Leeds fans who were banging the bus and it was all a bit intimidating. As the bus pulled up I looked out the window and noticed a big guy from Kinning Park, Stuart Daniels, standing in among hundreds of Leeds fans. He looked at me, unzipped his jacket so you could see his Rangers badge on his shirt – and saluted! It was hilarious but at the same time brilliant. It was as if to say, "Okay, we are outnumbered but here I am reporting for duty." You couldn't make it up.

'But what a night,' McCoist continues. 'The term "Battle of Britain" gets used all the time now but that was a proper Battle of Britain. We were never over-confident but we fancied our chances. We would have fancied ourselves against anyone that year. Once again the gaffer called it right. He was worried more about everyone getting carried away at the home game. He knew we could defend and get a goal in the away game, although I don't think he believed we were going to score the way they did at Ibrox, so early in the game. There were some great performances down there that night, from the keeper Andy Goram outwards and we won 2–1 again. The first person in the dressing room to congratulate us? Alex Ferguson.'

McCoist readily admits that 'you can't beat the European

nights' and reels off other favourites. 'The noise at the home game against Dynamo Kiev in 1987 equalled the noise of the Leeds game,' he recalls. 'They were one of the best sides I ever played against and we did well to lose only 1–0 in the first game over there. That Dynamo Kiev side were effectively the Russian national team and included players such as Rats, Belanov, Kutznetzov, Baltacha, Chanov in goals and Blokhin; they were a top team. Chanov made a mess of it for the first goal by Falco. I made it 2–0 after half-time and then they battered us for 15 minutes. As everyone knows Souness brought the touchline in a bit that night – I think he should have brought it in a little bit further. With 15 minutes to go, I was shouting at the dugout for a tin of paint, I was going to bring them in further myself. About ten years later we beat Alania Vladikavkas 7–2 over in Russia after winning 3–1 at Ibrox and I will never forget the home fans singing "Glasgow Rangers". Walter will tell you about when we scored our sixth or seventh goal, their coach got up and walked out the stadium. Not to the dressing room. Right out. He must have thought, "I've seen enough of this."

'On the other side of things, I can't forget the game against Levski Sofia a few years previous to Alania when Todorov scored in the last seconds for them. We were drawing 1–1 over there in the second leg and on the brink of going through 4–3 on aggregate, and then in the 93rd minute he hit a shot. I can still see it. I can remember it as if it was yesterday and the sickening feeling. The ball dipped, hit the bar and post and then went in. And that was us out the Champions League. Everybody sunk to their knees in despair.'

However, McCoist's biggest regret during his time as a Rangers striker came after the two-legged win over Leeds United had taken them into the last eight. Rangers had to face French champions Marseille, Belgian side Club Brugge and CSKA Moscow in Group A, with the winners going through to the final against the winners of Group B. McCoist missed the opening game against Marseille at Ibrox as Rangers came back from 2–0 down to draw 2–2, but returned for the rest of the campaign. A 1–0 away win over CSKA Moscow (played in Bochum, Germany due to the severity of the Russian winter) was followed by a double header against Brugge from where a 1–1 draw in Belgium was followed by a 2–1 win at Ibrox, courtesy of Scott Nisbett's infamous fluke goal. The downside to that victory was Mark Hateley's sending off which kept him out of the next game against Marseille in France. Both clubs were level on points and a win for either side would put them in the final. However, the game ended 1–1 and ultimately, it was Marseille who went on to face AC Milan in the final.

'It is selfish of me to say this but my biggest regret would probably be that myself and Mark did not get a crack at Marseille together,' said McCoist. 'I don't mean that Mark and I were the team, far from it. The success of that time was the team but we were a wee team within that team. I missed the first game – which was an epic – with a calf injury and Mark was suspended for the return game. I would love to have known what would have happened if we had both played. Wee Durranty scored a great goal over there but it was 1–1. We were just one more goal away from the final.

'For two years Hateley was out of this world,' McCoist continues. 'But in the first year that Maurice Johnston was at Rangers I think he was in the top three strikers in the world. It is an incredible statement to make but I really believe it. He was absolutely unbelievable. He was a more educated player having been to France. The thing that both players had in common was an incredible appetite. Great players that they were, they worked very hard. Mark was an old-school centre forward, a battering ram, although I'm loathe to call him that because although he was powerful, he could take the ball to feet and play. We were absolutely flying at that time of that Champions League campaign. I think we scored over 120 goals between us in two seasons, which was unbelievable. I used to go out knowing that one of us would score and I didn't have that feeling a lot in my career. We didn't lose a game in that European campaign. It was a brilliant run and we gave it our best shot. It might not have happened but I would have loved a crack at Marseille with Mark.'

On 22 February 2011, Rangers confirmed that McCoist would take over as manager when Walter Smith stepped down at the end of the season. It was revealed that McCoist, who would become only the 13th manager in Rangers' history, had agreed a one-year rolling contract, with Kenny McDowall as his assistant. At the press conference McCoist said: 'I was lucky enough to play for the club for 15 years, but this is an absolute dream and a privilege.' McCoist's demeanour becomes more serious when outlining what he believes will be the basic tenets of his management style, while giving a nod to his spat with Souness. 'You have to be fair and honest,' he said. 'As long as any decision you make is honest the players and fans will accept that. Arguably, the most important job in management is keeping the players that aren't playing happy. I've been there when the team is read out at half past one and you aren't in it. You can say what you like about the modern-day player, about their poor attitude or whatever, but they want to play. They train all week to play and if they don't they are disappointed. But leaving players out doesn't scare me. As long as the decision you make is an honest one. It might turn out to be wrong but as long as you can live with yourself. And that's what all my managers did.'

McCoist becomes even more serious as he assesses the potential problems of management in an ever-changing football landscape. 'The biggest problem the club is going to face is financial constraints and that will have a big effect,' he said. 'Gone are the days of spending £8 to £10 million on players. The way ahead for the club is shrewd signings and bringing boys through. As a facility Murray Park is better than most. But the real success is getting young kids in the first team, not winning youth cups. That's nice but secondary. The prospects of players like Jamie Ness and Kyle Hutton are brighter than a few years ago. There is a real acceptance that we have to bring boys through and that's great because they know they will get a chance. From the point of view of the fans, we hope there is a realisation that it's going to be tough. It's going to get worse before it gets better. But one thing is, I want to do everything here. This is my club.

'I am not daft,' he continues. 'I know the situation the club is in. It's probably not an ideal situation but it's not something that scares me. One of the pluses is that Rangers fans have an appreciation of what's happening and they know we won't buy our way out of trouble and buy our way to success. We have to be very shrewd. You can't plan for how it's going to be when you take over. You just have to play the cards you are dealt and get on with it.'

After recalling all the great European nights that he enjoyed as a player, McCoist is aware that they might be a bit harder to come by for the fans in the future. However, he remains confident that he and the club will get continued support from the punters who cheered him on when he was knocking in the goals. 'We are definitely off the pace with regards the top teams in the Champions League,' he admits. 'You have a chance on a one-off basis but on a consistent basis there is no way Rangers or Celtic can be expected to compete with Man United, Bayern Munich, Barcelona, Real Madrid or AC Milan, it is just not possible. In the January transfer window of 2011 there was over £100 million spent on three players in England while we were trying to get loan players and free transfers in. That is the reality of the situation. Some fans won't accept it but the vast majority of Rangers fans are intelligent enough to look at the broader picture and see what's happening and I don't have any doubts that they will continue to be loyal. They have been for a hundred years.'

 BIBLIOGRAPHY

John Allan, *The Story of the Rangers* (Desert Island Books, 1996 – originally published by RFC in 1923).

William Allison (ed.), *The Rangers Players' Story* (RFC, 1962).

William Allison, *Rangers – The New Era* (RFC, 1966).

John Burrowes, *Frontline Report* (Mainstream, n.d.).

Bob Crampsey, *The First 100 Years* (Scottish Football League, 1990).

David Downing, *Passovotchka* (Bloomsbury, 1999).

Neil Drysdale, *Silver Smith* (Birlinn, 2011).

Iain Duff, *Follow On – 50 Years of Rangers in Europe* (Fort, 2006).

Iain Duff, *Temple of Dreams* (Breedon Books, 2008).

Iain Duff, *Follow Follow. Classic Rangers Old Firm Clashes* (Mainstream, 2010).

David Edgar, *21st Century Blue* (DB Publishing, 2010).

Ronnie Esplin, *Down the Copland Road* (Argyll, 2000).

Ronnie Esplin and Alex Anderson, *Barcelona Here We Come* (Argyll, 2002).

Ronnie Esplin and Alex Anderson, *The Advocaat Years* (Argyll, 2004).

Ronnie Esplin (ed.), *Ten Days That Shook Rangers* (Fort, 2005).

Ronnie Esplin and Graham Walker (eds.), *It's Rangers For Me?* (Fort, 2007).

Ronnie Esplin and Graham Walker (eds.), *Rangers: Triumphs, Troubles, Traditions* (Fort, 2010).

John Fairgrieve, *The Rangers* (Robert Hale, 1964).

Barry Ferguson (with Iain King), *Blue: The Life and Times of Barry Ferguson* (Mainstream, 2007).

Ken Gallacher (ed.), *Playing For Rangers* (Stanley Paul, 1964).

Ken Gallacher, *Slim Jim Baxter* (Virgin, 2002).

John Greig, *A Captain's Part* (Stanley Paul, 1968).

John Greig (with Jim Black), *My Story* (Headline, 2005).

Stephen Halliday, *Rangers. The Official Illustrated History* (Weidenfeld and Nicolson, 1989).

Stephen Halliday, *Rangers. The Waddell Years* (Chameleon Books, 1999).

Willie Henderson, *Forward with Rangers* (Stanley Paul, 1966).

Lindsay Herron, *The Official Rangers Hall of Fame* (RFC, 2010).

Simon Inglis, *The Football Grounds of Britain* (Collins Willow, 1996).

Simon Inglis, *Engineering Archie* (English Heritage, 2005).

Sandy Jamieson, *Graeme Souness* (Mainstream, 1997).

Grant Jarvie and Graham Walker (eds.), *Scottish Sport in the Making of the Nation* (Leicester University Press, 1994).

Willie Johnston (with Tom Bullimore), *Sent Off At Gunpoint* (Know the Score, 2008).

Derek Johnstone, *Rangers – My Team* (Souvenir Press, 1979).

Hugh Keevins and Kevin McArra, *100 Cups* (Mainstream, 1985).

Stephen F. Kelly, *Graeme Souness. A Soccer Revolutionary* (Headline, 1994).

Bob MacCallum, *The Best of the Blues* (Mainstream, 2001).

Bob MacCallum, *Rangers' Fifty Flags* (Grange, 2003).

David McCarthy and Keith Jackson, *Lorenzo Amoruso: LA Confidential – The Autobiography* (First Press Publishing, 2002).

Robert McElroy and Bob Ferrier, *Rangers. The Complete Record* (Breedon Books, 1996; second edition, 2005).

Robert McElroy, *The Spirit of Ibrox* (Lancaster Publishing, 1998).

Robert McElroy, *50 Years of Rangers in Europe* (The History Press, 2006).

Bob McPhail (with Allan Herron), *Legend – Sixty Years at Ibrox* (Mainstream, 1988).

Archie Macpherson, *Action Replays* (Chapman, 1991).

David Mason, *Rangers: The Managers* (Mainstream, 2000).

David Mason (ed.), *Rangers: A Match to Remember* (Mainstream, 2001).

Ian Morrison, *Rangers* (Hamlyn, 1988).

John Moynihan, *The Soccer Syndrome* (Sportspages, 1987).

Bill Murray, *The Old Firm* (John Donald, 1984; second edition 2000).

Bill Murray, *Glasgow's Giants* (Mainstream, 1988).

Bill Murray, *The Old Firm in the New Age* (Mainstream, 1998).

Gary Ralston, *Rangers 1872. The Gallant Pioneers* (Breedon Books, 2009).

Harry Reid, *The Final Whistle?* (Birlinn, 2005).

David Ross, *The Roar of the Crowd* (Argyll, 2005).

Hugh Savage, *Born up a Close* (Argyll, 2006).

Paul Smith, *Rangers Cult Heroes* (Know the Score, 2007).

Graeme Souness, *The Management Years* (Andre Deutsch, 1999).

Graham Speirs, *Paul Le Guen: Enigma* (Mainstream, 2007).

Hugh Taylor, *We Will Follow Rangers* (Stanley Paul, 1961).

Wray Vamplew, *Pay Up and Play the Game* (Cambridge University Press, 1988).

Graham Walker and Tom Gallagher (eds.), *Sermons and Battle Hymns* (Edinburgh University Press, 1990).

Graham Walker, 'The Ibrox Stadium Disaster of 1971', *Soccer and Society*, Vol. 5, No. 2, Summer 2004.

Stephen Walsh, *Voices of the Old Firm* (Mainstream, 1995).

John Williams, *Seven Years On: Glasgow Rangers and Rangers Supporters, 1983–90* (Sir Norman Chester Centre for Football Research, 1990).

Chick Young, *Rebirth of the Blues* (Mainstream, 1987).

George Young, *Captain of Scotland* (Stanley Paul, 1951).

Other Sources

Rangers Archives

Ibrox Disaster Archive, Mitchell Library Glasgow

Weir Group Papers, Glasgow University Business Archive

Rangers Supporters' Association Annuals, 1952–1967

Various newspapers (titles cited in text)

Follow Follow, Aye Ready, Number One fanzines

The *Rangers Historian*

The *Scottish Football Historian*

Scottish Sport

Rangers FC Handbooks

Rangers FC match programmes

'The Official History of RFC' (DVD)

'Ian Ferguson – The Last True Blue?' (DVD)

MANAGERS APPENDIX

William Wilton

Surname:	WILTON				**Appointed:**	27/05/1899		
Forenames:	WILLIAM				**Left Post:**	02/05/1920		

Birthplace: Largs
Birthdate: 09/06/1865

	Pld	W	D	L	F	A	Pts	Titles
League	826	545	133	148	208	946	122	10
League Cup	0	0	0	0	0	0		0
Scottish Cup	104	65	18	21	281	101		4
Europe	0	0	0	0	0	0		0
Competitive Total	930	610	151	169	236	104		

League Titles   1890/91, 1898/99, 1899/1900, 1900/01, 1901/02, 1910/11, 1911/12, 1912/13, 1917/18, 1919/20

League Cup Wins

Scottish Cup Wins   1893/94, 1896/97, 1897/98, 1902/03

European

Bill Struth

Surname:	STRUTH	
Forenames:	WILLIAM	

Appointed:	20/05/1920
Left Post:	15/06/1954

Birthplace:	Milnathort
Birthdate:	1875

	Pld	W	D	L	F	A	Pts	Titles
League	975	646	198	131	2325	960	1490	18
League Cup	70	45	10	15	161	70		2
Scottish Cup	139	101	21	17	353	110		10
Europe	0	0	0	0	0	0		0
Wartime League	210	155	30	25	600	222		7
Wartime Cup	33	24	6	3	88	35		2
Wartime League Cup	50	43	3	4	131	40		2
Competitive Total	1477	1014	286	195	3658	1437		

League Titles	1920/21, 1922/23, 1923/24, 1924/25, 1926/27, 1927/28, 1928/29, 1929/30, 1930/31, 1932/33, 1933/34, 1934/35, 1936/37, 1938/39, 1946/47, 1948/49, 1949/50, 1952/53
League Cup Wins	1946/47, 1948/49
Scottish Cup Wins	1927/28, 1929/30, 1931/32, 1933/34, 1934/35, 1935/36, 1947/48, 1948/49, 1949/50, 1952/53

European

Scot Symon

Surname:	SYMON		**Appointed:**	15/06/1954
Forenames:	JAMES		**Left Post:**	01/11/1967

Birthplace:	Errol
Birthdate:	09/05/1911

	Pld	W	D	L	F	A	Pts	Titles
League	446	295	81	70	112	479	671	6
League Cup	122	81	18	23	340	144		4
Scottish Cup	59	42	10	7	158	64		5
Europe	54	28	5	21	101	90		0
Competitive Total	681	446	114	121	172	777		

League Titles   1955/56, 1956/57, 1958/59, 1960/61, 1963/64

League Cup Wins   1960/61, 1961/62, 1963/64, 1964/65

Scottish Cup Wins   1959/60, 1961/62, 1962/63, 1963/64, 1965/66

European

Davie White

		Appointed:	01/11/1967
Surname:	WHITE	Appointed:	01/11/1967
Forenames:	DAVID	Left Post:	27/11/1969

Birthplace:
Birthdate: ??/??/1933

	Pld	W	D	L	F	A	Pts	Titles
League	74	51	13	10	190	81	115	0
League Cup	12	8	1	3	28	12		0
Scottish Cup	10	6	2	2	19	10		0
Europe	18	8	3	7	27	19		0
Competitive Total	114	73	19	22	264	122		

League Titles

League Cup Wins

Scottish Cup Wins

European

Willie Thornton

Surname: THORNTON **Appointed:** 27/11/1969
Forenames: WILLIAM **Left Post:** 08/12/1969

Birthplace: Winchburgh
Birthdate: 03/03/1920

	Pld	W	D	L	F	A	Pts	Titles
League	2	2	0	0	5	1	4	0
League Cup	0	0	0	0	0	0		0
Scottish Cup	0	0	0	0	0	0		0
Europe	0	0	0	0	0	0		0
Competitive Total	2	2	0	0	5	1		

League Titles

League Cup Wins

Scottish Cup Wins

European

Willie Waddell

Surname:	WADDELL	
Forenames:	WILLIAM	

Appointed:	08/12/1969
Left Post:	31/05/1972

Birthplace:	Forth
Birthdate:	07/03/1921

	Pld	W	D	L	F	A	Pts	Titles
League	86	46	15	25	165	94	107	0
League Cup	16	13	1	2	36	8		1
Scottish Cup	17	9	5	3	37	19		0
Europe	11	5	4	1	17	13		1
Competitive Total	130	73	25	32	255	134		

League Titles

League Cup Wins   1970/71

Scottish Cup Wins

European   1971/72

Jock Wallace

Surname:	WALLACE
Forenames:	JOHN MARTIN

Appointed:	31/05/1972 & 10/11/1983
Left Post:	23/05/1978 & 07/04/1986

Birthplace: Wallyford
Birthdate: 06/09/1935

	Pld	W	D	L	F	A	Pts	Titles
League	303	174	72	57	557	295	420	3
League Cup	72	51	11	10	177	66		4
Scottish Cup	33	23	4	6	82	34		3
Europe	22	8	4	10	30	33		0
Competitive Total	430	256	91	83	846	428		

League Titles   1974/75, 1975/76, 1978/79

League Cup Wins   1975/76, 1977/78, 1983/84, 1984/85

Scottish Cup Wins 1972/73, 1975/76, 1977/78

European

John Greig

Surname:	GREIG		Appointed:	24/05/1978
Forenames:	JOHN		Left Post:	28/10/1983

Birthplace:	Edinburgh
Birthdate:	11/09/1942

	Pld	W	D	L	F	A	Pts	Titles
League	189	81	52	56	286	215	214	0
League Cup	46	37	5	4	118	37		2
Scottish Cup	34	22	9	3	71	29		2
Europe	21	11	5	5	39	21		0
Competitive Total	290	151	71	68	514	302		

League Titles

League Cup Wins   1978/79, 1981/82

Scottish Cup Wins   1978/79, 1980/81

European

Tommy McLean

Surname:	McLEAN	
Forenames:	THOMAS	

Appointed:	28/10/1983
Left Post:	10/11/1983

Birthplace:	Larkhall
Birthdate:	02/06/1947

	Pld	W	D	L	F	A	Pts	Titles
League	2	0	0	2	1	5	0	0
League Cup	1	1	0	0	3	0		0
Scottish Cup	0	0	0	0	0	0		0
Europe	1	0	0	1	0	1		0
Competitive Total	4	1	0	3	4	6		

League Titles

League Cup Wins

Scottish Cup Wins

European

Graeme Souness

Surname:	SOUNESS		**Appointed:**	08/04/1986
Forenames:	GRAEME JAMES		**Left Post:**	16/04/1991

Birthplace: Edinburgh
Birthdate: 06/05/1953

	Pld	W	D	L	F	A	Pts	Titles
League	196	125	38	33	343	127	288	3
League Cup	25	24	0	1	76	20		4
Scottish Cup	17	8	4	5	33	11		0
Europe	22	10	6	6	34	23		0
Competitive Total	260	167	48	45	486	181		

League Titles   1986/87, 1989/90, 1990/91

League Cup Wins   1986/87, 1987/88, 1988/89, 1990/91

Scottish Cup Wins

European

Walter Smith

Surname:	SMITH
Forenames:	WALTER

Appointed:	19/04/1991 & 10/01/2007
Left Post:	31/05/1998 & 16/05/2011

Birthplace:	Lanark
Birthdate:	24/02/1948

	Pld	W	D	L	F	A	Pts	Titles
League	447	303	84	60	939	369	902	10
League Cup	44	39	0	5	113	33		6
Scottish Cup	54	39	9	6	123	40		5
Europe	79	23	26	30	89	95		0
Competitive Total	624	404	119	101	126	537		

League Titles	1990/91, 1991/92, 1992/93, 1993/94, 1994/95, 1995/96, 1996/97, 2008/09, 2009/10, 2010/11
League Cup Wins	1992/93, 1993/94, 1996/97, 2007/08, 2009/10, 2010/11
Scottish Cup Wins	1991/92, 1992/93, 1995/96, 2007/08, 2008/09
European	

Dick Advocaat

Surname:	ADVOCAAT	**Appointed:**	01/06/1998
Forenames:	DIRK NICOLAAS	**Left Post:**	12/12/2001

Birthplace: The Hague, Holland
Birthdate: 27/09/1947

	Pld	W	D	L	F	A	Pts	Titles
League	128	88	20	20	290	106	287	2
League Cup	11	9	0	2	26	8		1
Scottish Cup	13	12	0	1	38	5		2
Europe	43	22	11	10	73	39		0
Competitive Total	195	131	31	33	427	158		

League Titles   1998/99, 1999/2000

League Cup Wins   1998/99

Scottish Cup Wins   1998/99, 1999/2000

European

Alex McLeish

Surname:	McLEISH	
Forenames:	ALEXANDER	

Appointed:	13/12/2001
Left Post:	31/05/2006

Birthplace:	Barrhead
Birthdate:	21/01/1959

	Pld	W	D	L	F	A	Pts	Titles
League	172	120	31	21	364	134	391	2
League Cup	15	13	1	1	44	12		3
Scottish Cup	18	13	2	3	42	13		2
Europe	30	9	10	11	38	37		0
Competitive Total	235	155	44	36	488	196		

League Titles   2002/03, 2004/05

League Cup Wins   2001/02, 2002/03, 2004/05

Scottish Cup Wins   2001/02, 2002/03

European

Paul Le Guen

| Surname: | LE GUEN | Appointed: | 01/06/2006 |
| Forenames: | PAUL | Left Post: | 04/01/2007 |

Birthplace: Pencran, France
Birthdate: 01/03/1964

	Pld	W	D	L	F	A	Pts	Titles
League	23	11	6	6	35	22	39	0
League Cup	2	1	0	1	2	2		0
Scottish Cup	0	0	0	0	0	0		0
Europe	6	4	2	0	10	4		0
Competitive Total	31	16	8	7	47	28		

League Titles

League Cup Wins

Scottish Cup Wins

European

Ian Durrant

Surname:	DURRANT	**Appointed:** 04/01/2007
Forenames:	IAN CHARLES	**Left Post:** 10/01/2007

Birthplace: Glasgow
Birthdate: 29/10/1966

	Pld	W	D	L	F	A	Pts	Titles
League	0	0	0	0	0	0	0	0
League Cup	0	0	0	0	0	0		0
Scottish Cup	1	0	0	1	2	3		0
Europe	0	0	0	0	0	0		0
Competitive Total	1	0	0	1	2	3		

League Titles

League Cup Wins

Scottish Cup Wins

European

Ally McCoist

Surname:	McCOIST		**Appointed:**	16/05/2011
Forenames:	ALISTAIR		**Left Post:**	

Birthplace: Bellshill
Birthdate: 24/09/1962

	Pld	W	D	L	F	A	Pts	Titles
League	0	0	0	0	0	0	0	0
League Cup	0	0	0	0	0	0		0
Scottish Cup	0	0	0	0	0	0		0
Europe	0	0	0	0	0	0		0
Competitive Total	0	0	0	0	0	0		

League Titles

League Cup Wins

Scottish Cup Wins

European

INDEX

Aberdeen 52–3, 72, 107, 108, 109, 111–12, 113, 119, 127, 128, 135, 136, 140, 142, 152, 171, 182, 244, 249
Advocaat, Dick 31, 32, 148, 149–50, 152, 153–7, 158–62, 170, 183, 204, 216, 218–19, 300
Airdrie 50, 137, 138
Albertz, Jorg 142, 143, 150, 152
Amoruso, Lorenzo 145, 146, 148, 150, 156, 159
Archibald, Sandy 35, 37, 47
Arsenal 29, 30, 60–1, 62–3, 66, 67, 224

Ball, Michael 158
Barcelona 104
Baxter, Jim 71, 72, 73–4, 77–8, 81, 89, 100, 101, 124, 208, 209, 225
Bayern Munich 93, 130, 153, 196–8, 210–12, 213
Beasley, DaMarcus 181, 182
Berwick Rangers 91, 210
Bo Andersen, Erik 141, 143
Boli, Basile 140–1, 203
Boozegate incident 177–8
Bougherra, Madjid 184, 188
Bowie, James 24, 32, 34–5, 68, 272, 273
Boyd, Kris 166, 167, 168, 179, 182, 185, 186, 188, 219, 220
brake clubs 253, 255, 257
Brand, Ralph 71, 76, 79, 82, 84, 208, 209
Brown, George 38, 58, 272, 273
Burnbank 14
Butcher, Terry 4, 118, 122, 125, 128, 151

Cairns, Tommy 36
Caldow, Eric 30, 43, 208–9
Campbell, Peter 9, 10–11, 12–13, 14, 15, 23
Caniggia, Claudio 158
Carroll, Roy 181
Celtic 2, 6–7, 17–18, 19, 20, 22, 29, 36, 37, 38, 39–40, 43, 47–8, 57, 65, 71, 75, 77, 78, 89–90, 91, 93, 94, 95–6, 98, 100, 103, 105, 107, 108, 109–10, 112, 113–14, 121, 123–4, 126–7, 128, 132–4, 137, 139, 141–2, 143, 144, 146, 147, 152, 155, 157, 158, 164, 165, 170, 171, 172, 181, 182, 185, 188, 189, 190, 192, 210, 225, 236, 256, 257, 259, 277, 278
Champions League 5, 142, 146, 149, 153, 157, 171, 182, 184, 189, 202, 203, 204, 205, 206, 215–16, 275
Chapman, Herbert 29, 30, 60
Charity Cup 16, 37, 57
CIS Cup 164, 172, 182, 186, 187, 190
Clement, Jeremy 163, 180
Clyde 18, 27, 28
Conn, Alfie 104
Cooper, Davie 4, 108, 109, 110, 112, 116, 119–20, 121, 123–4, 124, 250
Cousin, Daniel 181, 185, 217–18
Cuellar, Carlos 181, 184
Cunningham, Andy 35, 46, 55–6, 57

Darcheville, Jean-Claude 181, 185, 217, 219
Davis, Harold 70, 73, 75–6, 78, 79, 84, 208
Davis, Steven 184, 188, 190
Dawson, Jerry 38
de Boer, Ronald 154, 159, 172, 173
Dibble, Andy 144–5
Diouf, El-Hadji 185, 188
Drinkell, Kevin 127, 134
Drummond, Jock 21
Dumbarton 19
Duncanson, Jimmy 39
Dundee United 2, 40, 50, 72, 76, 81, 89, 107, 119, 124, 135, 136, 140, 146, 156, 164, 170, 179, 182, 186, 187, 190, 191, 278
Dunfermline 72, 96, 144, 164, 170, 177, 215
Durie, Gordon 139, 142, 144
Durrant, Ian 121, 123–4, 125, 127, 146, 177, 303
Dynamo Kiev 84, 195, 199–200, 281

East Fife 51, 52
Ehiogu, Ugo 179, 180
Empire Exhibition Cup 39
English, Sam 38–9, 48
Europa League 184, 189, 205
European Cup 71, 74, 75, 77, 85, 91, 92, 108, 115, 124–5, 130, 137, 138, 147, 196, 198–9, 200, 207–9, 212–13

European Cup-Winners' Cup 31, 74, 85, 93, 98, 100, 103, 112–13, 196–8, 208, 210–12, 212, 215
European Golden Boot 137

FA Cup 16–17
Falco, Mark 125, 199
Falkirk 165, 186
fanzines 262–3
Ferguson, Alex 94, 97, 99, 102, 119, 120, 173, 280
Ferguson, Barry 148–9, 154, 156, 159, 165, 166–7, 168, 172, 177–9, 187
Ferguson, Derek 121, 149
Ferguson, Duncan 138–9
Ferguson, Ian 125, 134, 136, 138, 146, 147, 277
Findlay, Bob 52
Fleck, Robert 121, 125
Fleming, Jimmy 36, 37, 47, 48, 56, 62
Flo, Tore Andre 157–8
Forrest, Jim 71, 91–2, 210
Forsyth, Tom 105, 107, 110
Founders Trail 9–11
Francis, Trevor 122

Gallacher, Mary 'Tiny' 222–3, 225–6, 232–3
Gascoigne, Paul 141, 142, 143, 144, 145, 146
Gillick, Torry 27, 67, 70–1
Goram, Andy 137, 143, 146
Gough, Richard 125, 132, 139, 140, 143, 145, 146, 151, 178, 277
Gow, Alan 181, 187
Gray, Dougie 37, 41
Greig, John 4, 59, 70, 75, 82, 84, 85, 90, 100, 103, 105, 107, 110, 111, 113, 114, 115, 116, 119, 120, 123, 154, 211, 214–15, 234, 250, 296

Hamilton, Tom 36, 47
Hampden riot (1909) 22
Hateley, Mark 114–15, 122, 135, 136, 137, 138, 203, 282
Heart of Midlothian 49, 72, 76, 98, 107, 121, 134, 137, 142, 144, 146, 151–2, 159, 171, 191
Henderson, James 268
Henderson, Martin 107
Henderson, Willie 71, 77, 78, 83, 84, 211
Hibernian 40, 41, 50–1, 65, 78, 99, 105, 107, 109, 113, 140, 156, 164, 169–70, 171, 188, 207
Hillsborough disaster 249, 250
hooliganism 65, 99, 102–3, 139, 255–6, 258–9
Hope, David 102, 243, 274
Hubbard, Johnny 43, 72
Hynd, Roger 93, 210, 211

Ibrox Disaster (1902) 22, 223, 235–6
Ibrox Disaster (1971) 103, 104, 230, 234–5, 239, 241–3, 244–9, 250–1, 254
Ibrox Park 222–6
  attendances 236, 237
  catering 226
  construction and rebuilding programmes 17, 104, 120, 126, 223, 224–5, 231–2, 235, 236
  crowd management 228, 229–30, 235, 237–8, 239, 240–2
  non-football events 230
  safety 230, 237–8, 243–4, 245
  stadium tours 222, 232–3
  Trophy Room 226–8, 232–3
Inter-Cities Fairs Cup 94, 98, 99
Inverness 164, 165, 191

Jackson, Colin 107, 110, 113, 114, 213
James, Alex 61, 62
Jardine, Sandy xi–xii, 9, 59, 93, 105, 107, 110, 197, 207, 209–12, 213–14, 215, 216, 221, 228
Jelavic, Nikica 188, 189, 190, 192
Johansen, Kai 90, 92, 95, 211
Johnston, Allan 154
Johnston, Maurice 31, 118–19, 124, 128, 129, 134, 137, 282
Johnston, Willie 98, 99, 100, 104, 211, 214
Johnstone, Derek 103, 107–8, 111, 112, 114, 115, 121

Kanchelskis, Andrei 151, 157
Kennedy, Stewart 105, 107
Kichenbrand, Don 72
Kilmarnock 2, 19, 48, 53, 72, 93, 94, 144, 156, 164, 170, 191, 208
Kinnear, Davie 65
Kinning Park 14, 16, 17
Konterman, Bert 154, 155

Lafferty, Kyle 184, 186, 188, 192
Latapy, Russell 158, 159
Laudrup, Brian 140, 141, 142, 143, 144, 146
Lawrence, John 93, 94, 96–7, 100, 121, 210, 227, 244, 273–4
Le Guen, Paul 148, 162–8, 175, 177, 178, 179, 302
league restructuring 7
Leeds United 98, 138, 200–1, 202, 279–80
Leitch, Archibald 223, 224, 236
Lennon, Neil 6, 188
Letizi, Lionel 163, 164, 180
Loving Cup 227

McAllister, Gary 200–1
McAuley, Bob 59

McBeath, William 9, 10–11, 12–13, 14, 23
McCall, Stuart 137, 146
McCandless, Billy 'Bucksy' 36, 37, 46
McCann, Neil 151, 152
McCloy, Peter 107, 214
McCoist, Ally 2, 121, 125, 126, 127, 137, 140, 145, 146, 177, 188, 199, 276–84, 304
McCulloch, Lee 181, 185, 188, 220
MacDonald, Alex 99, 107, 108, 110, 111, 112, 113, 115, 198, 215
McDonald, Scott 180–1
McGregor, Allan 164, 177–8, 188, 191
McGrory, Jimmy 29, 38, 48
McInnes, Derek 141, 145
MacKay, John Wallace 16, 268
McKinnon, Ronnie 83–4, 211
McLean, George 91–2, 210
McLean, Tommy 104, 107, 110, 115, 297
McLeish, Alex 159, 161, 162, 169–74, 301
McLelland, John 120
MacMillan, Ian 71, 75, 82
McNeil, Moses 9, 10–11, 12–13, 14, 15, 23–4
McNeil, Peter 9, 10–11, 12–13, 14, 23
McPhail, Bob 26, 36, 37–8, 46, 47, 48, 49, 55, 61, 63
McPherson, John 21
McStay, Paul 132–3
McSwegan, Gary 138, 145, 203
Maley, Willie 29, 30
Marlborough, Lawrence 121, 274
Marshall, James 37, 62
Matthews, Stanley 50, 64
Meiklejohn, Davie 28, 35, 37, 46, 47–8, 49, 62, 75
Mendes, Pedro 184, 185, 186, 187
Millar, Jimmy 85, 90, 208, 225
Miller, Alex 107, 111
Miller, Charlie 144
Miller, Kenny 154, 156, 164, 184–5, 187, 189
Mols, Michael 152, 153, 155, 172
Morton, Alan 29, 35–6, 37, 46, 48, 56, 59, 70–1, 76, 260, 272
Moscow Dynamo 66–8, 81, 213, 237
Motherwell 22, 37, 49, 72, 107, 112, 116, 136, 140, 144, 164, 166, 169, 171, 180–1, 191, 206, 241
Muirhead, Tommy 26, 37, 46
Murray, Sir David 1, 126, 131, 133, 135, 142–3, 157–8, 159–60, 162, 163, 167, 174, 175, 176, 187, 231, 273, 274, 275
Murray Park 5, 111, 158, 161

Naismith, Steven 181, 192
Negri, Marco 145–6
Nicholson, Billy 49
Niven, George 52, 53
North-Eastern League 64

Novo, Nacho 185, 186, 188, 218, 220, 265
Numan, Arthur 151, 159

Old Firm rivalry 6, 17–18, 22, 39–40, 65–6, 128–9, 225, 248, 249, 256–7
O'Neill, Martin 155, 160, 161, 169, 174

Papac, Sasa 163, 188, 192
Parlane, Derek 104, 107, 115, 197, 213
Partick Thistle 48, 98, 109
Penman, Andy 94, 95, 96
Persson, Orjan 94, 96
Porrini, Sergio 145, 150
Prodan, Daniel 151
PSV Eindhoven 115, 190, 205

Queen of the South 182, 185

racism 125
Rae, Gavin 166
Raith Rovers 98, 144
Rangers FC
    boardroom politics 32, 267–75
    charitable work 268
    debts 4, 18, 161–2, 187, 275
    founders and early years 9–24
    Protestant identity 12, 18, 32, 256, 258
    Russian tour 80–8, 195
    sectarianism 31, 99, 102, 118–19, 122, 128, 129–30, 256–8, 259–60, 261
    Treble winners 40, 51, 52, 69–70, 111, 112, 137–8, 152, 170
    under Alex Mcleish 162, 169–74, 301, 304
    under Bill Struth 26–68, 290
    under David White 98–100, 292
    under Dick Advocaat 32, 148, 149–62, 204–5, 218–19, 300
    under Graeme Souness 31, 116–17, 118–19, 122–31, 133–5, 199–200, 298
    under Ian Durrant 177, 303
    under Jock Wallace 31, 104–13, 116, 119, 120–2, 295
    under John Greig 113–16, 119, 120, 296
    under Paul Le Guen 148–9, 162–8, 302
    under Scot Symon 30, 71–98, 208–12, 291
    under Walter Smith 32, 135–47, 175–93, 216–18, 299
    under William Wilton 21, 23, 28, 289
    under Willie Thornton 100, 293
    under Willie Waddell 31, 101–4, 212–14, 294
    US and Canadian tour 54–9
    wages 4, 21, 72, 81
    wartime football 50, 64–6
    youth development operations 5, 95, 123, 283–4

see also Ibrox Park; supporters
Rangers Supporters' Association 263, 270
Reyna, Claudio 151, 204, 205
Ricksen, Fernando 154, 155, 157, 164
Ritchie, Billy 76, 79, 83, 208
Ritchie, Paul 154
Roberts, Graham 4, 122, 125
Robertson, David 137, 144
Russell, Bobby 106–7, 108–12, 113, 114–17

St Johnstone 139, 152, 156–7, 164, 165, 177
St Mirren 49, 83, 136, 137, 166, 187, 242
Salenko, Oleg 141
Scott, Alex 79, 83, 207, 208, 209
Scottish Cup 18, 19, 22, 35, 36, 37, 43, 45–9,
    51, 52–3, 71, 72, 76, 78, 83, 90, 91, 98, 99,
    101, 103, 105, 107, 108, 112, 113, 128,
    130, 137, 138, 142, 144, 146, 152, 170,
    171, 177, 182, 186, 187, 190, 210
Scottish FA 80, 127, 176
Scottish League 18–19, 21, 23, 37, 39, 40–1,
    43, 71, 78, 81, 89, 90, 98, 105, 142, 144,
    152
Scottish League Cup 51, 71, 72, 76–7, 90,
    95–6, 97, 100, 103, 107, 108, 111, 112,
    113, 121, 123, 124, 128, 137, 138, 140,
    144, 146, 152, 156, 170, 171, 177
Scottish Premier League (SPL) 1–2, 7, 157,
    166, 170, 171, 182, 186, 187–8, 189, 191,
    192, 199, 218, 275
Sebo, Filip 163, 165
Second World War 50, 64–6
Shaw, Jock 51, 67
Simpson, Billy 30, 43, 53
Simpson, Jimmy 38
Sionko, Libor 163
Smith, Alex 94, 211
Smith, Dave 94, 211, 214
Smith, Gordon 2, 108, 111, 112, 114, 198
Smith, Jimmy 36, 38, 49, 50, 58, 61, 67
Smith, Walter 2, 31, 32, 123, 133, 135–7, 138,
    140, 141, 143, 145, 146, 149, 150, 175–6,
    177, 178–9, 180, 183–6, 187, 188, 190,
    191–3, 207, 216, 219, 221, 299
Souness, Graeme 4, 31, 116, 118–19, 124,
    125, 126, 128, 129, 130, 131, 133, 135,
    199, 200, 226, 231, 274, 277, 279, 281,
    298
Spackman, Nigel 134
Stein, Colin 97, 99, 104, 105, 213, 214
Stein, Jock 78, 89, 96, 102
Steven, Trevor 122, 134–5, 137
Struth, Bill 24, 25–35, 37, 43–4, 46, 51, 52,
    53, 54, 58–9, 63, 64, 65, 66, 71, 225, 232,
    237, 256, 272, 273, 290

supporters 252–66, 275
    bus trips 263–4
    chants and songs 260, 261–2
    profile 236, 246–7, 254–5
    supporters' groups 262, 263
Svensson, Karl 163, 180
Symon, Scot 30, 31, 39, 44, 51, 53, 71, 73–6,
    81, 83, 86, 89–90, 92, 93, 94, 95, 96, 97–8,
    211, 225, 226, 227, 240, 291

Taylor, Matt 104, 274
Third Lanark 22, 41, 42, 49
Thompson, Steven 169, 171–2, 173–4
Thomson, John 35, 38
Thomson, Kevin 180, 187, 188
Thornton, Willie 27, 40–1, 51, 52, 65, 100,
    107, 227–8, 293

UEFA Cup 146, 151, 153, 157, 159, 162, 165,
    168, 177, 181, 182–3, 186–7, 196, 199,
    204, 215, 216–17, 265
Ure-Primrose, Sir John 268–9, 270
Urquhart, Billy 115

Vallance, Tom 11, 14, 15, 24
van Vossen, Peter 141, 143
Velicka, Andrius 184
Vidmar, Tony 204, 205

Waddell, Willie 31, 39, 40, 51, 67, 101–4, 109,
    212, 226, 230, 231, 243, 248, 259, 260,
    294
Wallace, Jock 31, 91, 101, 104, 105, 109, 110,
    112, 113, 116, 119, 120–2, 213, 226, 250,
    295
Wallace, Rod 151, 152
Walters, Mark 122, 125, 127, 137
Webster, Andy 179, 184
Weir, David 179–80, 188
White, David 95, 96, 98, 100, 101, 292
Whittaker, Steven 181, 188, 217
Whyte, Craig 1–8, 191
Wilkins, Ray 122, 126
Williamson, Billy 51–2, 67–8
Willoughby, Alex 93, 98, 210
Wilson, Davie 71, 73, 82–3, 86, 89, 90, 209
Wilton, William 21, 22–3, 28, 34, 268, 289
Wolverhampton Wanderers 78–9, 87, 208
Woodburn, Willie 39, 41–2, 51, 260
Woods, Chris 4, 122, 137

Young, George 28, 31, 41, 42, 44, 51, 52–3,
    65, 68, 75, 263